Female Transgression in Early Modern Britain
Literary and Historical Explorations

Edited by

RICHARD HILLMAN
Université de Tours, France / Centre d'Études Supérieures
de la Renaissance-CNRS

and

PAULINE RUBERRY-BLANC
Université de Tours, France / Centre d'Études Supérieures
de la Renaissance-CNRS

ASHGATE

Published by
Ashgate Publishing Limited
Wey Court East
Union Road
Farnham
Surrey, GU9 7PT
England

Ashgate Publishing Company
110 Cherry Street
Suite 3-1
Burlington, VT 05401-3818
USA

www.ashgate.com

British Library Cataloguing in Publication Data
A catalogue record for this book is available from the British Library

The Library of Congress has cataloged the printed edition as follows:
Female Transgression in Early Modern Britain : Literary and Historical Explorations /
    edited by Richard Hillman and Pauline Ruberry-Blanc.
    pages cm
  Includes bibliographical references and index.
    ISBN 978-1-4724-1045-0 (hardcover: alk. paper)—ISBN 978-1-4724-1046-7 (ebook)—
ISBN 978-1-4724-1047-4 (epub)
    1. English literature—Early modern, 1500–1700—History and criticism. 2. Women
and literature—Great Britain—History. 3. Women in popular culture—Great Britain—
History. 4. Women—Great Britain—Social conditions. I. Hillman, Richard, 1949– editor
of compilation. II. Ruberry-Blanc, Pauline, editor of compilation.
    PR428.W63F46 2014
    820.9'9287—dc23

2013047654

ISBN 9781472410450 (hbk)
ISBN 9781472410467 (ebk – PDF)
ISBN 9781472410474 (ebk – ePUB)

MIX
Paper from responsible sources
FSC
www.fsc.org FSC® C013985

Printed in the United Kingdom by Henry Ling Limited,
at the Dorset Press, Dorchester, DT1 1HD

Contents

List of Figures and Tables

Figures

Tables

Notes on Contributors

Marisha Caswell (Visiting Assistant Professor, Algoma University, Sault Ste. Marie, Ontario):

Marisha Caswell works chiefly on the social, cultural, legal and gender history of early modern England. Her work is centred on the use of legal records, especially those relating to the criminal courts, as a way to illuminate larger aspects of society. Her dissertation examines the experiences of married women in the criminal courts of the Northern Circuit from 1640–1760. In addition to contributing to the conference 'Women and Crime in the British Isles and North America since 1500' (Lyons, France, September 2008), she has presented papers in several other venues, including the I. H. R. Women's History Seminar (London, October 2008) and the Berkshire Conference on the History of Women (Minneapolis, MN, June 2008).

Pascale Drouet (Professor of English, Université de Poitiers):

Pascale Drouet's doctoral thesis was published in 2003 as *Le vagabond dans l'Angleterre de Shakespeare, ou l'art de contrefaire à la ville et à la scène* (Harmatton), and she has recently produced a large-scale study of the motif of banishment in Shakespeare's work: *Mise au ban et abus de pouvoir : essai sur trois pièces tragiques de Shakespeare* (Presses de l'Université Paris-Sorbonne, 2012). This is also the subject of an edited collection, *La mise au ban dans l'Europe de la Renaissance* (with Yan Brailowsky) (Presses Universitaires de Rennes, 2010). Other editorial projects include *'The true blank of thine eye': Approches critiques de King Lear* (with Pierre Iselin) (Presses Universitaires de France, 2009) and *The Spectacular in and around Shakespeare* (Cambridge Scholars Publishing, 2009). She is also the author of numerous articles on Shakespearean drama and related subjects.

Frédérique Fouassier-Tate (Senior Lecturer in English, Centre d'Études Supérieures de la Renaissance-CNRS, Université François-Rabelais, Tours):

Frédérique Fouassier-Tate is a specialist in the English theatre of the Renaissance with a particular interest in feminist approaches, as well as in the history of ideas. Her doctoral thesis concerned the representation of female sexual transgression on the early modern English stage. She is the author of numerous articles on subjects ranging from theatrical portrayals of Mary Magdalene and Joan of Arc to the English configuration of syphilis as the 'French disease' and the geography of places of pleasure and power in early modern London. Her publications include 'Mary Magdalene on Stage: "The Sinner in the City" and the Persistent Remnant of Catholic Culture in an Anglican Society', in *The Outsider Within: Figures de la médiation*, ed. Richard Hillman and André Lascombes, collection Theta, vol. 7 (online at http://umr6576.cesr.univ-tours.fr/publications/Theta7), and '"The French Disease" in Elizabethan and Jacobean Drama', in *Representing France and the French in Early Modern English Drama*, ed. Jean-Christophe Mayer (University of Delaware Press, 2008), 193–206.

Richard Hillman (Professor of English, Centre d'Études Supérieures de la Renaissance-CNRS, Université François-Rabelais, Tours):

The main specialty of Richard Hillman, co-editor of the present volume, is the English theatre of the Renaissance, a field in which he has published numerous articles and seven monographs. Among the latter, the most recent, *Shakespeare, Marlowe and the Politics of France* (Palgrave, 2002), *French Origins of English Tragedy* (Manchester University Press, 2010) and *French Reflections in the Shakespearean Tragic: Three Case Studies* (Manchester University Press, 2012), testify to the increasing concentration of his research on links between England and France. He has also produced translations, with introduction and notes, of several early modern French plays: *L'histoire tragique de la Pucelle de Domrémy*, by Fronton Du Duc, Carleton Renaissance Plays in Translation, No. 39 (Dovehouse Editions, 2005); *La tragédie de feu Gaspard de Colligny*, by François de Chantelouve, together with *La Guisiade*, by Pierre Matthieu, Carleton Renaissance Plays in Translation, No. 40 (Dovehouse Editions, 2005); *Coriolan*, by Alexandre Hardy (Presses Universitaires François-Rabelais, 2010 [online]); and *Les Visionnaires*, by Desmarets de Saint-Sorlin (online at http://umr6576. cesr.univ-tours.fr/publications/Visionaries). He is co-editor of the Theta series of volumes on Tudor theatre published online by the Centre d'Études Supérieures de la Renaissance, Tours (http://umr6576.cesr.univ-tours.fr/publications/Scene_ europeenne).

Jennine Hurl-Eamon (Associate Professor of History, Trent University, Peterborough, Ontario):

Jennine Hurl-Eamon's research interests focus on early modern England, especially with regard to gender, crime and criminal justice, and plebeian marriage and family life. Among her numerous publications are the following: *Marriage and the British Army in the Long Eighteenth Century: 'The Girl I Left Behind Me'* (Oxford University Press, 2014); *Gender and Petty Violence in London, 1680–1720* (Ohio State University Press, 2005); '"Spiralling out of Control?" Female Violence in Eighteenth-Century London and New Mexico' (with Sonya Lipsett-Rivera), in *Assaulting the Past: Violence and Civilization in Historical Context*, ed. Katherine

D. Watson (Cambridge Scholars Publishing, 2007), 179–202; '"I Will Forgive You if the World Will": Wife Murder and Limits on Patriarchal Violence in London, 1690–1750', in *Violence, Politics and Gender in Early Modern England*, ed. Joseph P. Ward (Palgrave Macmillan, 2008), 223–48; and 'The Fiction of Female Dependence and the Makeshift Economy of Soldiers, Sailors, and Their Wives in Eighteenth-Century London', *Labor History* 4 (2008): 481–501.

Krista Kesselring (Associate Professor of History, Dalhousie University, Halifax, Nova Scotia):

Krista Kesselring's research interests primarily concern early modern Britain and the issues of law and crime, protest, gender and women's histories. She is engaged in a long-term project on felony forfeitures in English law, c. 1170–1870. In addition to numerous journal articles and book chapters, she has published the following major monographs: *Mercy and Authority in the Tudor State* (Cambridge University Press, 2003) and *The Northern Rebellion of 1569: Faith, Politics and Protest and Elizabethan England* (Palgrave Macmillan, 2007).

Anne-Marie Kilday (Professor in Criminal History, Oxford Brookes University):

Anne-Marie Kilday researches and publishes on the history of violent crime and the history of female criminality, beginning with the early modern period. Her extensive publications in this field include *Histories of Crime: Britain 1600–2000*, edited with David Nash (Palgrave Macmillan, 2010); *Women and Crime in Enlightenment Scotland* (Boydell and Brewer, 2007); *Cultures of Shame: Exploring Crime and Morality in Britain 1700–1900*, edited with David Nash (Palgrave, 2010); *A History of Infanticide in Britain, c. 1600 to the Present* (Palgrave, 2013); *The Violent North? Crime in Scotland 1660 to the Present* (Routledge, forthcoming 2015); and *Crime, Law and Religion in Britain since 1600: A Curious Relationship*, edited with David Nash (Palgrave, forthcoming 2015). She is on the editorial board of the e-journal *Crimes and Misdemeanours: Deviance and the Law in Historical Perspective*.

Diane Purkiss (Associate Professor of English, Keble College, Oxford University):

Diane Purkiss received a BA with first-class Honours from the University of Queensland and a PhD from Merton College, Oxford. She became Lecturer in English at the University of East Anglia in 1991, and Lecturer in English at the University of Reading in 1993. In 1998, she became Professor of English at Exeter University, before taking up her current post at Keble College in 2000.

Her major publications include *The Witch in History: Early Modern and Late Twentieth Century Representations* (Routledge, 1996); *Troublesome Things: A History of Fairies and Fairy Stories* (Allen Lane, 2000); *Literature, Gender, and Politics during the English Civil War* (Cambridge University Press, 2005); and *The English Civil War: A People's History* (HarperCollins, 2006). She has also edited *Women, Texts and Histories 1575–1760* (Routledge, 1992), with Clare Brant; *Renaissance Women: Elizabeth Cary's* Tragedie of Mariam *and* Edward II *and Aemilia Lanyer's* Salve Deus Rex Judaorum (William Pickering, 1994); and *Three Tragedies by Renaissance Women:* Iphigeneia at Aulis, *by Lady Jane Lumley,* The Tragedie of Antonie, *by Lady Mary Sidney,* The Tragedy of Mariam, *by Elizabeth Cary, Viscountess Falkland* (Penguin, 1998).

Pauline Ruberry-Blanc (Senior Lecturer in English, Centre d'Études Supérieures de la Renaissance-CNRS, Université François-Rabelais, Tours):

Pauline Ruberry-Blanc, co-editor of the present volume, has published a number of articles in English and French on medieval, Tudor and Jacobean drama, as well as a monograph on the development of English tragicomedy from the 'Vice drama' of the mid-fifteenth century to Shakespeare's late plays: *L'univers tragi-comique du théâtre shakespearien et ses précédents sur la scène Tudor* (Publications de l'Université Jean Moulin-Lyon 3, 2007). She is the editor of *Selfhood on the Early Modern English Stage* (Cambridge Scholars Publishing, 2008) and co-editor of the Theta series of volumes on Tudor theatre published online by the Centre d'Études Supérieures de la Renaissance, Tours (http://umr6576.cesr.univ-tours.fr/publications/Scene_europeenne). Recently, her work has focused increasingly on early modern codes of conduct.

James Sharpe (Professor of History, University of York):

James Sharpe's initial research was on the history of crime in seventeenth-century England, which resulted in a PhD thesis subsequently published as *Crime in Seventeenth-Century England: A County Study*. He went on to broaden his research in this field, completing a number of essays and articles, a general book on crime in early modern England and a short survey of punishment in England from c. 1550 to the 1980s. In 1996, he published *Instruments of Darkness*, a major work on the history of witchcraft in England over the period c. 1550–1750. Latterly, his interest in crime and law enforcement has led him to work on a wide variety of court records, which are frequently the only source for examining the attitudes of the middling and lower sorts in the early modern period. He has been director of an ESRC-funded project on violence in early modern England.

Acknowledgements

The editors wish to thank their colleague and friend Krista Kesselring, who preferred to remain an unofficial member of the editorial team, for her invaluable expertise, and willingness to share it, regarding the historical contributions to this volume. She is also responsible for locating the engraving by Wenceslaus Hollar and proposing the design for the cover. Thanks are due as well to Erika Gaffney of Ashgate for her astute editorial guidance and, especially, for her unstinting encouragement of this project from its inception to its realization.

Chapter 8, by Anne-Marie Kilday, is a précis of work previously published in the monograph *Women and Violent Crime in Enlightenment Scotland*. It is reproduced here with the kind permission of The Boydell Press.

The cover illustration is adapted from the engraving 'Winter' by Wenceslaus Hollar, which is employed courtesy of The Thomas Fisher Rare Book Library, University of Toronto.

Introduction

Richard Hillman and Pauline Ruberry-Blanc

This is a collection of wide-ranging reflections by both established and younger scholars, based in England, Canada and France, on the subject of female transgression in early modern Britain – that often casually denominated time and place, the boundaries of which are at once precise and dauntingly ample. Our broad objective as editors is to foster the dialogue which has been underway for some years now between the analysis of fictional representations of female transgression and the interpretation of recorded facts. This collection contains five essays in each of two categories, and our hope is that their arrangement will stimulate further thought and research along interdisciplinary lines.

The categories merit a word of explanation, as do the relations between them. We have formalized the headings as, respectively, 'Imag(in)ing Female Transgression and Transgressors' and 'Reading (into) the Social Picture'. The aim is to accentuate the dynamic interchange between fiction and fact that informs literary and socio-historical analysis alike. Such interchange is, of course, widely taken for granted in recent scholarship. For although the evidence of literature (and, behind it, of myth) privileges the shaping role of narrative, while the social record stands primarily as a body of data to be evaluated, this is a boundary that thinking within both disciplines has been crossing for some time – more or less circumspectly, sometimes uneasily, but with no sense of transgression.

In evolving within itself, each of the traditional disciplines has in effect moved towards the other. For their part, literary historians have found it increasingly important to attend to the social realities which underpin literature and myth, and with which the latter are inevitably engaged. Such realities are indeed the inescapable reference points of both Old and New Historicists (or Cultural Materialists), the principal difference being that, for these schools, they are not fixed and stable but themselves infused with meaning, and hence subject to inflection, by the discursive mediations mandated by culture and ideology. Such mediations are especially evident, and more readily measurable, when 'literature' encounters its ambient culture physically in the theatre; hence, no doubt, the dominance of theatrical instances in criticism of this kind – in the present volume, as in such important precursor treatments of the subject as that of Frances Dolan.[1]

---

[1]   Frances E. Dolan, *Dangerous Familiars: Representations of Domestic Crime in England* (Ithaca, NY: Cornell University Press, 1994). See also Dolan's treatment of the variable representation of female violence in 'Tracking the Petty Traitor Across Genres', in *Ballads and Broadsides in Britain, 1500–1800*, ed. Patricia Fumerton, Anita Gerrini, Kris McAbee et al. (Farnham, Surrey: Ashgate, 2010), 149–72.

From the other side, most currently practising historians and social analysts (certainly those included in this book) are highly sensitive to the discursive mediation – 'representation', in Hayden White's influential formulation – of even the 'hardest' factual evidence. White and Paul Ricœur (the latter especially by way of his mimetic theories) were already conditioning approaches to archival material at least by the 1980s.[2] To a great extent, such thinking has become the norm: it is common to approach female criminality in terms of 'literature' of all sorts, and more broadly of storytelling.[3] Joan W. Scott played a catalytic role here in arguing for the discursive production of subjectivity and agency.[4] At the same time, the resistance of most historians to the post-structuralist tendency to subordinate realities to their representation, if not wholly to dissolve them discursively, has also been registered – with particular force by Garthine Walker, whose solution is

---

[2]   See, e.g., Natalie Zemon Davis, *Fiction in the Archives: Pardon Tales and Their Tellers in Sixteenth-Century France* (Stanford, CA: Stanford University Press, 1987), 3. For White, see esp. 'The Historical Text as Literary Artifact', in *The Writing of History: Literary Form and Historical Understanding*, ed. Robert H. Canary and Henry Kozicki (Madison: University of Wisconsin Press, 1978), 41–62, and *The Content of the Form: Narrative Discourse and Historical Representation* (Baltimore, MD: Johns Hopkins University Press, 1987); for Ricœur, *Time and Narrative*, trans. Kathleen McLaughlin and David Pellauer, 2 vols (Chicago: University of Chicago Press, 1984–85), vol. 1, 180–92. Ricœur posits a threefold dynamic whereby 'first-order entities', already imbued with significance by way of their cultural contexts, are effectively recycled through an authorial imagination into forms which, in turn, are inevitably read back into the current environment by their interpreters. The particular attraction of this model, arguably, is its heuristic openness to concentration on one aspect or another of the mimetic process. The theoretically pivotal volume of Canary and Kozicki notably contained, as well, an important essay by Lionel Gossman, 'History and Literature: Reproduction or Signification' (3–39), who has continued to reflect usefully on the problematic; see Lionel Gossman, *Between History and Literature* (Cambridge, MA: Harvard University Press, 1990), in which his 1978 essay is reprinted, together with a range of later commentaries taking account of the post-structuralist critiques that White has attracted for positing a distinction between 'literary or poetic language and "literal" or scientific language' (Gossman, 'The Rationality of History', in *Between History and Literature*, 306).

[3]   See the important reflection on the issue, and application of the principle, by Laura Gowing, *Domestic Dangers: Women, Words, and Sex in Early Modern London* (Oxford: Clarendon Press, 1996), esp. 41–48 on 'legal narratives'. For further examples, see Joy Wiltenburg, *Disorderly Women and Female Power in the Street Literature of Early Modern England and Germany*, Feminist Issues: Practice, Politics, Theory (Charlottesville: University Press of Virginia, 1991); Sandra Clark, *Women and Crime in the Street Literature of Early Modern England* (Basingstoke, Hampshire: Palgrave Macmillan, 2003); Susan C. Staub, *Nature's Cruel Stepdames: Murderous Women in the Street Literature of Seventeenth Century England* (Pittsburgh, PA: Duquesne University Press, 2005); and Randall Martin, *Women, Murder, and Equity in Early Modern England*, Routledge Studies in Renaissance Literature and Culture, 10 (London: Routledge, 2008).

[4]   Joan W. Scott, 'The Evidence of Experience', *Critical Inquiry* 17.4 (1991): 773–97.

to privilege Bakhtin's notions of heteroglossia and multivocality, which come, in effect, to praise the factual, not to bury it.[5]

What more precisely, then, do we hope to gain by harking back, in our organization of this volume, to an arguably outmoded divide between literary historians and the 'real' kind? Most fundamentally, we seek to signal the fact – and to invite reflection on it – that the disciplines, despite their *rapprochement* along the axis of discursivity, continue by and large to pursue divergent preoccupations associated with different orders of 'raw material'. The two approaches highlighted by our titles, therefore, can claim to be taken as methodological mirror-images of each other – or views from opposite sides of the interpretative lens – and indeed we hope that readers will be stimulated to think about method as well as content in terms of complementarity.

Such thinking might start from the premise that the methodological divergences obviously existing between most literary scholars and most social scientists should not be blurred but rather acknowledged, and in such a way as to highlight the areas of productive intersection. After all, neither perspective can wholly do without, or remain innocent of, the other. Our two categories of study thus announce their shared epistemological assumptions and adherence to the same broad field of research (hence their right to presence within the same physical collection!), while encouraging attention to the degrees of focus offered by individual essays on matters of fact or procedures of mediation.

We would also suggest that, while the material available for analysis to both is necessarily discursive in nature, ranging from myths, on the one hand, to court records, on the other, our juxtaposition highlights a common factor currently less in vogue, both because it is less tangible and because it risks evoking forms of 'humanist' thinking now widely derogated as excessively subjective. We wish, with due circumspection, to recuperate, across the multiple forms of discursive mediation, the role of imagination in producing, just as the term implies, images of human behaviour, whether fictional or factual. Hence our preference for the variable and inclusive category of 'transgression', as opposed to the more restrictive one of 'crime', although the latter continues to dominate in scholarly studies. 'Transgression', like crime, is discursively mediated – it can be measured only by what is written or reported – but it stands in a closer (indeed intimate) relation to imagination. Insofar as it implies the crossing of boundaries, it denotes a process, rather than a fixed state. As such, it throws into relief the interventions of subjective judgement and invites a destabilizing interrogation of what it means, not just to cross those boundaries, but to put them in place.

What emerges from this collection overall, in our view, is, if not a complete picture of female transgression in the period (hardly a practical or necessarily a desirable objective), at least a series of provocative and mutually revealing

---

[5]   Garthine Walker, *Crime, Gender and Social Order in Early Modern England*, Cambridge Studies in Early Modern British History (Cambridge: Cambridge University Press, 2003), esp. 5–6.

snapshots – some panoramic, some close up, and taken from a variety of angles. Those angles continue to reflect, we readily acknowledge, one persistent disciplinary divide that carries the weight of consensus: what constitutes 'early modern' for literary historians tends to be bounded at the end of the seventeenth century, if not before, while most social historians extend the period by another hundred years or so. This is a question no doubt deserving interrogation in itself – such as it has notably received recently, indeed, from Merry Wiesner-Hanks.[6] Wiesner-Hanks is chiefly concerned, however, to redeem the category of 'Renaissance' – or, as most English-speaking scholars now prefer, early modern – conventionally dated from 1500, from assimilation into the Middle Ages.[7] This is a position which our essays serve to bolster, implicitly or explicitly, by documenting forms of female subjectivity and agency distinct from medieval antecedents. Within each of our two sections we have arranged essays in the chronological order, approximately, of the material they deal with, but also, insofar as is possible, in such a way as to proceed from more general issues to narrower topics and so allow our readers' 'reading back' to flow in a variety of clearly defined channels.

I

The broad thesis that cultural sectors of profound taboo increasingly attach themselves to women in the early modern period in ways that evolve towards criminal stigmatization is illustrated, in various ways, by the five essays comprising Part I of this collection. First, Richard Hillman takes up *Pericles* (c. 1607), Shakespeare's dramatic adaptation (probably with George Wilkins) of the venerable Apollonius of Tyre romance, of which numerous versions exist from the early medieval period, with a late Hellenistic novel doubtless lying behind them. Father-daughter incest serves as the mainspring of the plot, posing both a physical and a less tangible moral danger to the hero. As has been widely recognized, the motif carries a strong mythical charge. Commentators have neglected, however, a sharp departure from the sources. The intensity of the play's treatment of incest is actually reinforced by making Antiochus's daughter, not the unequivocal victim of paternal aggression, as in all the medieval precursor texts – including the fourteenth-century version of John Gower, formally acknowledged within the play as its immediate source – but the willing partner of her father in a mutual crime.

Hillman proposes that the playwrights may have taken their cue on this point from a contemporary retelling of the Apollonius story by François de Belleforest in his *Histoires tragiques* (vol. 7), where the French popular author likewise faces the challenge of adapting his medieval *exemplum* to early modern cultural conditions. The latter are partly stylistic, entailing the more 'realistic' expectations of the

---

[6]   Merry E. Wiesner-Hanks, 'Do Women Need the Renaissance?', in *Gender and Change: Agency, Chronology and Periodisation*, ed. Alexandra Shepard and Garthine Walker (Chichester: Wiley-Blackwell, 2009), 109–32.

[7]   Wiesner-Hanks, 'Do Women Need the Renaissance?', esp. 116–25.

public. But there is an ideological component as well. As both the Continental *histoire tragique* and the English theatre abundantly demonstrate, the fictional criminalization of women, especially by way of their sexual behaviour, reflects a broad misogynistic tendency, which, in turn, registers cultural anxieties such as are apt to surface when a culture is undergoing profound change. At the same time, even in rendering the story's women more actively responsible for evil – and this effect extends beyond the incestuous daughter to a murderous older woman analogous to Lady Macbeth – the versions of Belleforest and Shakespeare develop them as agents and subjects. This matches both authors' treatment of the vitally important positive female figures of the story. In the two early-modernizing versions, the virtuous wife and daughter of the protagonist are developed well beyond the passive emblematic figures found throughout the medieval tradition: their capacity symbolically to redeem the bereft protagonist from death to life is enriched by their endowment with will, desire, wit and intelligence.

Certainly, the redemptive actions of the women in these texts, like female crimes, are circumscribed within traditional notions of femininity: the wish-fulfilment they embody is the other side of the misogynist coin, whose more common face is a troubled and anxious one. Still, the extension of agency for better and for worse testifies to a broad reimagining of the feminine in the early modern period. In their very instability and contradictions, these texts mark a distinct transition from the medieval categories of sinner and saint towards the modern ones of the degenerate female criminal, on the one hand, the 'angel in the home', on the other. These are, needless to say, stereotypes that govern social judgements, and with them legal determinations, as to what constitutes female transgression.

Likewise returning to medieval – frankly mythical – roots as a source, and drawing on them to gauge cultural evolution, Diana Purkiss next traces the transformation of primitive anti-Semitism into the early modern obsessive fear of witches. Indeed, Purkiss suggests that the displacement of the Jew by the witch as a figure of evil was one of the distinctive imaginative features of the Reformation era. Obviously, the process entailed a broad re-gendering of transgression: the stereotypical evil Jew was masculine, witches (in the overwhelming majority) feminine.

Illustrating this process of displacement involves, as in Hillman's essay, an interest in Lady Macbeth, but Purkiss is particularly concerned with the treatment of bodies in Shakespeare's tragedy. Four buried sets of 'stories' about bodies and markings in the play are explored: the story of relics, fragments and 'rubbish'; the story of child-murder as a means to supernatural power; the story of the hard body, impervious to feeling, and its power to do violence to other bodies; and the way in which all these stories exchange themselves between papists, Jews and witches, groups defined as misusers of bodies. *Macbeth* thereby becomes readable as an interrogation of the ways in which heaven and earth touch at the point of the dead body, marking its substance forever with the will of the supernatural. It is also a record in the sense of being a criminal record, as stories of Jewish child-murder, host-theft and witches' murder of infants coalesce in the single criminally signed figure of Lady Macbeth.

The exploration of witch figures is sustained by Pauline Ruberry-Blanc in her study of a play from the 1620s based on a recent sensational criminal case. *The Witch of Edmonton*, co-authored by Thomas Dekker, John Ford and William Rowley, stages the transgression of (and around) Elizabeth Sawyer, who was tried and condemned as a witch and executed at Tyburn in April 1621, some months before the play was performed. This essay is premised on the existence of two divergent but complementary critical approaches: one emphasizing the historical/ sociological causation of the female criminality portrayed, the other privileging the demonological dimension in relation to contemporary beliefs. Ruberry-Blanc proposes a synthesis of these approaches imbricating documented folkloric elements with both aspects of the play. Central to her discussion, as to the dramatic experience itself, is the staging of the devil in the guise of a large black dog.

In this view, the social picture presented by the play – essentially, that of a poor and ugly old woman blamed for economic and personal losses in the rural milieu of Edmonton – is complicated and enriched by a metaphysical dimension developed through the relation between the witch and the diabolic animal. The latter proves to have a 'real' counterpart in East Anglian folklore, according to 'eye-witness' records. These intersect with contemporary published accounts of Sawyer's case, where a dog is specified as being her 'familiar'. The playwrights, however, fundamentally transform this material, using it to engage supernatural machinery surprisingly reminiscent of Christopher Marlowe's dramatic treatment of the intellectual sorcerer, Dr Faustus, and offering a similar challenge to received doctrines, both religious and social.

Next, with an essay by Frédérique Fouassier-Tate, the focus shifts from the witch to the most common type of female sexual transgressor – the prostitute. Fouassier-Tate studies the paradox at the heart of the construction of the figure of the prostitute in Renaissance England. The official discourse of the period uses negative definition to ostracize the prostitute. She is carefully described as being everything the official discourse is not, whether in terms of space, religion or social status. She thereby stands out as the negative pole indispensable to the definition of the positive, dominant values. If the prostitute has to be ostracized, it is because she is dangerously similar, since she stands for the world of the body, for potentially anarchic forces constantly threatening to overflow, which the official discourse bears within itself. Given the weight of her negative dimension, the prostitute naturally emerges as a convenient scapegoat. The perception of the – often stereotyped – character of the prostitute is further complicated by the fact that the world of the theatre (except for its audiences) was an exclusively male one in Renaissance England. The prostitute often appears as a source of laughter in plays, but if laughter excludes, it is also potentially subversive, and playwrights were far from always endorsing the values of the official discourse.

The final contribution, by Pascale Drouet, to 'Imag(in)ing Female Transgression and Transgressors' is also concerned with the dramatic fictionalization of an actual woman – this time, however, a fictionalization which absolves a 'real' criminal (and sexual transgressor) by making her not only the touchstone of satirical social commentary but also the effective instrument of orderly social relations, even of romantic fulfilment within a comic scheme. This is to harness subversively, in a sense, the cultural energy attached to transgressive behaviour, which in the real world tends to lead, as in the case under study, to less exalted – and certainly not comic – outcomes.

'Moll Cutpurse' was the underworld nickname of a certain Mary Frith, but the sobriquet inadequately conveys the whole range of the historical person's eccentric attitudes and illegal practices. Frith was accused, and at times convicted, of thieving, but also of a range of other criminal and social transgressions. The highly theatrical confession of her offences against convention, which resulted in her imprisonment in Bridewell, was recorded in *The Consistory of London Correction Book* as early as January 1611. In the same year, Thomas Middleton and Thomas Dekker's city comedy, *The Roaring Girl, or Moll Cut-Purse*, was performed at the Fortune Theatre, thereby transmitting a portrait of Frith and her persona to posterity. A couple of years after her death, in 1662, her misdemeanours were revived in an anonymous volume containing both a biography and a supposed autobiography: *The Life and Death of Mistress Mary Frith, alias Moll Cutpurse,* and *Moll Cutpurse's Diary.*

How was Frith represented, romanticized, appropriated and capitalized upon in the Jacobean play and the Restoration volume, both of which stray from the historical data known to us? This essay first concentrates on the fleeting references to her chastisement in both *The Roaring Girl* and *The Life and Death of Mistress Mary Frith* to show to what extent the facts are watered down, displaced, subverted or appropriated; in so doing, it addresses the relationship between punishment and performance, and unveils the implicit ideologies of the respective playwrights and authors. The focus then shifts to the various phases of the reversal strategy employed: Moll as a mediator between the city and its underworld, as a protector of the oppressed, as a castigator of male crimes (even a virtual warrior-woman!), and finally as a conservative subject. The objective is to trace the ways in which the original criminal figure, Protean and elusive, gives way, through the operations of mimesis, to a sort of popular mythical construct. During her lifetime, at least, interpreters of that construct had a rare opportunity to read myth back into, and against, reality, according to the third stage in Ricœur's theory of mimetic process.

II

'Reading (into) the Social Picture' begins with three essays concerned with female violence – a form of transgressive behaviour which, if generally less imaginatively engaging than sexual deviation, more concretely preoccupied the judicial system and certainly also became the object of discursive representation, beginning with the statutes themselves. Marisha Caswell first deals with the effect of marital status on the judicial treatment accorded to two forms of female offences in early modern London: husband-murder and infanticide. To modern eyes, the former crime is readily assimilable to other forms of homicide, which may sometimes appear justified, while the latter – and the figure of Hetty Sorel in George Eliot's *Adam Bede* may stand as typical of its post-romantic fictional representation – appears as one of the most horrific female transgressions. We learn, however, that the early modern period did not view matters in this light, and that, even though the principle of coverture was not supposed to apply (see the chapter by Krista Kesselring on this legal doctrine), marital status played an important role in homicide trials.

A comparison of married women accused of these crimes reveals some interesting statistics. According to the records of the Old Bailey (both the Old Bailey Papers and the Ordinary's Accounts), 18 married women were accused of infanticide under the 1624 statute, and juries acquitted all of them solely because they were married. Conversely, a woman's marital status transformed the killing of her husband from murder into a form of treason (however 'petty'), and women accused of this crime faced the highest conviction rate for married women accused of homicide. Thus a woman's marital status excused her actions in one case, but exacerbated them in another. Moreover, the influence of marital status went further than these statistics. The treatment, perceptions and experiences of these women were also influenced by larger understandings about acceptable behaviour, while what was acceptable was, in turn, determined in large part by marital status.

James Sharpe at once broadens the issue to include female violence more generally (though the concentration is still on murder) and narrows the field of enquiry by concentrating on the records of the Cheshire Court of Great Sessions between 1600 and 1800 (supplemented by the archives of the Cheshire Quarter Sessions and, from the mid-eighteenth century, reports of violent crime in Cheshire newspapers). His conceptual framework owes much to the insight of anthropologist David Riches that in studying violence we must consider three groups of people: perpetrators, victims and witnesses. The significance of this last group is frequently missed by historians of crime, yet it is witnesses who are likely to prove the richest source of discursive material, not only telling us what (supposedly) happened but inevitably shaping their narratives according to cultural biases – often with a large imaginative overlay, as in the 'eye-witness' accounts of supernatural phenomena discussed by Ruberry-Blanc.

Sharpe's findings concern, in the first instance, the ways in which women contributed peripherally, rather than as principal participants, to the judicial investigation of cases of infanticide, in which distinctively female forms of knowledge were often indispensable. As it emerges through the surviving narratives, their role, which he designates as 'pre-official', points to the existence of a community of female interests and exchanges which this archetypically female crime was especially likely to activate.

The sense of such a community as integral to the social fabric is sustained by the second and third parts of Sharpe's study. These entail analysis of the depositions of women initially in cases of homicide with women as victims, then in cases involving the killing of men by men. The Cheshire materials reveal a distinct female voice in the representation of violent behaviour. They also shed light on the role women played in attempting to defuse (or on occasion encourage) acts of violence, and in encouraging prosecution.

Finally, within this sequence concerned with women and violence, Anne-Marie Kilday shifts the field of enquiry to Scotland and likewise explores issues of culture and gender by way of judicial archives. The notions of femininity promulgated in early modern England through treatises and pamphlet literature helped to develop stereotypical and gendered ideas about how women should behave within the confines of polite and public society – a point amply made by the studies of Fouassier and Drouet. Obviously, similar recommendations were made north of the border, whose gist was to impose characteristics such as submissiveness, gentility, domesticity and maternity on all women regardless of age or class. Indeed, the actions and sermons of the Church of Scotland are well known for promoting such ideals throughout 'North Britain' with particular rigour and insistence.

One might have supposed that the presence of this extra-judicial arm in Scotland would have had the result of rendering the behaviour of women relatively non-violent, by comparison with that of men. Such a conclusion would conform, moreover, to the general tendency among historians of English criminality to downplay the importance of female violence, on the grounds both of the smaller number of women accused of such crimes and of the lesser degree of brutality involved in their perpetration.

This essay calls such a conclusion into question, at least with regard to the experience of women in lowland Scotland. Employing records of the Scottish Justiciary Court to examine violent female criminality between 1750 and 1815, it reconfigures and challenges the assumption that criminal women were timid, non-threatening and commonly acting at the behest of men. Case studies of homicide and assault, in particular, are used as a basis for comparing the level of violence in male and female criminality. The special provisions of the Scottish legal system are taken into account, and the transgressive behaviour of the women involved is considered in the context of the social and economic factors prevailing in their environment. The evidence from these Scottish cases is strong against assuming less aggressiveness in female than in male criminal behaviour, and it is equally apparent that Scottish women deserve closer attention than they have so far received in the growing body of literature dealing with crime and criminality in the pre-modern period.

The way in which female deviance was perceived by society is also the preoccupation of Jennine Hurl-Eamon in an essay which returns to the issue of transgressive sexuality and its consequences – notably, the production of illegitimate children. Like prostitution, bastardy itself was not a crime, but it cast a criminal pall over those associated with it. This essay looks at the social and legal contexts of bastardy through the lens of one particular group – military couples – and against the background of popular stereotypes.

Again, we discover a significant and revealing divergence between the reality and its representation. Common soldiers and their women were frequently portrayed as behaving with a sexual licence and debauchery that would naturally lead to illegitimate pregnancy. Such unwed mothers were furthermore regarded as prone to malicious allegations against innocent men. This essay argues that the real circumstances of military bastards' conception could be quite different from external impressions. Contemporary testimony given to parish poor relief officials shows that low-ranking soldiers often entered into long-term relationships with women who considered themselves their wives in all but law. The fruit of such liaisons were bastards only in the eyes of the state, and military men often accepted their offspring and remained with the women through repeat pregnancies. This particular group of bastard-bearing women considered themselves to be in permanent, faithful relationships, in stark contrast to the women impregnated by officers or even most civilian men. From their own testimony to bastardy examiners, their petitions to the state, and, to a lesser extent, their autobiographies, soldiers' female companions offer an interpretation of illegitimacy markedly distinct from the standard.

The final essay in this collection, by Krista Kesselring, continues to consider the relation between legal theory and social practice, but steps back to look at a situation in which women were sanctioned for the offences of others. Throughout much of English history, the law punished felons not just with death but also with the forfeiture of their land and possessions. Operating in conjunction with the legal notion of coverture, which vested a wife's property in her husband, forfeiture for felony had devastating effects on the wives of male convicts. Kesselring's essay explores the consequences of the confluence of these two legal practices in the long centuries before forfeiture's abolition in 1870, with particular focus on the early modern period. It discusses the ways in which this confluence affected both the creation and the enforcement of criminal law: concerns about protecting the dower of the widows of criminals prompted legislation as early as 1547 that changed the centuries-old practice of forfeiture, but did similar concerns manifest themselves in jury verdicts, serving as yet another factor in 'jury nullification' – perhaps the most radical act of interpretation possible – of an unbending criminal law?

The essay also investigates the intersection between legal fact and the discourse it generated by discussing wives' strategies for evading or mitigating forfeiture: from the desperate woman who argued that she had only cohabited with and never properly married her murderer-lover, to the women who engaged in elaborate fraudulent conveyances of their marital property, scattered court records show women of the early modern period artfully subverting the strictures of coverture and forfeiture. Ultimately, the essay establishes the centrality of women themselves to discussions of this ancient and long-lived criminal punishment, which effectively imposed transgression upon them. From the sixteenth century through to the nineteenth, the effects of felony forfeiture on the wives of offenders generated interpretive responses, serving as the basis for both the main defences and the key criticisms of forfeiture: for some, it was precisely the effects on wives that justified the retention of a practice founded in feudalism but now reformulated as an effective deterrent; for others, these effects offered the surest evidence that forfeiture was an unjust punishment that penalized the innocent rather than the guilty.

III

With the concluding piece by Kesselring, the essays in this volume complete the tracing, in one sense, of a lengthy (if tortuous) trajectory, passing from more-or-less fanciful popular imaginings about transgressive women to a 'higher' level of discourse composed of considered social and political responses to real questions of justice. To be reminded that criminal forfeiture was abolished only in 1870, however, so that only then did women cease in effect to be criminalized for the behaviour of their husbands, is to be struck by the stubborn persistence of imaginative factors in the criminal treatment of women throughout the early modern period – if not beyond. More particularly, it is to confirm (if confirmation were needed) that women's transgressive behaviour has historically been conceived, measured, conditioned – and often constructed – in relation to their place within patriarchal societies. It seems prudent, finally, to renounce any claim to have traced a trajectory and simply to reaffirm our opening metaphor: that of a series of richly complementary snapshots, whether fiction or fact provides foreground or background. The images themselves are capable, no doubt, of being arranged in different orders and patterns, but they unmistakably belong to the same album – one that chronicles a richly reflective aspect of the cultural history of early modern Britain.

Works Cited

Secondary Sources

Clark, Sandra. *Women and Crime in the Street Literature of Early Modern England.* Basingstoke, Hampshire: Palgrave Macmillan, 2003.

Davis, Natalie Zemon. *Fiction in the Archives: Pardon Tales and Their Tellers in Sixteenth-Century France.* Stanford, CA: Stanford University Press, 1987.

Dolan, Frances E. *Dangerous Familiars: Representations of Domestic Crime in England.* Ithaca, NY: Cornell University Press, 1994.

———. 'Tracking the Petty Traitor across Genres'. In *Ballads and Broadsides in Britain, 1500–1800.* Edited by Patricia Fumerton, Anita Gerrini, Kris McAbee et al. Farnham, Surrey: Ashgate, 2010. 149–72.

Gossman, Lionel. *Between History and Literature.* Cambridge, MA: Harvard University Press, 1990.

———. 'History and Literature: Reproduction or Signification'. In *The Writing of History: Literary Form and Historical Understanding.* Edited by Robert H.

Canary and Henry Kozicki. Madison: University of Wisconsin Press, 1978. 3–39.

———. 'The Rationality of History'. In *Between History and Literature*. Cambridge, MA: Harvard University Press, 1990. 285–324.

Gowing, Laura. *Domestic Dangers: Women, Words, and Sex in Early Modern London*. Oxford: Clarendon Press, 1996.

Martin, Randall. *Women, Murder, and Equity in Early Modern England*. Routledge Studies in Renaissance Literature and Culture, 10. London: Routledge, 2008.

Ricœur, Paul. *Time and Narrative*. Translated by Kathleen McLaughlin and David Pellauer. 2 vols. Chicago: University of Chicago Press, 1984–85.

Scott, Joan W. 'The Evidence of Experience'. *Critical Inquiry* 17.4 (1991): 773–97.

Staub, Susan C. *Nature's Cruel Stepdames: Murderous Women in the Street Literature of Seventeenth Century England*. Pittsburgh, PA: Duquesne University Press, 2005.

Walker, Garthine. *Crime, Gender and Social Order in Early Modern England*. Cambridge Studies in Early Modern British History. Cambridge: Cambridge University Press, 2003.

White, Hayden. *The Content of the Form: Narrative Discourse and Historical Representation*. Baltimore, MD: Johns Hopkins University Press, 1987.

———. 'The Historical Text as Literary Artifact'. In *The Writing of History: Literary Form and Historical Understanding*. Edited by Robert H. Canary and Henry Kozicki. Madison: University of Wisconsin Press, 1978. 41–62.

Wiesner-Hanks, Merry E. 'Do Women Need the Renaissance?'. In *Gender and Change: Agency, Chronology and Periodisation*. Edited by Alexandra Shepard and Garthine Walker. Chichester: Wiley-Blackwell, 2009. 109–32.

Wiltenburg, Joy. *Disorderly Women and Female Power in the Street Literature of Early Modern England and Germany*. Feminist Issues: Practice, Politics, Theory. Charlottesville: University Press of Virginia, 1991.

PART I
Imag(in)ing Female Transgression and Transgressors

Chapter 1
Criminalizing the Woman's Incest: *Pericles* and Its Analogues

Richard Hillman

This essay ventures warily into a vast cultural issue by way of a narrow textual, or rather intertextual, study. Such a procedure may be common these days, but it is as well to be sensitive to the risks and limitations: I prefer to treat the limited evidence with circumspection, and not to push it too far. For at stake, finally, is nothing less than a paradigm shift from medieval to early modern conceptions of female transgression – and more broadly of agency – as this may be traced, I propose, through intertextual presences within a Jacobean dramatic text, one which amounts, more clearly than most, to a palimpsest comprising past and contemporary narrative inscriptions. On the question of periodization, a vexed one for many scholars, I take comfort (if not refuge) in the defence of a meaningful cultural shift offered by Merry Wiesner-Hanks, who resolutely answers her own question – 'Do Women Need the Renaissance?' – in the affirmative.[1] On the other hand, Wiesner-Hanks is not particularly concerned to link the cultural narrative to an evolution in the narrative (much less the dramatic) representation of female figures, and, given the exceptionally rich opportunity presented by the intertexts in question here, it is this link I seek to develop.

Critics of *Pericles* (c. 1607[2]), Shakespeare's dramatic adaptation (probably in collaboration with George Wilkins) of the venerable story of Apollonius of Tyre,[3] have long been fascinated by the incest motif. By way of the episode initiating the action, the motif serves as the mainspring of the adventure plot that ensues:

---

[1] Merry E. Wiesner-Hanks, 'Do Women Need the Renaissance?', *Gender and Change: Agency, Chronology and Periodisation*, ed. Alexandra Shepard and Garthine Walker (Chichester: Wiley-Blackwell, 2009), 109–32.

[2] The Quarto text, on which all subsequent versions are based, dates from 1609, and the play was probably staged shortly before. It is not included in the 1623 First Folio of Shakespeare's collected works, a fact which has encouraged debate and conjecture about the work's authorship. This issue does not concern me here, but I accept the premise of collaboration and refer to the authors in the plural.

[3] See Elizabeth Archibald, *Apollonius of Tyre, Medieval and Renaissance Themes and Variations: Including the Text of the* Historia Apollonii Regis Tyri *with an English Translation* (Cambridge: Cambridge University Press, 1991), for a valuable survey of the story's circulation, from the late classical period and throughout the Middle Ages, in its numerous variant forms, although many details necessarily remain uncertain.

Pericles, Prince of Tyre, risks his life at Antioch in an attempt to found a royal dynasty by marrying the beautiful daughter of King Antiochus; to gain her, he has to answer a dangerous riddle – his predecessors have paid for their failure with their lives – but the true answer which he discovers also reveals the incestuous relation of the father and daughter. Thereupon Pericles must flee for his life, symbolically abandoning, along with his kingdom, his very identity, all sense of self. This is, then, the first and foremost of a long succession of lessons in love and life administered, like most effective lessons in romance, through painful loss but finally recompensed, as the genre will also have it, through restoration. In finally recovering his supposedly deceased daughter and wife, Pericles dispels the shadow of death and corrects the perverse confusion of human and sexual bonds enacted by Antiochus and his daughter, who, meanwhile, are duly destroyed by a divinely dispatched lightning bolt.

As presented in the dramatic version, the episode is enriched by insistent overtones of the Fall of Man, through female and ultimately diabolic seduction, into the knowledge of good and evil – and, pointedly, into mortality. The play presents a brash young prince dazzled by specious beauty ('As heaven had lent her all his grace' [I.0.24]), self-assured to the point of defying mortality itself ('Think death no hazard in this enterprise' [I.i.5]), and *knowing* his mortal limits less profoundly than he claims: 'Antiochus, I thank thee, who hath taught / My frail mortality to know itself' (42–43).[4] As Pericles approaches the 'golden fruit ... dangerous to be touched' and guarded by 'death-like dragons' (29, 30), his language ominously implicates him in the dynamic of seduction by sin set in motion by father and daughter, acting in discordant concert:

> You gods that made me man, and sway in love,
> That have inflamed desire in my breast
> To taste the fruit of yon celestial tree
> Or die in the adventure, be my helps,
> As I am son and servant to your will,
> To compass such a boundless happiness. (20–25)

Pagan though the setting remains, the dramatic hero's encounter with incest thus gains impact from a conspicuous overlay of Christian mythology.

This effect is part of the 'early modernizing' tendency the present essay seeks to document, but it works by enhancing the taint of taboo and the force of folklore already attached to the incest motif, which is central within the Apollonius narrative tradition generally.[5] Recently, Deanne Williams has usefully reopened

---

[4]   The play is cited throughout from William Shakespeare and George Wilkins, *Pericles*, ed. Suzanne Gossett, The Arden Shakespeare, 3rd ser. (London: Thomson Learning, 2004).

[5]   See Arthur R. Heiserman, *The Novel before the Novel: Essays and Discussions about the Beginnings of Prose Fiction in the West* (Chicago: University of Chicago Press, 1977), 216.

the play along its fraught incestuous fold by invoking this tradition, although she may overstate (if not outright mistake) what she calls the 'important departure from the play's sources' represented by Pericles's less-than-forthright response to Antiochus, which she takes to provide a significant connection to the subsequent action.[6] The sources in question, as formally recognized by criticism, are two. They are, most influentially, the fourteenth-century poetic rendition by John Gower included in his vast dream-vision compilation, *Confessio Amantis*. This version generally follows the line laid down by the *Historia Apollonii Regis Tyri*.[7] Comparison with *Pericles* is not merely authorized but imposed by the deployment of the poet 'John Gower' himself to serve as Chorus within the play. Now widely acknowledged as a subordinate source, especially for the tribulations of the hero's daughter, is the Elizabethan novelistic reworking by Laurence Twyne, *The patterne of painefull aduentures* (putatively first published in 1576, reissued in 1594 and 1607); the latter was based, not on Gower's version, but, with basic fidelity, on the widely diffused thirteenth-century narrative incorporated in the *Gesta Romanorum* (from which Gower also took some details).[8] *Pace* Williams, on the point of the hero's response to the riddle of Antiochus, there is, in fact, an essential concordance between the dramatic version and the traditions of the *Historia* and *Gesta*, as represented by Gower and Twyne, respectively.[9]

---

[6] Deanne Williams, '"Papa Don't Preach": The Power of Prolixity in *Pericles*', *University of Toronto Quarterly* 71 (2002): 603.

[7] On the versions that Gower was – and claimed to be – adapting (notably the *Pantheon* of Godfrey of Viterbo), see G. C. Macaulay, ed., *The English Works of John Gower*, 2 vols, Early English Text Society Extra Series (London: Oxford University Press for the EETS, 1900), vol. 2, 536–38; cf. Archibald, *Apollonius*, 192–93. Macaulay's edition is used throughout for citations from *Confessio Amantis* (by book and line numbers).

[8] The edition cited in this essay is *The patterne of painefull aduentures. Containing the most excellent, pleasant and variable historie of the strange accidents that befell vnto Prince Apollonius, the Lady Lucina his wife, and Tharsia his daughter, etc.* (London: Valentine Simmes, 1607). On the recognized borrowings from Twyne, see especially F. D. Hoeniger, introduction to *Pericles*, by William Shakespeare, The Arden Shakespeare, 2nd ser. (London: Methuen, 1963), xvi, and Roger Warren, introduction to *A Reconstructed Text of Pericles, Prince of Tyre*, by William Shakespeare and George Wilkins (text prepared by Gary Taylor and Macd. P. Jackson), The Oxford Shakespeare (Oxford: Oxford University Press, 2003), 14–16. Still, Hoeniger (introduction, xvi, n. 2) allows for the possible influence of some other version of the *Gesta*, as does Archibald, *Apollonius*, 1991, 214. There is general agreement that the cognate novel of George Wilkins, *The painfull aduentures of Pericles prince of Tyre Being the true history of the play of Pericles, as it was lately presented by the worthy and ancient poet Iohn Gower* (London: T. P[urfoot] for Nat. Butter, 1608), derives from a combination of Twyne with reminiscence of the theatrical performance. I have not found it useful to include the work systematically in the present discussion.

[9] In order to maintain that 'it is the hero's utter refusal to testify to the incest at Antioch that supplies the motivation for the play as a whole', Williams draws a particular distinction with what she calls the 'fearless verbal exposition of the riddle' ('"Papa Don't

There is, however, another striking departure from the sources which commentators have not made much of. In keeping with the biblical allusions, with their insinuation of female culpability, the play makes Antiochus's daughter the willing partner of her father in a mutual act of transgression. Elsewhere, by contrast, she is unequivocally his victim. Not just in Gower's and Twyne's versions but across the narrative tradition, the sexual initiation of the daughter is depicted straightforwardly as a rape. Concomitantly, her suffering, shame and despair – to the point of inducing thoughts of suicide – are powerfully evoked. The play, however, entrusts the episode to the choric mediation of Gower, who makes it a matter of seduction ('provoke' and 'entice' are his key words), then complicity, offering no suggestion at all of the daughter's victimization or even reluctance:

> the father liking took
> And her to incest did provoke.
> Bad child, worse father, to entice his own
> To evil should be done by none.
> But custom what they did begin
> Was with long use account' no sin. (I.0.25–30)

The moral blindness of both parties is clearly presented as both cause and effect of their 'sin', and we are thereby prepared to see the tainting of the hero by his contact with the incest as more than symbolic or mythical. Rather, it points up his own need for better judgement, finer discrimination, which painful experience must supply. For Pericles, too, has his perspicacity numbed by sensuality – to the point

---

Preach"', 603) by Gower's Apollonius. The lines she cites, however – 'Unto the king he hath ansuerd / And hath rehersed on and on / The pointz' (8.420–22) – more probably mean that the prince began his answer by repeating the terms of the riddle (see *OED* under 'rehearse'); when the solution is actually proffered –

> and said therupon:
> 'The question which thou hast spoke,
> If thou wolt that it be unloke,
> It toucheth al the privete
> Betwen thin oughne child and thee,
> And stand al hol upon you tuo'. (8.422–27)

– it is not notably more explicit or confrontational than in the other versions, including that of *Pericles*: 'Few love to hear the sins they love to act. / 'Twould braid yourself too near for me to tell it' (I.i.93–94). Antiochus is no less definite in the play than elsewhere that a wrong answer – not no answer at all – has been provided ('Your exposition misinterpreting' [113]). Nor is Gower's hero 'fearless' in the aftermath – on the contrary:

> This yonge Prince forth he wente,
> And understod wel what it mente,
> Withinne his hert as he was lered,
> That forto maken him afered
> The king his time hath so desmaied.
> Whereof he dradde and was espaied,
> Of treson that he deie scholde. (8.441–47)

where he mistakes desire for love, virtue for vice, death for life. He is deluded into a faith in the eternal perfection ('ever', 'never') of this notably fallen specimen of frail and contingent human nature by what he hears, as Antiochus calls, 'Music! / Bring in our daughter, clothed like a bride' (I.i.6–7), and especially by what he sees, although his conditional formulation points to the truth despite himself:

> See where she comes, apparelled like the spring,
> Graces her subjects, and her thoughts the king
> Of every virtue gives renown to men;
> Her face the book of praises, where is read
> Nothing but curious pleasures, as from thence
> Sorrow were ever razed, and testy wrath
> Could never be her mild companion. (13–19)

Such a confident display of learning and morality for the purpose of showing, with irony, how seriously the hero has got it wrong marks a distinct passage beyond the medieval pattern. Humanist principles bearing on self-knowledge and folly are suddenly at stake. This new dimension, I suggest, is not necessarily the spontaneous innovation of the English playwrights, anticipating the expectations of spectators 'born in these latter times / When wit's more ripe' (I.0.11–12), as Gower is made to say apologetically. It may conceivably represent instead their response to a recent retelling of the Apollonius story by a French author who likewise took up the challenge of adapting the medieval *exemplum* to early modern cultural conditions. The text in question, which has generally been dismissed as irrelevant to *Pericles*,[10] when it has been mentioned at all, is the extensive prose redaction of François de Belleforest (1530–83) in volume 7 of his *Histoires tragiques*, a collection first published in 1582 and reprinted several times, most lately in 1604.[11] It seems to me that this version has light to shed, if not necessarily

---

[10] No dissent is recorded from the categorical declaration of Hoeniger, 'no trace of influence can be found' (introduction, xvii). Archibald includes Belleforest's as a version that the author(s) of *Pericles* 'may have known' (*Apollonius*, 214) but does not elaborate, although she summarizes his version as 'notable both for its strong interest in psychological realism, especially in the love scenes, and for its emphasis on classical details' (208). The precise sources of Belleforest have not been identified, and, as will be apparent, I am inclined to credit him with significant innovation.

[11] The publication history of all seven volumes of the vastly popular *Histoires tragiques* of Belleforest is dauntingly complex, given their (sometimes unauthorized) reissue in various forms. See Michel Simonin, *Vivre de sa plume au XVIᵉ siècle, ou, La carrière de François de Belleforest*, Travaux d'Humanisme et Renaissance, 268 (Geneva: Droz, 1992), esp. 216–18, 283–84 and 312. Not all the editions purporting to be of volume 7 contain the Apollonius story. Except as otherwise indicated, I will be citing, by page numbers, *Histoires tragiques contenant plusieurs choses dignes de memoire, de ce qui s'est passé & de notre temps, mises en lumière, Par François de Belle-Forest, Comingeois, TOME SEPTIEME* (Rouen: Adrian de Launay, 1604), 'Histoire CXVIII', 109–206, as the

as a source, at least as an intertext, on the approach to female transgression taken by the English dramatists.

By the early 1600s, writers for the English theatres, including Shakespeare, had been making liberal use for some time of the *histoires tragiques* in wide European circulation. Of course, the form was recognizably Italian in origin, and direct English translations from that language were sporadically available (notably, a minority of the stories in William Painter's collection, *The Palace of Pleasure* [1566–67]), but its diffusion, development and proliferation came primarily by way of France, as was freely acknowledged by English adapters.[12] As early as 1559, Belleforest had taken up the project, initiated by Pierre Boaistuau (1500–1566), of translating, freely embellishing and supplementing what he saw as the cruder inventions of Mattheo Bandello; the genre proved central to his practice and self-image as a professional modern author over 30 years: with a keen sense of the genre's adaptability to the tastes of the time, he devoted himself at once 'à la poétique et à la morale qui l'informent [to the poetics and the moral orientation that inform it]',[13] and he was as prolific as he was skillful. His production ran to a total of some 120 *histoires*, depending on how one counts (the counting is not facilitated by the shifting numbers assigned in the various editions).

As for Shakespeare's use of Belleforest elsewhere, the latter's name recurs in scholarly indexes and introductions but as often as not records uncertainty, given the frequent availability of the same or similar material in other places; the jury remains out even on the question of whether Shakespeare had recourse to Belleforest's treatment of the story of Hamlet (from volume 5) in reworking the old play.[14] I am convinced that consultation of Belleforest played some role in the composition of *Pericles*, and although I readily admit that there is no 'smoking gun', there is uniquely, besides numerous other resemblances which cannot be developed here, a mutual sexual crime, as well as a notably naive prince, despite his trappings of sophistication. For although Belleforest's Apollonie is initially labelled as 'autant vertueux que sçauant [as virtuous as learned]' (114), his

---

latest edition conceivably available to Shakespeare; it is listed as no. 274 in Simonin's bibliography.

[12] The point is extensively documented by René Pruvost, *Matteo Bandello and Elizabethan Fiction*, Bibliothèque de la Revue de littérature comparée, 113 (Paris: H. Champion, 1937), whose meticulous survey amounts, as he states, to 'a study ... of a French rather than of an Italian influence' (5).

[13] Simonin, *Vivre de sa plume*, 218.

[14] See Harold Jenkins, introduction to *Hamlet*, by William Shakespeare, The Arden Shakespeare, 2nd ser. (London: Methuen, 1982), 96. Ann Thompson and Neil Taylor, introduction to *Hamlet*, by William Shakespeare, The Arden Shakespeare, 3rd ser. (London: Thomson Learning, 2006), 66–77, confine themselves to speculation (Shakespeare 'may possibly have read', 'may have known', 'may have read Belleforest in French'). By contrast, Andrew Hadfield, *Shakespeare and Republicanism* (Cambridge: Cambridge University Press, 2005) does not mince words: 'This French collection, used by many English writers in the late sixteenth century, was undoubtedly Shakespeare's principal source' (187).

determination to gain the princess of Antioch flirts with serious vices – not only the blind desire of youth but a desire to possess, which stems from rivalrous pride. Belleforest takes pains to establish this quite independently of the incest, which at this point has been mentioned but not yet recounted:

> Lequel ayant ouy parler de l'extreme beauté de la fille du Roy Antiochus, & de la grande pursuitte que plusieurs faisoient pour l'auoir en mariage en deuint extremément amoureux: & comme il fut en la premiere ardeur de son adolescence, il ne pensoit aussi qu'aux moyens de paruenir à la jouyssance de chose si rare, sans aduiser au peril qui s'offroit par trop euident à ceux qui aspiroient aux nopces de ceste belle Princesse, & lequel danger procedoit de l'occasion que ie vous vay descrire.

> [He, having heard tell of the extreme beauty of the daughter of King Antiochus, and of the great endeavour that many undertook to have her in marriage, fell strongly in love with her; and since he was in the first burning of his adolescence, he also thought only of the means of arriving at the enjoyment of such a rare object, without considering the peril, all too apparent, faced by those who aspired to the hand of that beautiful princess, and what danger followed from this circumstance I will recount to you.] (114)

The prince's great learning, moreover, which in traditional versions does him great credit and stands him in good stead, does not here amount to much, since the interpretation of the riddle, as Belleforest sardonically comments (doubling the irony through a suggestive allusion), was 'si manifeste, qu'il n'y falloit point autre Oedipus pour l'esclarcir [so obvious that another Oedipus was hardly needed to elucidate it]' (122).

As for the incest itself, Belleforest's treatment confirms that the very raison d'être of the *histoire tragique* is sensationalism, an imperative that tends to transform the Horatian principle of combining delight with instruction into an uneasy blend of titillation and preaching. In his introduction, Belleforest spends a good page-and-a-half deploring incest as a sign of man's degeneration into sensual sinfulness from his first state of perfection; it thus becomes, as in *Pericles*, charged with the symbolic weight of the Fall. He excuses his need to introduce the subject at all and assures the reader (somewhat contradictorily) that he will not linger on it because he has dealt with it fully in other volumes (111). In fact, the father's compulsive attraction to and eventual rape of his daughter are then narrated at length with a remarkable (but typical) combination of prurience and emotional authenticity.

The rape itself, then, is hardly elided, as in *Pericles*. Its immediate aftermath, however, is channelled into an unequivocally culpable and diabolical complicity. This transformation is effected by way of a figure present in all the narrative accounts but not in the play – namely, the Princess's nurse, who shares the same intimacy as Juliet does with hers in Shakespeare's tragedy. In fact, the latter parallel proves surprisingly to the point.

In all the analogues, the nurse enters the girl's chamber to discover her in tears and desperate. The old woman dissuades her from killing herself; her advice is to endure the abuse because it cannot be resisted. The premise remains the unwillingness of the girl – commonly underlined in the Latin versions by variants of 'invita'[15] – and, except in Belleforest, the nurse is at least passively a positive figure, since she prevents a suicide. Gower's version is less direct on the point than others ('With that sche swooneth now and eft, / And evere wissheth after deth' [8.332–33]), but there is no ironic critique when, in keeping with the *Gesta* redactions, he refers to the nurse's 'confortinge' (8.336), any more than when Twyne recounts that she, 'weying that the young Lady gaue inkling of remedy by death, which shee much feared, beganne to asswage her griefe with comfortable wordes' (sig. Bᵛ).[16]

In Belleforest, by striking contrast, the nurse becomes an elderly 'Dame d'honneur' (117) whose lecherous disposition and immorality attract an ironic application of that title. True, in this version alone she is faced, like Friar Lawrence when he offers Juliet his 'desperate ... remedy' (*Rom.*, IV.i.52–76)[17] – or, indeed, like the Friar and the Nurse together when Romeo raises his own 'desperate hand' (III.iii.108) – with the threat of a real knife. In dramatic fashion, Belleforest's nurse wrests the knife away, then dissuades the lady 'de cette furieuse & mal conseillee volonté [from that mad and ill-advised intention]' (119).[18] In 'la consolant [consoling her]', this confidante, too, begins with the recommendation

---

[15] See *Historia Apollonii Regis Tyri*, ed. Gareth Schmeling, Bibliotheca scriptorum Graecorum et Romanorum Teubneriana (Leipzig: B. J. Teubner, 1988), redactions A, B and C, ch. 2 (2, 46, 85); Archibald, *Apollonius*, 114; and *Narratio eorum que contigerunt Apollonio Tyrio*, ed. Marcus Welser (Augsburg: Augustae Vindelicorum ad insigne Pinus, 1595), sig. A3ᵛ.

[16] The tradition appears clearly in *Gesta Romanorum* (Louvain: John of Westphalia, 1480), sig. aaᵛ, and one of its French versions, *Le violier des histoires romaines: ancienne traduction françoise des Gesta Romanorum*, ed. G. Brunet, Bibliothèque elzévirienne, 66 (Paris: P. Jannet, 1858), which is particularly insistent on the point: 'Elle la revocqua par doulces et aymables parolles de son propos insensé [She recalled her by means of sweet and gentle words from her mad intention]' (326).

[17] With the exception of *Pericles*, I cite Shakespearean texts from *The Riverside Shakespeare*, ed. G. Blakemore Evans, J. J. M. Tobin et al., 2nd ed. (Boston: Houghton Mifflin, 1997).

[18] The repeated threats of self-stabbing in *Romeo and Juliet* (which foreshadow Juliet's ultimate suicide) are only partially and dimly anticipated in Shakespeare's immediate source, Arthur Brooke, *The Tragicall Historye of Romeus and Juliet (1562)*, in *Narrative and Dramatic Sources of Shakespeare*, ed. Geoffrey Bullough, 8 vols (London: Routledge; New York: Columbia University Press, 1964), vol. 1, 284–363; this is my edition of reference, cited by line numbers. In Brooke, no dagger is actually presented until Juliet kills herself with that of Romeus. It is tempting to take the physical intervention of the Nurse in Lawrence's cell, as prescribed in the First Quarto's stage direction ('He offers to stab himself, and Nurse snatches the dagger away' [III.iii.108 SD]), as a transformed reminiscence of the action in Belleforest.

of resignation: 'Ma dame, puis que la chose est faite, le conseil en est pris, & n'y a plus moyen de la reparer qu'en la souffrant patiemment [since the thing is done, counsel on the point has already been taken (i.e., is superfluous), and there is no longer any means of redressing it than by putting up with it patiently].' So much is paralleled, for instance, in Gower:

> To lette hir fadres fol desir
> Sche wiste no recoverir:
> Whan thing is do, ther is no bote,
> So suffren thei that suffre mote. (8.337–40)

But Belleforest's character proceeds to take a distinctive and sinister further step. First, she makes excuses for the father on the grounds of his royal status and the compelling power, even the possible divine inspiration, of his passion. Then, at once cynically and salaciously, she urges the Princess not merely to forego resistance but to exploit the situation for her own sexual pleasure. As Shakespeare's character advises Juliet to take Paris in the place of Romeo, who 'is dead, or 'twere as good he were / As living here and you no use of him' (III.v.225–26), so 'cest Megere infernale sollicita cest pauure Dame à souffrir l'inceste, & à prendre plaisir au forfait plus nuisible que la mort qu'elle vouloit se donner [that hellish Fury exhorted this poor lady to permit the incest, and to take pleasure in a crime more harmful than the death that she wished to give herself]' (120). Given the context, the epithet 'infernale' matches the execration of Juliet, who likewise would prefer death: 'Ancient damnation! O most wicked fiend' (III.v.235). But in Belleforest the execration is not the lady's, and the implication is that she finally matches her will to her father's, as in *Pericles*, and not simply out of fear, as is unmistakable in Gower ('sche dorste him nothing withseie' [8.347]).

The stereotype of the aged bawd had already served in Arthur Brooke's *The Tragicall historye of Romeus and Juliet*, where Juliet's nurse gives essentially the same advice concerning Paris and the narrator condemns her as 'naughty' (2312) for her 'wicked words' (2310). The element is an addition to Brooke's source (Boaistuau's version of the *histoire tragique* of Bandello) and part of the character's lubricious vivacity, which has long been recognized as largely Brooke's contribution.[19] What tends to confirm that Shakespeare's adaptation of

---

[19] See, e.g., Pruvost, *Matteo Bandello*, 132–33. Still, the portrait is outlined by Boaistuau – sufficiently to suggest that his 'dame d'honneur' may have tinted (or tainted) Belleforest's. (Boaistuau's narrative, after all, had been incorporated in Belleforest's first volume of *Histoires tragiques*.) The nurse's association with the desire of the heroine develops from the point when the latter, eager to identify the young man she has encountered, 'appella une vieille dame d'honneur qui l'avoit nourrie et eslevée de son laict [summoned an old waiting-woman who had nourished and raised her with her milk]' (Pierre Boaistuau, *Histoires tragiques*, ed. Richard A. Carr, Société des textes français modernes [Paris: H. Champion, 1977], 72). The culmination is the woman's urging the couple to bed (81). She is herself finally banished from Verona for concealing the marriage (118–19) – a passive

Brooke was inflected by Belleforest's story of Apollonius is his displacement of the Nurse's counsel from its position in the poem. There it is offered repeatedly ('dayly' [2312]) when neither wanted nor needed: Juliet has already received the potion from Friar Lawrence and is simply buying time by deluding her entourage.[20] Shakespeare moves the detail where it is dramatically effective in establishing Juliet's isolation – namely, to the moment of crisis immediately after the confrontation with her enraged father, who imposes a hasty marriage with Paris. The Nurse's intervention is thereby associated with Capulet's assault, which, besides unwittingly raising the spectre of bigamy, resounds with overtones of sexual aggression quite accessible to contemporary audiences. (*The Atheist's Tragedy* puts the point starkly: 'Why, what is't but a rape to force a wench / To marry, since it forces her to lie / With him she would not?'[21]) As for Juliet, her pain and need are acute, as with the daughter of Antiochus: 'Comfort me, counsel me!'; 'Hast not a word of joy? Some comfort, nurse' (*Rom.*, III.v.208, 211–12). 'Counsel' and 'comfort' are the key terms in the exchange (cf. III.v.230, 239). Neither occurs in Brooke's equivalent, except in the contrary sense: 'The secret counsell of her hart [from]²² nurce childe seekes to hide' (Brooke, 2290). And in flagrant contradiction of the promise of 'comfort' ('Faith, here it is ... ' [*Rom.*, III.v.212]), the response by Shakespeare's Nurse, like that of her 'consolant' counterpart in Belleforest, urges resignation ('since the case now stands as now it doth' [216]) as a springboard to counseling 'sin' (236).

The 'forfait [crime]' of the rapist-father in Belleforest – for this was the nurse's original word for it (120) – is thereby blended with that of the complicit daughter to produce a composite transgressive act. And since the instigator is herself a woman – one, moreover, who stands in the fraught role of maternal substitute – at stake is a criminal perversion of femininity that lends depth and urgency to the challenge posed to the hero's discrimination. As both the Continental *histoire tragique* and the English theatre abundantly and notoriously demonstrate, such criminalization of women, in particular by way of their transgressive sexuality, reflects a broad misogynistic tendency within early modern culture. The instances of Belleforest and *Pericles* also suggest, however, that this is, paradoxically, a step in the direction of rendering women responsible by endowing them with

---

complicity in sexual aberrance anticipating that actively urged in Brooke and Shakespeare, as well as by Belleforest's analogous figure.

[20]   See Brooke, *Romeus*, 2294–309.

[21]   Cyril Tourneur, *The Atheist's Tragedy, or, The Honest Man's Revenge*, ed. Irving Ribner, The Revels Plays (London: Methuen, 1964), I.iv.129–31.

[22]   'From' is my emendation of 'the', the reading of the 1562 edition printed by Bullough and of the other early editions; the resulting sense is clear and the diction is quite consistent with Brooke's, which is often metrically mandated. The need for correction is confirmed by the invention of a compound noun, 'The nurse-childe' (fol. 76ᵛ), which makes no better sense than the original, in the revised version of 1587 (*The tragicall historie of Romeus and* Juliet, *Contayning in it a rare example of true constancie: with the* subtill counsels and practices of an *old Fryer, and their ill euent* [London: R. Robinson, 1587]).

subjectivity and agency. And from this point of view, *Pericles* goes Belleforest a step further by eliminating the abetment of the nurse altogether in favour of an autonomous act of corrupted will on the daughter's part.

The pattern appears even in the treatment of the jealous foster-mothers who, in all versions of the Apollonius story, attempt the murder of the protagonist's daughter, when she proves more attractive and accomplished than her own. The play takes the fairy-tale stepmother figure of the tradition and makes her a recognizably human monster, albeit in cameo, on the formidable lines of Lady Macbeth – and likewise at the expense of her husband's manhood. 'I do shame / To think of what a noble strain you are / And of how coward a spirit' (IV.iii.23–25), Dionyza retorts scornfully to her husband Cleon, when he expresses horror at her deed. There is a primal, nature-altering force, as well as psychological plausibility, in her wilful insistence on her jealousy as a legitimate motive, an act of protective love:

> She did distain my child, and stood between
> Her and her fortunes. None would look on her,
> But cast their gazes on Marina's face,
> Whilst ours was blurted at and held a malkin
> Not worth the time of day. It pierced me through,
> And though you call my course unnatural,
> You not your child well loving, yet I find
> It greets me as an enterprise of kindness
> Performed to your sole daughter. (31–39)

Similarly, with the depersonalized moralizing of the fourteenth-century Gower – 'Bot wo worthe evere fals envie!' (8.1334) – may be contrasted Belleforest's near expression of awe: 'Voyez quelle est la force d'vne enuie, & ialousie feminine [See what strength there is in a woman's envy and jealousy].' There is, in this conception of a specifically feminine capacity for moral transgression, the stuff of tragic heroism such as Shakespeare develops it also (if again sketchily) in the figure of the wicked queen of *Cymbeline*.

It is equally notable, moreover, that, in what we may think of as the two early-modernizing versions, the protagonist's wife and daughter are developed well beyond the passive exemplars of virtue that are recurrent in the medieval tradition. There is no space to expand the point here, but it suffices to cite the initiatives displayed by both Thaisa and Marina at key junctures for moving the plot towards resolution, even if that resolution is inevitably measured by the symbolic restoration of identity to the hero. Thaisa, after the tournament at Simonides's court, marks the unknown knight out as her future husband regardless of her father's preference (which happens to coincide with her own – the spectre of Capulet-like outrage being generically dispelled, as 'wishes fall out as they're willed' [V.ii.16]). For her part, Marina forcefully deters and converts the customers of the brothel, then persuades the bawd to let her try an alternative course. That course leads to the encounter with her unknown father, where her persistence in the face of his impassivity, even hostile violence, produces the key revelations of identity.

Certainly, in both the play and the *histoire tragique*, women's redemptive actions, like women's crimes, remain sexually stereotyped, charged with the anxieties that especially attach themselves to the feminine at moments of cultural transition. Nevertheless, agency is unmistakably being extended along both opposing moral axes, and this balance implicitly situates female transgression within a larger dynamic of demystification and social contextualization. This may seem a peculiar phenomenon to pinpoint within the revival of romantic and fantastic tale-telling, in both narrative and dramatic forms, that swept over Europe in the late sixteenth and early seventeenth centuries. But one key to that revival may be precisely the impulse to rewrite romance according to new cultural imperatives, which were beginning to hold female transgressors accountable in a profound way, rather than simply to project stereotypes upon them. Nor can the concomitant emergence of positive agency for women be dismissed as a mere concession to tragicomic form. After all, when, for *Romeo and Juliet*, Shakespeare grafted onto Brooke's 'naughty' Nurse the propensity of Belleforest's 'Dame d'honneur' for inducing transgression at a critical moment, he also endowed a 13-year-old girl with the tragedy-engendering capacity to refuse – to assume identity, fidelity and desire alone, at the risk of her life, and to call a spade a spade: 'Ancient damnation! O most wicked fiend.'

Works Cited

Primary Sources

Belleforest, François de. 'Histoire CXVIII'. In *Histoires tragiques contenant plusieurs choses dignes de memoire, de ce qui s'est passé & de notre temps, mises en lumière, Par François de Belle-Forest, Comingeois, TOME SEPTIEME*, 109–206. Rouen: Adrian de Launay, 1604.

Boaistuau, Pierre. *Histoires tragiques*. Edited by Richard A. Carr. Société des textes français modernes. Paris: H. Champion, 1977.

Brooke, Arthur. *The tragicall historie of* Romeus and Juliet, *Contayning in it a rare example of true constancie: with the subtill counsels and practices of an old Fryer, and their ill euent.* London: R. Robinson, 1587. STC 1356.9.

———. *The Tragicall Historye of Romeus and Juliet* (1562). In *Narrative and Dramatic Sources of Shakespeare*. Edited by Geoffrey Bullough, 8 vols, vol. 1 (Early Comedies, Poems, *Romeo and Juliet*). London: Routledge; New York: Columbia University Press, 1964. 284–363.

Gesta Romanorum. Louvain: John of Westphalia, 1480.

Gower, John. *The English Works of John Gower*. Edited by G. C. Macaulay, 2 vols. Early English Text Society Extra Series. London: Oxford University Press for the EETS, 1900.

Historia Apollonii Regis Tyri. Edited by Gareth Schmeling. Bibliotheca scriptorum Graecorum et Romanorum Teubneriana. Leipzig: B. J. Teubner, 1988.

Narratio eorum que contigerunt Apollonio Tyrio. Edited by Marcus Welser. Augsburg: Augustae Vindelicorum ad insigne Pinus, 1595.

Shakespeare, William. *The Riverside Shakespeare*. Edited by G. Blakemore Evans, J. J. M. Tobin et al. 2nd ed. Boston: Houghton Mifflin, 1997.

Shakespeare, William, and George Wilkins. *Pericles*. Edited by Suzanne Gossett. The Arden Shakespeare, 3rd ser. London: Thomson Learning, 2004.

Tourneur, Cyril. *The Atheist's Tragedy, or, The Honest Man's Revenge*. Edited by Irving Ribner. The Revels Plays. London: Methuen, 1964.

Twyne, Laurence. *The patterne of painefull aduentures. Containing the most excellent, pleasant and variable historie of the strange accidents that befell vnto Prince Apollonius, the Lady Lucina his wife, and Tharsia his daughter, etc.* London: Valentine Simmes, 1607.

Le violier des histoires romaines: ancienne traduction françoise des Gesta Romanorum. Edited by G. Brunet. Bibliothèque elzévirienne, 66. Paris: P. Jannet, 1858.

Wilkins, George. *The painfull aduentures of Pericles prince of Tyre Being the true history of the play of Pericles, as it was lately presented by the worthy and ancient poet Iohn Gower*. London: T. P[urfoot] for Nat. Butter, 1608.

Secondary Sources

Archibald, Elizabeth. *Apollonius of Tyre, Medieval and Renaissance Themes and Variations: Including the Text of the* Historia Apollonii Regis Tyri *with an English Translation*. Cambridge: Cambridge University Press, 1991.

Hadfield, Andrew. *Shakespeare and Republicanism*. Cambridge: Cambridge University Press, 2005.

Heiserman, Arthur R. *The Novel before the Novel: Essays and Discussions about the Beginnings of Prose Fiction in the West*. Chicago: University of Chicago Press, 1977.

Hoeniger, F. D. Introduction to *Pericles*, by William Shakespeare. The Arden Shakespeare, 2nd ser. London: Methuen, 1963. xiii–xci.

Jenkins, Harold. Introduction to *Hamlet*, by William Shakespeare. The Arden Shakespeare, 2nd ser. London: Methuen, 1982. 1–159.

Pruvost, René. *Matteo Bandello and Elizabethan Fiction*. Bibliothèque de la Revue de littérature comparée, 113. Paris: H. Champion, 1937.

Simonin, Michel. *Vivre de sa plume au XVIᵉ siècle, ou, La carrière de François de Belleforest*. Travaux d'Humanisme et Renaissance, 268. Geneva: Droz, 1992.

Thompson, Ann, and Neil Taylor. Introduction to *Hamlet*, by William Shakespeare. The Arden Shakespeare, 3rd ser. London: Thomson Learning, 2006. 1–137.

Warren, Roger. Introduction to *A Reconstructed Text of Pericles, Prince of Tyre*, by William Shakespeare and George Wilkins (text prepared by Gary Taylor and Macd. P. Jackson). The Oxford Shakespeare. Oxford: Oxford University Press, 2003. 1–80.

Wiesner-Hanks, Merry E. 'Do Women Need the Renaissance?'. *Gender and Change: Agency, Chronology and Periodisation.* Edited by Alexandra Shepard and Garthine Walker. Chichester: Wiley-Blackwell, 2009. 109–32.

Williams, Deanne. '"Papa Don't Preach": The Power of Prolixity in *Pericles*'. *University of Toronto Quarterly* 71 (2002): 595–622.

Chapter 2
Body Crimes:
The Witches, Lady Macbeth and the Relics

Diane Purkiss

What were once norms can become crimes with frightening speed. Events, words, practices which are normal in religion, particularly, can abruptly become deadly just because they are so laden with significant power and meaning by the very stamp of authority which once authenticated them. Witchcraft, I shall argue, is among other things a dumping ground for such power-imbued norms. *Macbeth* is a play filled with bodies ineradicably signed with choices made and their visible consequences. But it is also filled with bodies that bear the marks of a recently created cultural unconscious. Once, the play sometimes seems to know, once there was a space for the body as functioning in and incorporated into a coherent culture. That culture has now been sealed over by history and can now be remembered only as a senseless and/or demonic inversion of what once was cogent and holy. The bodies of *Macbeth* are like an archaeological site; layers of sedimented story and layers of unreadable rubbish disclose themselves. The bodies in the play are inscribed with almost – but not quite – indecipherable signs of a past which has now been registered as 'the supernatural' rather than as 'religion'. What had recently been a cohesive, comprehensible and sophisticated way of understanding and speaking with the dead had become illegitimate, extracurricular, and thus could be the subject of poetry as never before because it became a way of talking slantwise, sideways, about black and deep desires. I will be exploring four buried sets of stories about bodies and markings in the play: the story of relics, fragments and 'rubbish'; the story of child-murder as a means to supernatural power, a story which is transferred from Jews to witches; the story of the hard body, impervious to feeling, and its power to do violence to other bodies; and the way all these stories exchange themselves between papists, Jews and witches, groups defined as misusers of bodies.

But to unravel at least some of that discourse implies a need to sit on exactly the same historical fault lines on which the play sits, which implies a willingness to look backwards as well as looking around. In this chapter I want to challenge what have become the complacent assumptions of historicists about chronology and to argue that poetry, including drama, may contain alluvial deposits of material and stories about material which go back much further than their author's direct historical experience, even than his or her direct reading. Books themselves contain sedimentations of the past. The topic of 'the body' carries a false immediacy, but actually thinking and reading the body is a process determined by historical forces which precede our own bodies by decades, even centuries. The chronologies historicists now often assume – of near-contemporaneity, grounded in the question, 'Could Shakespeare have known this book?' – mean that we risk overlooking the way art is equipped to respond more flexibly to history than polemic can. Historicization has come too often to ignore the long slow-burning fuse of myth and folklore in favour of faster-moving print discourses, even where these seem less relevant. And given how little we know about what Shakespeare really knew, can we really say that he didn't know anything?

These bodies of folkloric material are relevant because they continue to surface in print culture, and in Shakespeare's own reading, especially his perusal of three bodies of texts – the writings of Samuel Harsnett, which we know he read at around this time, Lucan's *Pharsalia*, with its frightening necrophiliac night-hags, and Donne's exposition of his papist family – while the motifs of paganism were paradoxically kept in circulation by the very Reformers who had hoped to stamp them out. These writings lay a powder-trail which leads back to older and darker stories which underlie and deepen – perhaps even unfairly deepen – the witch stories Shakespeare reinvents and sets in motion.

Macbeth is a play whose poetry is firmly founded on an epistemic change in thinking about the body, a change which in part gives it its charge. The first marker of that change is the decline and fall of the relic as object of worship and desire. A relic is a physical object permanently saturated by the power or personality of a saint. Because it is always already metonymic of the saint, it becomes a way to love him or her; the relic can be kissed, fondled, held, journeyed for, as one might also do for love. The saint's body, and to a lesser extent items which have been in contact with that body, bear the mark of the saint's bodily value; they are inscribed with the saint's holiness, which can be 'caught' by the venerating believer. The ultimate relic is the Eucharist, which in medieval thought *is* bodily, and which could convey the sacrificed Christ into the body of the believer. Like a relic, it could be devoured by the longing gaze of love, and then held to the lips like a lover's hand. More aggressively, of course, it was eaten – eaten even more, all the more – when believers saw in it the body of a baby, a child, a beautiful young knight.

Macbeth is littered with a transposed discourse of the body as relic, the body as lightning rod between God and earth. The fissured response to the fragments of bodies evoked by Protestant denunciations of relics becomes a way of marking off *which* bodies are illegitimately supernatural and which are holy, and the play fully explores the horror thus evoked. But for others the relic was a physical manifestation of love. The love of children for a father's ring or coat naturally extends to his body, said Aquinas, which allows us to venerate saints' bodies, too. And yet Jack Goody argues that the cult of relics was always 'characterised not only by attraction but also by repulsion, by an attachment to the dead as well as a distancing from death, which readily becomes associated with our death'.[1]

---

[1]   Jack Goody, *Representations and Contradictions: Ambivalence towards Images, Theatre, Fiction, Relics and Sexuality* (Oxford: Blackwell, 1997).

Relic-gathering and relic veneration required a deep transgression of normal rules for dealing with dead bodies. The constant troping of relics as, in Polycarp's words, 'more precious than precious stones' and the construction of reliquaries encrusted with jewels draw attention to the problem that relics are often liable to fill the sacred space with objects likely to arouse disgust. Statues surrounding relics are a way of rendering the material immaterial. The gold arm that surrounds the browned arm bones symbolizes their holy transfiguration, the light that suffuses them. But it also draws attention to the disparity between the engineered sheen and the mortal decay that overtakes the body within. The intrinsic paradox of the materiality of relics was problematic long before the Reformation. Vigilantius said, 'they worship with kisses I know not what heap of dust in a mean vase surrounded by precious linen'.[2] Jerome complained that Vigilantius had 'opened his stinking mouth, casting a load of filthy rubbish before the relics of saints', but Vigilantius was himself anxious that the saints were being conflated with filthy rubbish. Fakes were also a worry from the beginning. Martin of Tours exposed the tomb of a thief being venerated.

Just how problematic – how criminal – all this could become is visible in the following story. Rectors in the Lake District during the late Elizabethan period were dismayed to discover among their congregations both magic-users and papist sympathizers. There were people who kept the fast for St Anthony, or who wore beads; there was also a woman who buried 'a quick newt, a dog, and a quick cock', and a woman who was a healer 'for the fayries'. Finally, there was also a woman named Agnes Watson, who was reported because she 'kept a dead man's scalp'. The interesting thing about Agnes is that we cannot be certain which list to put her in; was she keeping the scalp because it was a relic of some kind? People did keep particularly sacred items after the Henrician Reformation and well into Charles's reign. Or was she keeping the scalp as a grisly trophy for use in necromancy?

That we cannot know the identity of this body part is instructive, because it points towards the ideological and cultural overlap between relics, on the one hand, and the materials of necromancy, on the other. (Necromantic use of body parts, in fact, antedates the cult of relics by many centuries.) In this story, the scalp is an isolated fragment in many senses; it is plainly metonymic, but we do not know anything of the whole from which it is taken, and hence we cannot know the power with which it is invested. Conversely, the fact that it is a *fragment* points to a link between the dismembering of the dead and iconoclasm. This linkage always troubled equations between the iconoclasts and forces of Good. In some respects, relics and their powers could be understood as a licensed form of necromancy, one in which fragments of the bodies of the dead are reanimated to curative, vatic or other miraculous purposes.

In order to understand more fully how that overlap worked and also how it came to seem frightening that bodies could be thus used, I want to consider the

---

[2]   Saint Jerome, *Lettres*, ed. Jérôme Labourt, vol. 4 (Paris: Les Belles Lettres, 1955), 201; cited by Goody, *Representations*, 91.

idea of the fetish. The word 'fetish' derives from the Portuguese word *feitica*, meaning saints' body parts. A fetish is an object specially created to carry social power. It tends to be metonymic – like the lucky rabbit's foot, which carries the luck and magic of the animal with it. The witches in *Macbeth* are fetish- and hence relic-makers, collecting and deploying fragments of personhood. The fetish allows power over the thing with which it is linked, but in a manner which is apt to collapse. The violent removal of body parts from worship – perhaps taken together with the renunciation of the doctrine of the transubstantiation – may have reinforced the civilizing process that was going on around the body and its parts, creating new categories of dirt that could then be regarded with repugnance. The nausea aroused by the dead was especially strongly stimulated by relics; indeed, Catholic Robert Bellarmine remarked that 'there is nothing that they [the Protestants] shudder at and abhor more than ... the cult of relics'.[3] Calvin's *Treatise on Relics* began the revulsion:

> [people] not only turned from God, in order to amuse themselves with vain and corruptible things, but even went on to the execrable sacrilege of worshipping dead and insensible creatures, instead of the one living God. Now, as one evil never comes alone but is always followed by another, it thus happened that where people were seeking for relics, either of Jesus Christ or the saints, they became so blind that whatever name was imposed upon any rubbish presented to them, they received it without any examination or judgment; thus the bones of an ass or dog, which any hawker gave out to be the bones of a martyr, were devoutly received without any difficulty.[4]

The association between relics and disgust was built gradually – rather, relics' grisliness was slowly uncovered and laid bare as the licence to transgress broke down. Whereas earlier denunciations of false miracles had focused on forged documents, as Langland had with his document covered with the seals of bishops, Reformers highlighted the animal origins of relics, following Chaucer and his 'sholder-boon / Which that was of an hooly Jewes sheep'.[5] Thomas More himself wrote of 'some old rotten bone'.[6] So relics are no longer metonymically linked

---

[3]   Robert Bellarmine, *Disputationes de controversiis christianae fidei adversus hujus temporis haereticos*, 4 vols (Ingolstadt: A. Sartorius, 1601), vol. 2, 826; cited by Simon Ditchfield, 'Martyrs on the Move: Relics as Vindicators of Local Diversity in the Tridentine Church', in *Martyrs and Martyrologies: Papers Read at the 1992 Summer Meeting and the 1993 Winter Meeting of the Ecclesiastical History Society*, ed. Diana Wood, Studies in Church History, 30 (Oxford: Blackwell for the Ecclesiastical History Society, 1993), 283.

[4]   John Calvin, *Treatise on Relics*, trans. Walerian Skorobohaty, Count Krasinski (Edinburgh: Johnstone and Hunter, 1854), www.godrules.net/library/calvin/176calvin4.htm (accessed 14 October 2012).

[5]   Geoffrey Chaucer, *The Canterbury Tales*, in *The Riverside Chaucer*, ed. Larry D. Benson, 3rd ed. (Boston: Houghton Mifflin, 1987), 'The Pardoner's Prologue', ll. 350–51.

[6]   Thomas More, *A Dialogue of Comfort against Tribulation*, ed. Frank Manley, vol. 12 of *The Yale Edition of the Works of St. Thomas More* (New Haven, CT: Yale University Press, 1977), 98.

to the divine, but to death and to animality, and later Calvin seeks to erase the prior marking of these bones and other bodily fragments by relabelling them as 'rubbish', unmarked bones which have been picked and discarded: 'even the smallest Catholic church has a heap of *bones* and other small *rubbish* [emphasis mine]';[7] rubbish is precisely that which has no name. Links with filth are apparent when Shaxton condemned 'stinking boots, mucky combs, ragged rochets, rotten girdles, pyld purses, great bullocks' horns, and locks of hair, and filthy rags, gobbets of wood, under the name of parcels of the holy cross'.[8] Erasmus singled out the monks' collection of linen rags, with which, 'they say, the holy man wiped the sweat from his face or neck, the dirt from his nose'.[9] Lollard attacks began this trend, describing 'worme-eten bonys ... olde ragges'.[10] Samuel Harsnett was similarly sickened by the bits of the English martyrs used in a Jacobean rite of exorcism: '*Campians* thumbe, put into *Fids* mouth ... what wonders they wrought with these poor she-deuils: how these made them to vomite, scritch, and quackle, like Geese that had swalowed downe a gagge.'[11] The association often made by Reformers between relics and the female rituals of childbirth strengthened the sense that there was something messy about the whole business of the religious and powerful body part. Thomas Cromwell's 1538 Proclamation explicitly outlawed 'offering of money, candles, or tapers to images and relics, or kissing or licking the same'.[12] The phrase exposes the implicit eroticization of veneration practices which focus on bodies and their apposition.

If an image comes to signify a body, it will partake of that body's capacity to arouse and (conversely) disgust, a fetishism paradoxically increased by the dismemberment of iconoclasm itself. The politically fraught symbol that was also the living woman Elizabeth Barton was described in terms of her own effort to make relics. Her fraudulent napkin, said to be stained by the devil's spittle, was said to be faked when Barton took soot 'and mingled it with a stinking thing, you wot

---

[7] Calvin, *Treatise*.

[8] *Visitation Articles and Injunctions of the Period of the Reformation*, 3 vols, ed. Walter Howard Frere and William McClure Kennedy (London: Longmans, Green, 1910), vol. 2, 38–39, 218, 224.

[9] Desiderius Erasmus, *The Colloquies of Erasmus*, trans. Craig R. Thompson (Chicago: University of Chicago Press, 1965), 288–89, 293–97, 301.

[10] *The Works of a Lollard Preacher: The Sermon 'Omnis plantacio', the Tract 'Fundamentum aliud nemo potest ponere' and the Tract 'De oblacione iugis sacrificii'*, ed. Anne Hudson, Early English Text Society Original Series, 317 (Oxford: Oxford University Press, 2001), 231; cited by Peter Marshall, *Religious Identities in Henry VIII's England* (Aldershot: Ashgate, 2006), 134.

[11] Samuel Harsnett, *A declaration of egregious popish impostures to with-draw the harts of her Maiesties subiects from their allegeance, and from the truth of Christian religion professed in England, vnder the pretence of casting out deuils, etc.* (London: James Roberts, 1603), 120.

[12] *Visitation Articles and Injunctions*, 3 vols, ed. Walter Howard Frere and William McClure Kennedy (London: Longmans, Green, 1910), vol. 2, 37 (The Second Royal Injunctions of Henry VIII).

what I mean'.[13] Barton's spectacular dealings with the devil, which might endanger her because they could be interpreted as witchcraft, are thus reread as a sign of the dirty female body. She is 'devilish' precisely because she 'passeth all others in devilish devices'. In contemplating this kind of figure with horror, the Reformers were half-consciously teaching their followers to 'read' relics as signifiers of necromancy. Erasmus also linked saints' lives with 'old wives tales': 'no educated or serious-minded person can read them without disgust.'[14] The witches' Sabbath involved disgusting food of the kind stigmatized elsewhere as relics/rubbish – bones of discarded animals, infants whose *hands* had been removed 'like sucking pigs' – along with other animals: horsemeat, hare, buck, ravens, crows, toads and frogs.[15] This list recalls not only the cauldron scene but also the allegations made about the true origins of fraudulent relics. Martha Nussbaum defines disgust as 'a shrinking from contamination that is associated with a human desire to be non-animal. That desire, of course, is irrational in the sense that we know we will never succeed in fulfilling it'.[16] This is effortlessly expressed through the wish to read what was once holy as merely animal. In his history of the devil, Robert Muchembled argues that there is a point where smell becomes acutely problematic, and when bodily and animal smells became a problem, they were often linked with the evil one.[17] Smell also became an index of truth about body and its evils, and hence disguising it with perfume was also sinful and duplicitous, associated with the duplicity of femininity.[18] At the very moment when cities were reorganizing

[13]   *The Statutes of the Realm, etc.*, ed. A. Luders et al., 11 vols (London, 1810–28), vol. 3, 448, 450. See also 'The Sermon against the Holy Maid of Kent and Her Adherents, Delivered at Paul's Cross, November the 23rd, 1533, and at Canterbury, December the 7th', ed. L. E. Whatmore, *English Historical Review* 58.232 (1943): 469–70; on Barton, see Diane Watt, *Secretaries of God: Women Prophets in Late Medieval and Early Modern England* (Woodbridge: D. S. Brewer, 1997), and Ethan H. Shagan, *Popular Politics in the English Reformation*, Cambridge Studies in Early Modern British History (Cambridge: Cambridge University Press, 2003), 61–88.

[14]   Desiderius Erasmus, *The Correspondence of Erasmus: Letters 1658–1801* (1526–27), trans. Alexander Dalzell, ed. Charles G. Nauert, vol. 12 of The Collected Works of Erasmus (Toronto: University of Toronto Press, 2003), 5.250.

[15]   Michael Kunze, *Highroad to the Stake: A Tale of Witchcraft*, trans. William E. Yuill (Chicago: University of Chicago Press, 1987), 276.

[16]   Martha C. Nussbaum, *Hiding from Humanity: Disgust, Shame, and the Law* (Princeton, NJ: Princeton University Press, 2004), 74.

[17]   Robert Muchembled, *A History of the Devil: From the Middle Ages to the Present*, trans. Jean Birrell (Cambridge: Polity, 2003), 221.

[18]   There have been a plethora of academic works on the topic of the rise of disgust. See William Miller, *The Anatomy of Disgust* (Cambridge, MA: Harvard University Press, 1997); Nussbaum, *Hiding from Humanity*; William A. Cohen and Ryan Johnson, eds, *Filth: Dirt, Disgust, and Modern Life* (Minneapolis: University of Minnesota Press, 2005); Emily Cockayne, *Hubbub: Filth, Noise, and Stench in England, 1600–1770* (New Haven, CT: Yale University Press, 2007). On smell, see especially Ruth Brown, 'Middens and Miasma:

themselves to exclude tanneries and shambles, the body was also reorganized as a site where smell and impingement signified moral corruption. So the filth and garbage of relics were denounced through a kind of deconstruction which sought to break links between the relic and the saint it metonymically represented. To see how all this works in more detail, we can turn to the cauldron scene in *Macbeth*, ultimately readable as an extended commentary on the cult of relics and also as a commentary on Protestant commentaries.

This is, after all, natural, for relics were seen by their critics as problematically overlapping with necromancy: 'The vilest witches and sorcerers of the earth … are the priests that consecrate crosses and ashes, water and salt, oil and cream, boughs and bones, stocks and stones.'[19] Jewel called the *agnus dei* a 'conjuration'; Pilkington called St Agatha's letters 'sheer sorcery', while the use of consecrated bells in a storm was 'witchcraft'.[20] The Lollards had spoken of 'the witch of Walsingham', referring to the powerful image of the Virgin venerated there. The Feast of the Invention of the Cross was said to be hymned by 'magic spells'. Litanies were regarded as 'nothing but an impure mass of conjuring and charming', while other prayers were also condemned as 'conjuring of God'.[21] Incantatory prayers, like relics, are gestured at in *Macbeth* and also attacked by Reformers. All of these issues were still urgent matters for dispute in the early seventeenth century. The Jesuit mission still proclaimed and used the power of relics, and there was some regret for their heyday, due to a lack of relics to cure possession.[22] Relics were kept in York Minster as late as 1695, and in countless parish churches, too.[23]

The parallels between relics and the ingredients of necromancy are made obvious in *Macbeth*'s cauldron scene. Like relics, the ingredients in the witches' cauldron of prophecy are decontextualized *bits* of animal and human bodies, detached pieces of what were once living things. The cauldron of death is an image of ruins, fragments, shards – bits of *things*, bits that suggest a whole that can never be reconstructed but can persistently be desired. We see the body parts that go into the cauldron not as part of larger wholes, but *as fragments*, in the same way that we do not see the whole beasts whose bones make up the rubbish, or the whole saint whose individual bones have become relics. And yet they are still metonyms

---

A Portrait of Seventeenth-Century Village Life in Banburyshire', *Cake and Cockhorse* 6.1 (2003): 2–8; Mark Jenner, 'Civilization and Deodorization? Smell in Early Modern English Culture', in *Civil Histories: Essays Presented to Sir Keith Thomas*, ed. Peter Burke, Brian Howard Harrison and Paul Slack (Oxford: Oxford University Press, 2000), 127–44; and Dominique Laporte, *The History of Shit*, trans. Nadia Benabid and Rodolphe El-Khoury (Cambridge, MA: MIT Press, 2000).

[19]   James Calfhill, *An Answer to John Martiall's Treatise on the Cross*, ed. Richard Gibbings for the Parker Society (Cambridge: The University Press, 1846), 17.

[20]   Keith Thomas, *Religion and the Decline of Magic* (London: Penguin, 1971), 60.

[21]   Thomas, *Religion*, 70–71.

[22]   Thomas, *Religion*, 583.

[23]   Thomas, *Religion*, 83.

of stories, still marked with those stories which prove more ineradicable than the Reformers might have hoped.

Let us take the most striking, the 'finger of birth-strangled babe / Ditch-delivered by a drab' (IV.i.30–31).[24] It recalls one of London's most prized relics, treasured carefully throughout the Edwardian Reformation and deployed as soon as Mary's reign began. This was the finger of one of the Holy Innocents, returned to St Stephen Walbrook in 1553.[25] Holy Innocents' Day was especially controversial with Reformers, because of its strong links with a particular form of misrule, the custom of electing a choirboy to be a boy bishop.[26] This transgressive rite was one in which children took on adult powers, so it is directly relevant to *Macbeth*'s cauldron scene, in which child-apparitions take power over adult Macbeth. Henry VIII specifically banned such child carnivals.[27] But what might such a story suggest about the *cauldron* except misprision? The witches' powers seem to derive not from our *knowledge* of these stories but from our forgetting of them, even our repression of them. Rubbish is also that which we would rather forget, and when relics become rubbish, the marked body resituates itself as unmarked. In this context, the witches' trafficking in relics is freighted with all the disgust Reformers intended to evoke. Relics have become rubbish, silent and storyless, heaped together apparently at random with other disgust-evoking street-sweepings. And it was when they became rubbish that their devotees became criminals.

But elsewhere, the play interests itself further in the notion that *any* kind of *body* might turn out to be a relic. Lady Macbeth, as we shall see, turns herself into a love-relic of a dead child, who is also her relic-sacrifice to gain necromantic powers. And it is in the eroticization of the relic that we begin to see another kind of imbrication of the once-sacred and the bodily. From an early stage, martyrological venerations could be troped or even practised through the register of the erotic. Lucilla in the fourth century CE is said to have kissed the bone of a martyr. Yet this kind of practice becomes acutely problematic when the licit supernatural is reimagined as illicit necromancy. The ritual kiss in witchcraft representations resembled veneration of relics. More significantly, a number of medieval romances set out to explore the way in which love makes every dead body into a relic.

---

[24] References are to William Shakespeare, *Macbeth*, ed. Nicholas Brooke, The Oxford Shakespeare (Oxford: Clarendon Press, 1990).

[25] Eamon Duffy, *The Stripping of The Altars: Traditional Religion in England 1400–1500* (New Haven, CT: Yale University Press, 1992), 384–85.

[26] Ronald Hutton, *The Stations of the Sun: A History of the Ritual Year in Britain* (Oxford: Oxford University Press, 1996), 100ff. Ritual and its disposal of the bodies of the faithful attracted criticism, too, and by the end of the Reformation era was often regarded as synonymous with fraud: see Edward Muir, *Ritual in Early Modern Europe* (Cambridge: Cambridge University Press, 2005), 175.

[27] Duffy, *Stripping of the Altars*, 186.

In Malory's *Le Morte Darthur*, the sorceress Hallewes threatens Lancelot. Hallewes inhabits a chapel, the Chapel Perilous, from which Lancelot must purloin what look like healing relics, a piece of cloth and a sword. But Hallewes threatens to turn the tables on him by making the knight himself into a relic. She offers to kiss him, and he declines; then she explains that if he had said yes, she would have preserved his dead body so as to be able to kiss and hold it in her arms every day:

> And Sir Launcelot, now I tell the: I have loved the this seven yere, [but] there may no woman have thy love but queen Guenyver; and sytthen I may not rejoyse the nother thy body on lyve, I had kepte no more joy in this worlde but to have thy body dede. Then wolde I have bawmed it and sered it, and so to have kepte hit my lyve dayes; and dayly I sholde have clypped the and kissed the, dispyte of queen Gwenyvere.[28]

It looks as if Hallewes longs for a love-relic. She plans to embalm Lancelot, dry him out, and then venerate him. This eerily necromantic ambition is also about the price of excessive love; a relic is actually a more manageable love-object than a living knight, though Hallewes makes it clear that it is her second choice. As Elisabeth Bronfen remarks, a corpse is both abject and object.[29] But her desires also mark her as a witch, and it is as such that Lancelot replies to her. 'Jesu preserve me frome youre subtyle crauftys!', replies Lancelot, which may either refer to the 'craft' of preservation or extend more generally to Hallewes and define her as a witch precisely because she is in the business of using and preserving bodies. The question is, why isn't memory enough for Hallewes? If love makes a relic of its object, then that relic should, Protestant thought tells us, be pure because mental. The act of venerating or kissing Hallewes would make Lancelot a relic.[30]

Hallewes's preservation of Lancelot as motivated by desire is expanded upon by Malory. His source, *Perlesvaus*, also called *The High History of the Holy Grail*, features a number of maidens already carrying knightly relics or questing for other relics. One maiden prepares three jewelled coffins for Gawain, Lancelot, and Percival, because they are the best knights in the world. She plans to kill them, then cut off their heads and place their bodies in the coffins. The otiose beheading signals the transformation of the knights from heroes to saints; saints' relics were often decapitated so the head alone could be presented for veneration,

---

[28] Thomas Malory, *Le Morte Darthur*, ed. Stephen H. A. Shepherd, Norton Critical Editions (New York: W. W. Norton, 2003), 1, 281, 3–20.

[29] Elisabeth Bronfen, *Over Her Dead Body: Death, Femininity and the Aesthetic* (Manchester: Manchester University Press, 1992), 12.

[30] Janet Knepper, 'A Bad Girl Will Love You to Death: Excessive Love in the Stanzaic *Morte Arthur* and Malory', in *On Arthurian Women: Essays in Memory of Maureen Fries*, ed. Bonnie Wheeler and Fiona Tolhurst (Dallas, TX: Scriptorium Press, 2001), 229–44. I am grateful to Carolyne Larrington for supplying this reference. See also Geraldine Heng, 'Enchanted Ground: The Feminine Subtext in Malory', in *Arthurian Women*, ed. Thelma S. Fenster (London: Routledge, 2000), 97–114.

as was the case with Thomas à Becket; earlier in *Perlesvaus*, we have met another maiden bearing a head encased in a reliquary and accompanying a cart in which lie the heads of 150 knights, some sealed in gold and silver, others in lead. Another maiden vows to love Lancelot in relic-like form:

> 'Ah, Lancelot,' said she, 'How hard and cruel you are to me! And it grieves me greatly that you have the sword and that things must go so well for you! For if you did not have it with you, you would never part from here of your free will, and I would have taken all my pleasure of you and had you taken back to my castle; and, powerless, you would never escape.'[31]

Here the passivity of the eroticized body mimics the stillness of the relic, just as erotic exhaustion mimics death. This passivity extends to relics as well; the physical power of the puissant knight can be appropriated by the desiring woman, just as the saint's power can be taken to work magic.

The relics here show the knight becoming an emblem of the saint, a saint of romance. There is a crossover between the desires set in motion by romances and those set in motion by veneration. The knight's survival in the face of many perils also makes him like a saint, since Jacopo de Voragine's *Legenda Aurea* often depicted saints' bodies magically resisting attempts to assault, hurt or kill.[32] By Malory's day, a woman's interaction with relics could be suspiciously erotic. Relics are characteristically venerated by kissing, so they do bring two bodies together. When that happens, the venerating or predatory woman becomes clearly marked as a sorceress.

The eroticization of both relics and images became acutely problematic for Reformers. As relics cross over from being distant objects of veneration to desirability, the idea of veneration as kissing and licking becomes problematically tinged with necrophiliac sexuality. Cromwell's 1538 Proclamation outlawing 'kissing or licking' makes worshippers sound very like the sorceress Hallewes. If an image comes to signify a body, it will partake of that body's capacity to arouse. This partially explains the new disgust the veneration of relics could arouse; it had become an eroticization of the dead. John Colet was repelled by kissing an arm with flesh still attached, and refused one of the fluid-stained rags as a gift.[33] The

---

[31] *Le haut livre du graal: Perlesvaus*, ed. William A. Nitze and T. Atkinson Jenkins (Chicago: University of Chicago Press, 1932); available in translation as *The High Book of the Grail: A Translation of the Thirteenth-Century Romance of Perlesvaus*, trans. Nigel Bryant (Cambridge: D. S. Brewer; Totowa, NJ: Rowman and Littlefield, 1978). This quotation comes from *Le Morte Darthur*, ed. Shepherd, translated by the editor from *Le haut livre du graal*, ed. Nitze and Atkinson-Jenkins, 1, 343–45, 8312–78.

[32] St Agnes, in particular, cannot be burnt, and her hair grows miraculously when she is taken to a brothel.

[33] John Colet, in Erasmus, *Colloquies*, trans. Thompson, 305, 308, 310. See also Peter Marshall, 'Forgery and Miracles in the Reign of Henry VIII', *Past and Present* 178 (2003): 39–73, and 'The Rood of Boxley, the Blood of Hailes and the Defence of the Henrician

Reformers were also troubled by the feminization, and even homoeroticization, of the body of Christ in the Eucharists that miraculously revealed themselves to be the male body of Jesus. In *Perlesvaus*, for example, the king sees the hermit 'holding in his hands a man, bleeding from his side, bleeding from his hands and feet and crowned with thorns'.[34] The 'Corpus Christi Carol' similarly places the Eucharist as a visible knight adored by a lady:

> And in that hall ther was a bede;
> Hit was hangid with gold so rede.
>
> And yn that bed ther lythe a knyght,
> His wowndes bledyng day and nyght.
>
> By that bedes side ther kneleth a may,
> And she wepeth both nyght and day.
>
> And by that bedes side ther stondith a ston,
> 'Corpus Christi' wretyn theron.[35]

This elliptical text fails to distinguish between the erotically worshipful lady and the Virgin, the church or the soul. The bleeding figure is doubly feminized, by its very bleeding and by being the passive object of the adoring gaze that is powerless to save or help, a gaze strongly reminiscent of the look to which Hallewes hopes to subject Lancelot. As Caroline Walker Bynum notes, the Jesus of the late Middle Ages was already a feminized figure.[36] Richard Rambuss has pointed to the sadomasochistic eroticization of Christ in Counter-Reformation poetry, but the same impulse can be unearthed in medieval texts, and especially in romances where the knight's struggles can metaphorize the struggles of Christ, as they do in *Perlesvaus*.[37] Finally, Alan Stewart has shown the powerfully homophobic use of slander in the reports of the Cromwellian Visitors on the monasteries.[38] The world of medieval piety was suddenly readable as erotic in a manner that especially

---

Church', *Journal of Ecclesiastical History* 46 (1995): 689–96. On the Protestant horror of the dead, see Andrew Spicer, '"Defyle not Christ's kirk with your carrion": Burial and the Development of Burial Aisles in Post-Reformation Scotland', in *The Place of the Dead: Death and Remembrance in Late Medieval and Early Modern Europe*, ed. Bruce Gordon and Peter Marshall (Cambridge: Cambridge University Press, 2000), 149–69.

[34] *Perlesvaus*, trans. Bryant, 9.

[35] 'Corpus Christi Carol', in *The Early English Carols*, ed. Richard Leighton Greene (Oxford: Clarendon Press, 1935).

[36] Caroline Walker Bynum, *Jesus as Mother: Studies in the Spirituality of the High Middle Ages* (Berkeley: University of California Press, 1982).

[37] Richard Rambuss, *Closet Devotions*, Series Q (Durham, NC: Duke University Press, 1998).

[38] Alan Stewart, *Close Readers: Humanism and Sodomy in Early Modern England* (Princeton, NJ: Princeton University Press, 1997), 44–52.

implicated one of Catholicism's most appealing features, its influence over and connections with the body.

When the host became a beautiful baby, a different kind of bodily closeness was evoked. Yet was it really so different? When Hallewes imagines herself tending Lancelot's body, the act is reminiscent not only of a lover but of a maternal, even a *pieta* figure. The maternalization of the cult of relics was disturbing too, the more so because it laid bare a potential core of maternal erotics. The overlap is enacted in the host, so that 'sometimes she happily accepted her Lord under the appearance of a child ... and sometimes in the pure and gorgeously embellished marriage bed of the heart'.[39] Wilburgis (d. 1289) took the host to her enclosure to help her avoid sexual temptation; it revealed itself as a beautiful baby who spoke to her in the words of the Song of Songs.[40] Gautier of Flos saw a baby in the host, while Dorothy of Montau internalized the beautiful babe as a mystical pregnancy. It is therefore in the host itself that the bodily overlap between erotics and maternity is sketched out. Hallewes's plan for Lancelot's body accompanies the presence in the chapel of a wounded body which recalls both Christ and the Fisher King, and her treatment of it is a work of extreme mourning. The images of baby, blood and breaking are knitted together in the Eucharist to make a disturbing eroticism also detectable when the same images are traced in *Macbeth*.

Then, too, Hallewes does not long survive her own frustrated inability to venerate the dead Lancelot. The good relic revives, but the eroticized kills in its absence. The image of the witch who has dealings with a dead body that ought properly to be sacred has origins which go beyond the cult of relics themselves. The witch who embraces and deploys dead and eroticized fragments also derives from the figure of the Jew as understood and depicted in legends and folklore. Carlo Ginzburg's story about anti-heretical and anti-witchcraft stereotypes in southwest Germany epitomizes the way the problematics of how the dead could be engaged supernaturally are tied in to questions of orthodoxy and heresy. In his tale, a heretic carried ashes of a dead child; whoever ate them became at once a member of the sect.[41]

In particular, both Jews and witches steal and desecrate hosts, turning the most precious relic of all into an object with which to perform magic, just as in any other ritual. The Nuremberg Chronicle links witches to Jews as criminals against Christendom. The witch and the Jew became interchangeable. Legends of Jewish desecration and child-murder were transferred holus-bolus from Jews to women.[42] As witches replaced Jews as problematic instances of persons whom the

---

[39] Jacques de Vitry on Mary of Oignies, cited by Bynum, *Jesus as Mother*, 59.

[40] Bynum, *Jesus as Mother*, 63. The Song of Songs is itself a text about longing and desire.

[41] Carlo Ginzburg, *Ecstasies: Deciphering the Witches' Sabbath*, trans. Raymond Rosenthal, ed. Gregory Elliot (London: Hutchinson Radius, 1990), 75.

[42] H. C. Erik Midelfort, *Witch Hunting in Southwestern Germany, 1562–1684: The Social and Intellectual Foundations* (Stanford, CA: Stanford University Press, 1972), 25–26.

church had failed to convert and contain, they also took over a variety of stories in which unbelievers gained power from an urge to kill and reuse Christ's body and those of Christians, images which lie behind Lady Macbeth's murderous desire for babies. Witches long for babies in order to turn them into a demonic equivalent of the salvific relic: 'we secretly steal them from their graves and cook them in a cauldron until the whole flesh comes away from the bones and becomes a soup.'[43]

Johann Weyer's *Catalogue of Popular Belief* was intended to expose such practices for what they really were – the delusions of common people. But R. Po-chia Hsia notes that the key manifestation is 'the greater emphasis on ritual child murders in witchcraft discourses of the late sixteenth century', as 'witches seemed to have replaced Jews as the most dangerous enemies within Christian society'.[44] It included the idea that witches kill children for ritual reasons, or dig up their bodies for ritual uses. One story in particular, the story which eventually became Hansel and Gretel, exchanged a Jewish child-stealing protagonist for a witch-figure. Take this Serbian version:

> Then there came along some Yids, and when they saw the fire, came up to the children and asked them what they were doing there and whether there was anyone with them, and when the children had told them what and how, the Yids told them to go along with them, saying that they would have a fine time at their house. The children agreed and went with the Yids, and the Yids took them to their house. They didn't have anyone else at home, only their mother, and when they came home, they shut the boy up to get fat and made the girl a servant to their mother. One day, when the boy had been well fed and was fat, the Yids went out on some errand and told their mother to roast him, and then when they came home in the evening from their work, they would eat him.[45]

In her book on Jewish child-murder libel and the Eucharist, Miri Rubin suggests further parallels between the lost children story that eventually becomes familiar to us as Hansel and Gretel and the stories of ritual child-murder. The basic story she records tells of a Jewish boy who secretly receives the Eucharist and is thrown into an oven by his furious father. The Virgin Mary protects the boy in the oven by covering him in her cloak. The boy and his mother convert to Christianity, and the father is put in the oven himself.[46] Rubin points out that the oven represents a womb from which the child is reborn. We can detect the faint, unexorcized shadow

---

[43] Johannes Nider, *Formicarius*, cited in Walter Stephens, *Demon Lovers: Witchcraft, Sex, and the Crisis of Belief* (Chicago: Chicago University Press, 2003), 241.

[44] R. Po-chia Hsia, *The Myth of Ritual Murder: Jews and Magic in Reformation Germany* (New Haven, CT: Yale University Press, 1988), 228.

[45] Vuk Stefanovic Karadzic, *Serbian Folk Tales*, cited in Stefan Ljubica, *From Fairy Tale to Holocaust* (excerpts), www.hic.hr/books/from-fairytale/part-01.htm (accessed 11 March 2014). On Hansel and Gretel, see Maria Tatar, *Off with Their Heads! Fairy Tales and the Culture of Childhood* (Princeton, NJ: Princeton University Press, 1992), 208–10.

[46] Miri Rubin, *Gentile Tales: The Narrative Assault on Late Medieval Jews* (New Haven, CT: Yale University Press, 1999).

of this story in *Macbeth* and its womblike cauldron, into which an innocent child is thrown, out of which a supernaturally endowed child emerges. But once more this rebirth is not benign, as it is in the original story. Rather, what was once the healing Christian magic of the Virgin has become an angry and violent witchcraft. Crucial to the connection is the figure of the cauldron, the instrument of punishment in Christopher Marlowe's *The Jew of Malta*. In that play, the cauldron is the means by which the Jew is finally excised from the play. His trace is locatable in the cauldron in *Macbeth*, where we find the 'Liver of blaspheming Jew' (IV.i.26) marking the cauldron as a site of Jewish punishment. The admixture of the Jew's trace with parts of the baby might seem incongruous, but it makes a kind of warped sense when read in the context of anti-Semitic stories in which the Jew is specifically labelled as the foe of Christian children. Usury in particular is represented as a man taking a baby away from its mother.[47] Similarly, a Paris Jew tests the divinity of the Eucharist in a cauldron of boiling water; the water turns the colour of blood. The point here is in part that children and the Eucharist are equally vulnerable. They can be appropriated to do magic. The boy in the original story as recounted by Rubin is himself a kind of Eucharist, baked in an oven like bread, then reborn from the Virgin. While the contents of the cauldron in the dramas are again an inversion – unappetizing – there is a sense in which the very replication of the register of a recipe calls the possibility of consumption of the contents into action. Another story tells of a Jew who refuses to swallow the host, keeping it for experimental purposes. He keeps it in his mouth and eventually spits it out of the cauldron of his body. It turns into an attractive little child on the palm of his hand.[48] Undeterred, he still tries to eat it, but it is too chewy. Similarly, Jews capture and murder a priest, whose heart contains 'a lovely little boy'.[49] Here the message is that of *Titus Andronicus* – eating people is wrong – and yet these vehemently anti-Semitic stories expose the central transgression of the transubstantiation and its implications, just as relics are laid bare as decaying bones.

There is a marked resemblance between the Hansel and Gretel story and the anti-Semitic legend of the blood libel, with witch substituted for Jewish man. In both cases there is a story of a beautiful child sacrificed to perverse desires, and such stories often contain the motif of a child who cannot be silenced, speaking blood, along with the Christological motif of a child made to suffer unjustly. All three are present in *Macbeth*: the sacrificed child in Lady Macbeth's baby, the children of the cauldron as the prophetic discovery of child-murder, and the unjustly murdered child in young Macduff. And there is a further link between witches and Jews across Shakespeare. This is the trope of the hard body of the villain implicitly compared with the softness of the victim: witchmarks had to be pricked. Similarly, it is necessary for Shylock actively to assert his own fleshly

---

[47]   Rubin, *Gentile Tales*, 26.
[48]   Rubin, *Gentile Tales*, 35.
[49]   Rubin, *Gentile Tales*, 36.

normalcy: 'If you prick us, do we not bleed?'[50] This hard body is the antithesis of the maternal softness and succour which could also seem difficult. Neither deliquescence nor too much rigour was acceptable.

In both the blood libel story and the story of the witches' murder of babies, the baby's body is a source of supernatural power. A third group of stories, stories of women selling their babies to the fairies in exchange for supernatural sight, ties in further with these. A Scottish woman called Bessie Dunlop believed she had given up her baby in exchange for fairy powers.[51] Like a saint's relic, Bessie's baby connects her to the Otherworld to which it goes. She exchanges it for magical powers. Though Shakespeare knew nothing about Bessie Dunlop, there's an ironic and fascinating way in which her story *is* reflected in *Macbeth*. At a simple level, the witches' treatment of a dead baby is usually read as merely and drearily infanticidal: the birth-strangled babe who goes into the potion.

But is it? For among the spirits to come out of the potion is the spirit of a child; is this a faint trace of the *aoros* summoned by the body of the dismembered baby? And what does that child speak about? Why, about inheritance, about patrilinearity, about the rights of the father. As if this is not enough, there is also a bloodstained baby, and the baby speaks of a birth that is not of woman, a hyper-masculine birth. And is there a faint analogy between Bessie's choice and Macbeth's? Bessie acquires occult powers by sacrificing not only her child, but her identity as that child's caring mother. Just so does Macbeth sacrifice the normal ties of human warmth, honour, troops of friends, for power. And when he metaphorizes these human feelings, he does so using the image of a baby: 'pity, like a naked new-born babe, / Striding the blast' (I.vii.21–22).

So it seems natural to turn back to Lady Macbeth's own metaphorization of those feelings, in which she keeps alluding, not narratively, but metaphorically, to a lost or dead baby, and once, crucially, to a baby she murdered herself. Let's look very closely at her most famous speech:

> I have given suck, and know
> How tender 'tis to love the babe that milks me;
> I would, while it was smiling in my face,
> Have plucked my nipple from his boneless gums
> And dashed the brains out, had I so sworn
> As you have done to this. (I.vii.54–59)

---

[50] William Shakespeare, *The Merchant of Venice*, in *The Riverside Shakespeare*, ed. G. Blakemore Evans, J. J. M. Tobin et al., 2nd ed. (Boston: Houghton Mifflin, 1997), III.i.64.

[51] See my discussion of Bessie Dunlop in 'Losing Babies, Losing Women: Attending to Women's Stories in Scottish Witchcraft Trials', in *Culture and Change: Attending to Early Modern Women*, ed. Margaret Mikesell and Adele Seeff (Newark: University of Delaware Press, 2003), 143–60.

This baby is figured in extreme and sensuous materiality. Shakespeare *delays* the violence to allow us to experience an erotic and bodily closeness; Lady Macbeth's resolute 'I would' is followed by an evocation of tenderness which defers the violent end and makes anticipation of it seem worse: 'while it was smiling in my face'. Now comes the stroke of real genius: 'Have plucked my nipple from his boneless gums'. For a heartbeat we think *this* is the act of untender, unmaternal resolution, the refusal of food. Lady Macbeth is, for a second, merely someone who restrains her child's greed for suckling; but then comes the terrific force of 'and dashed the brains out', delayed again and hence given added force by that initial 'and'. 'Dashed' is just the right word; imagine how much 'knocked' would reduce the force of the lines, losing that onomatopoeic sense of splattering that makes 'dashed' so untender.

Thus it is that the very senses that made us feel the baby so tenderly are now turned to a painful and fully bodily awareness of his destruction. The baby also becomes a kind of martyr. It is a Holy Innocent that recalls the birth-strangled babe of the cauldron and anticipates it. It is also a sacrifice – or rather, a fantasy about the sacrifice of a baby in order to make something much more fixed, a kind of monument to its death. Finally, the death of the baby prefigures the transformation of Lady Macbeth herself into a kind of relic through the figures of breast milk and bloodstains.

Lady Macbeth's other long speech is also haunted by something, the ghost of a dead baby, even if he only dies in story, and is a way of understanding Lady Macbeth's relations to the supernatural. For it is Lady Macbeth, not Macbeth, and not the Weird Sisters, who delivers the only authentic invocation to the powers of darkness in the play:

> Come, you spirits
> That tend on mortal thoughts, unsex me here,
> And fill me from the crown to the toe, top-full
> Of direst cruelty. Make thick my blood,
> Stop up th'access and passage to remorse,
> That no compunctious visitings of nature
> Shake my fell purpose, nor keep peace between
> Th'effect and it. Come to my woman's breasts
> And take my milk for gall, you murd'ring ministers,
> Wherever, in your sightless substances,
> You wait on nature's mischief. (I.v.39–49)

This speech is usually read as a renunciation of the sexed body. But what does that mean within the context of the play? The witches, of course, are unsexed – or rather their gender is to Banquo problematically undecidable – because they have beards. But what kind of marker are beards in women? They are markers of old age, when hair begins to grow in places coded as smooth in young women. What Banquo is seeing is a body unsexed by old age, and we shall see in a moment that this is how Lady Macbeth marks her body, too.

Old age brings the functions of the female body to a halt. Lady Macbeth is making, in effect, the same choice as Bessie Dunlop, but making it much more comprehensively. She is wishing for early menopause, and this is why she asks that her blood be made thick. A witch's blood was thought to be so thick with old age, so lacking in fire that it was impossible to extract it, and it was this idea which lay behind the notion that a witch's body could not be pierced by shot or by a pin. Like the Jew's body, the witch's body was hard, and insensible. Such hardness is inimical to the soft body of the mother. Yet this is the body Lady Macbeth desires for *herself*: a body that is dried and preserved, just what Hallewes wants to do with Lancelot, a body that is a dead end, not capable of multiplying. With her reproductivity denied, her hard body seems inimical to time, not unlike the body of a virgin. Her body now seems static, caught forever at the instant of her crime like that of an inverse martyr. The witch's body is thus like the body of the saint in being the way by which supernatural power transmits itself to other parts of the material world. (It is also interesting how often and how derogatorily the word 'old' is used in the critique of relics; they are 'old bones', as though being old means they are especially repugnant.) When witches are depicted, there is sometimes a strident contrast between the sexual poses they adopt and their withered bodies.

Similarly, Lady Macbeth offers to substitute gall for her breast milk. To early modern medicine, breast milk was impure blood from the womb that was made white and pure by the burning fires of maternal love, which also drew it upward through the body until it reached the breasts.[52] By contrast, the gall which Lady Macbeth substitutes for milk is a signifier indicating that her heart has failed in maternal love, as well as of the poison in which witches are thought to deal. In an era when babies were far more likely to die if not breastfed, she imagines herself murdering her child, via the trope of a refusal to feed it. Lady Macbeth's double refusal of breast milk marks her as a witch, too, because witches were beings who stole the milk of other animals and also mothers, substituting unnourishing blood for it. And she also imagines herself choosing not to feed the child, but to feed something else, to feed the familiar spirits she summons. Worse still, these spectral images of infanticide are haunted by the image of the female demons whose breast milk acted as poison to babies, especially the Jewish mother-demon Lilith.

This concern with the protocols of maternal love and their physical expression is also tied in to concerns with relics and their truth or value. So, too, it was when breast milk relics were also exposed as hard, perhaps as unfeeling. Fake breast milk, and especially the fraudulent breast milk of the Virgin Mary, was one of the most popular targets for Reformers keen to hunt out fake relics. Erasmus began the trend by his account of his visit to Walsingham. The shrine's premier relic was a crystal vial of this milk. In his colloquies, Erasmus complained that it was remarkable that a woman with only one child should have produced so

---

[52] Jacques Guillemeau, *Child-birth, or, The happy deliuerie of women, etc.* (Amsterdam: Theatrum Orbis Terrarum; New York: Da Capo Press, 1972).

many milky relics.[53] The East Anglian Visitors noted at least seven specimens of the Virgin's milk.[54] The fraudulent milk disconnected the relic from the body from which it supposedly came and the body on which it was supposed to act magically. That metonymy was based on an assumed metaphoricity, or likeness. But if it is fake, it deprives the believer of nourishment, just as Lady Macbeth herself does. Breast milk is revealed to be hard rather than liquid, indigestible rock rather than nourishing food. The revelation that it's hard rock mimics Lady Macbeth's murderous request.

Through her child-sacrifice, her wish to be prematurely ancient and withered, her summoning of familiars, and her story of sensuous child-sacrifice, Lady Macbeth is the play's only true witch. She also becomes a relic, or perhaps more accurately an anti-relic, of her own wicked deeds. In the play's final act, she is glimpsed again as the victim of a marked body whose marks cannot ever be erased, despite her neurotic efforts. Her shocked repetitive washings in the sleepwalking scene uncannily and chillingly replicate the many rituals of relic-devotion, but these ritual cleansings are ineffective because nothing can wipe out the stain of murder from her sight, nor its smell. Here all the themes being discussed in this essay come together. First, blood spots are simple signs of witchcraft. A witchmark in England was a demon's suckling place, but it could also be wounds or bruises found on waking that the witches could not explain. The devil left a secret mark on those who made a compact with him. Usually the mark took the form of some kind of sign of sexual congress with the devil, but in England it was more usually a sign of perverse nurturance, a misplaced teat from which devils rather than children were fed. The marks on Lady Macbeth's hands tie in her acts with her will to murder children through half-remembered stories of host-theft and child-murder. Just as Lady Macbeth has denied the supernatural power of Duncan's royal body, so that power manifests itself forcibly in her eyes by the reappearance of his blood, as it did for the child-murdering Jews, witches and infanticidal mothers of popular story and legend. The relic-like power of the blood Lady Macbeth sees and smells on herself has the ability to transcend death and to bring the living into close – too close – apposition with the dead. The appearance of blood upon hands is not only a common criminal sign, but especially associated with the Jewish blood libel. And the bloodstained bodies of Jews in these medieval legends are themselves hard, like the body for which Lady Macbeth longs. Finally, like Duncan, the host is always stabbed repeatedly in these legends, and the miraculous abundance of the host's blood is correlated with this multiple stabbing: 'A Jew has mutilated the / Host of the holy sacrament / By striking ten blows or more / And making it bleed abundantly.'[55]

At the same time, the finger that entered the witch's cauldron as perhaps their most elaborated upon ingredient is replicated here in Lady Macbeth's telltale

---

[53]   Erasmus, *Colloquies*, 288–89, 293–97, 301.

[54]   Marshall, 'Forgery and Miracles', 51.

[55]   Cited by Rubin, *Gentile Tales*, 163.

hand. Both fingers and hands were relics especially fraught with power.[56] The finger relics of Holy Innocents were echoed in the innocent baby slain by his guilty mother in *Macbeth*. In the same way, arm and hand relics of the great saints are among the most common of the Middle Ages, especially relics of the right hand. Healing miracles were celebrated with models of healed limbs, which went with the display of bones of ordinary people in ossuaries – there being a crucial distinction between the recent dead and 'clean bones'.[57]

As the body was progressively displaced by the very jewellers' arts which were supposed to represent it, the body's own resonances of mortality and disgust were displaced, too, and relics ceased to be a visible way of loving the dead, became the kinds of objects of disgust associated with necromancy. As that process occurred, visceral loathing was transferred to the body of the witch created by necromancy, which had all too much in common with the relics themselves, being fixed, static, infertile, hard, duplicitous, dead and disgusting because it was the body of an old and infertile woman. In *Macbeth*, this marked body, the body-as-relic, is set alongside and in some respects set against the fragmentary and inscrutable scraps of leftover personhood which constituted relics. Ironically, just as stories of Jewish child-murder, host-theft and witches' murder of infants coalesce in the single criminally signed figure of Lady Macbeth, so the same stories are scattered throughout the witches' 'readings' of the cauldron and its ingredients. The play is thus readable as an interrogation of the ways in which heaven and earth touch at the point of the dead body, marking its substance forever with the will of the supernatural. It is also a record in the sense of being a criminal record. Lovingly, it traces upon the body the frail lineaments of a past set of meanings which were being progressively discarded to make new ones.

Works Cited

Primary Sources

Bellarmine, Robert. *Disputationes de controversiis christianae fidei adversus hujus temporis haereticos*. 4 vols. Ingolstadt: A. Sartorius, 1601.

Calfhill, James. *An Answer to John Martiall's Treatise on the Cross*. Edited by Richard Gibbings for the Parker Society. Cambridge: The University Press, 1846.

Calvin, John. *Treatise on Relics*. Translated by Walerian Skorobohaty, Count Krasinski. Edinburgh: Johnstone and Hunter, 1854. www.godrules.net/library/calvin/176calvin4.htm (accessed 14 October 2012).

---

[56]   Of all body parts, right-hand reliquaries were the most common because the hand mimicked a bishop's blessing gesture. See Thomas P. F. Hoving, 'A Newly Discovered Reliquary of St Thomas Becket', *Gesta* 4 (Spring 1965): 28–30.

[57]   Brian Taylor, 'The Hand of St James', *Berkshire Archaeological Journal* 75 (1994–97): 97–102.

Chaucer, Geoffrey. *The Canterbury Tales*. In *The Riverside Chaucer*. Edited by Larry D. Benson. 3rd ed. Boston: Houghton Mifflin, 1987.

'Corpus Christi Carol'. In *The Early English Carols*. Edited by Richard Leighton Greene. Oxford: Clarendon Press, 1935.

Erasmus, Desiderius. *The Colloquies of Erasmus*. Translated by Craig R. Thompson. Chicago: University of Chicago Press, 1965.

———. *The Correspondence of Erasmus*: *Letters 1658–1801* (1526–27). Translated by Alexander Dalzell. Edited by Charles G. Nauert. Vol. 12 of The Collected Works of Erasmus. Toronto: University of Toronto Press, 2003.

Guillemeau, Jacques. *Child-birth, or, The happy deliuerie of women, etc.* Amsterdam: Theatrum Orbis Terrarum; New York: Da Capo Press, 1972.

Harsnett, Samuel. *A declaration of egregious popish impostures to with-draw the harts of her Maiesties subiects from their allegeance, and from the truth of Christian religion professed in England, vnder the pretence of casting out deuils, etc.* London: James Roberts, 1603.

Le haut livre du graal: Perlesvaus. Edited by William A. Nitze and T. Atkinson Jenkins. Chicago: University of Chicago Press, 1932.

The High Book of the Grail: A Translation of the Thirteenth-Century Romance of Perlesvaus. Translated by Nigel Bryant. Cambridge: D. S. Brewer; Totowa, NJ: Rowman and Littlefield, 1978.

Jerome (Saint). *Lettres*. Edited by Jérôme Labourt. Vol. 4. Paris: Les Belles Lettres, 1955.

Malory, Thomas. *Le Morte Darthur*. Edited by Stephen H. A. Shepherd. Norton Critical Editions. New York: W. W. Norton, 2003.

More, Thomas. *A Dialogue of Comfort against Tribulation*. Edited by Frank Manley. Vol. 12 of The Yale Edition of the Works of St. Thomas More. New Haven, CT: Yale University Press, 1977.

'The Sermon against the Holy Maid of Kent and Her Adherents, Delivered at Paul's Cross, November the 23rd, 1533, and at Canterbury, December the 7th'. Edited by L. E. Whatmore. *English Historical Review* 58.232 (1943): 463–75.

Shakespeare, William. *Macbeth*. Edited by Nicholas Brooke. The Oxford Shakespeare. Oxford: Clarendon Press, 1990.

———. *The Merchant of Venice*. In *The Riverside Shakespeare*. Edited by G. Blakemore Evans, J. J. M. Tobin et al. 2nd ed. Boston: Houghton Mifflin, 1997.

The Statutes of the Realm, etc. Edited by A. Luders et al. 11 vols. London, 1810–28.

Visitation Articles and Injunctions of the Period of the Reformation. 3 vols. Vol. 2. Edited by Walter Howard Frere and William McClure Kennedy. London: Longmans, Green, 1910.

The Works of a Lollard Preacher: The Sermon 'Omnis plantacio', the Tract 'Fundamentum aliud nemo potest ponere' and the Tract 'De oblacione iugis sacrificii'. Edited by Anne Hudson. Early English Text Society Original Series, 317. Oxford: Oxford University Press, 2001.

Secondary Sources

Bronfen, Elisabeth. *Over Her Dead Body: Death, Femininity and the Aesthetic.* Manchester: Manchester University Press, 1992.

Brown, Ruth. 'Middens and Miasma: A Portrait of Seventeenth-Century Village Life in Banburyshire'. *Cake and Cockhorse* 6.1 (2003): 2–8.

Bynum, Caroline Walker. *Jesus as Mother: Studies in the Spirituality of the High Middle Ages.* Berkeley: University of California Press, 1982.

Cockayne, Emily. *Hubbub: Filth, Noise, and Stench in England, 1600–1770.* New Haven, CT: Yale University Press, 2007.

Cohen, William A., and Ryan Johnson, eds. *Filth: Dirt, Disgust, and Modern Life.* Minneapolis: University of Minnesota Press, 2005.

Ditchfield, Simon. 'Martyrs on the Move: Relics as Vindicators of Local Diversity in the Tridentine Church'. In *Martyrs and Martyrologies: Papers Read at the 1992 Summer Meeting and the 1993 Winter Meeting of the Ecclesiastical History Society.* Edited by Diana Wood. Studies in Church History, 30. Oxford: Blackwell for the Ecclesiastical History Society, 1993.

Duffy, Eamon. *The Stripping of the Altars: Traditional Religion in England 1400–1500.* New Haven, CT: Yale University Press, 1992.

Ginzburg, Carlo. *Ecstasies: Deciphering the Witches' Sabbath.* Translated by Raymond Rosenthal. Edited by Gregory Elliot. London: Hutchinson Radius, 1990.

Goody, Jack. *Representations and Contradictions: Ambivalence towards Images, Theatre, Fiction, Relics and Sexuality.* Oxford: Blackwell, 1997.

Heng, Geraldine. 'Enchanted Ground: The Feminine Subtext in Malory'. In *Arthurian Women.* Edited by Thelma S. Fenster. London: Routledge, 2000. 97–114.

Hoving, Thomas P. F. 'A Newly Discovered Reliquary of St Thomas Becket'. *Gesta* 4 (Spring 1965): 28–30.

Hsia, R. Po-chia. *The Myth of Ritual Murder: Jews and Magic in Reformation Germany.* New Haven, CT: Yale University Press, 1988.

Jenner, Mark. 'Civilization and Deodorization? Smell in Early Modern English Culture'. In *Civil Histories: Essays Presented to Sir Keith Thomas.* Edited by Peter Burke, Brian Howard Harrison and Paul Slack. Oxford: Oxford University Press, 2000. 127–44.

Hutton, Ronald. *The Stations of the Sun: A History of the Ritual Year in Britain.* Oxford: Oxford University Press, 1996.

Knepper, Janet. 'A Bad Girl Will Love You to Death: Excessive Love in the Stanzaic *Morte Arthur* and Malory'. In *On Arthurian Women: Essays in Memory of Maureen Fries.* Edited by Bonnie Wheeler and Fiona Tolhurst. Dallas, TX: Scriptorium Press, 2001. 229–44.

Kunze, Michael. *Highroad to the Stake: A Tale of Witchcraft.* Translated by William E. Yuill. Chicago: University of Chicago Press, 1987.

Laporte, Dominique. *The History of Shit.* Translated by Nadia Benabid and Rodolphe El-Khoury. Cambridge, MA: MIT Press, 2000.

Ljubica, Stefan. *From Fairy Tale to Holocaust* (excerpts). www.hic.hr/books/from-fairytale/part-01.htm (accessed 11 March 2014).

Marshall, Peter. 'Forgery and Miracles in the Reign of Henry VIII'. *Past and Present* 178 (2003): 39–73.

———. *Religious Identities in Henry VIII's England.* Aldershot: Ashgate, 2006.

———. 'The Rood of Boxley, the Blood of Hailes and the Defence of the Henrician Church'. *Journal of Ecclesiastical History* 46 (1995): 689–96.

Midelfort, H. C. Erik. *Witch Hunting in Southwestern Germany, 1562–1684: The Social and Intellectual Foundations.* Stanford, CA: Stanford University Press, 1972.

Miller, William. *The Anatomy of Disgust.* Cambridge, MA: Harvard University Press, 1997.

Muchembled, Robert. *A History of the Devil: From the Middle Ages to the Present.* Translated by Jean Birrell. Cambridge: Polity, 2003.

Muir, Edward. *Ritual in Early Modern Europe.* Cambridge: Cambridge University Press, 2005.

Nussbaum, Martha C. *Hiding from Humanity: Disgust, Shame, and the Law.* Princeton, NJ: Princeton University Press, 2004.

Purkiss, Diane. 'Losing Babies, Losing Women: Attending to Women's Stories in Scottish Witchcraft Trials'. In *Culture and Change: Attending to Early Modern Women.* Edited by Margaret Mikesell and Adele Seeff, 143–60. Newark: University of Delaware Press, 2003.

Rambuss, Richard. *Closet Devotions.* Series Q. Durham, NC: Duke University Press, 1998.

Rubin, Miri. *Gentile Tales: The Narrative Assault on Late Medieval Jews.* New Haven, CT: Yale University Press, 1999.

Shagan, Ethan H. *Popular Politics in the English Reformation.* Cambridge Studies in Early Modern British History. Cambridge: Cambridge University Press, 2003.

Spicer, Andrew. '"Defyle not Christ's kirk with your carrion": Burial and the Development of Burial Aisles in Post-Reformation Scotland'. In *The Place of the Dead: Death and Remembrance in Late Medieval and Early Modern Europe.* Edited by Bruce Gordon and Peter Marshall, 149–69. Cambridge: Cambridge University Press, 2000.

Stephens, Walter. *Demon Lovers: Witchcraft, Sex, and the Crisis of Belief.* Chicago: Chicago University Press, 2003.

Stewart, Alan. *Close Readers: Humanism and Sodomy in Early Modern England.* Princeton, NJ: Princeton University Press, 1997.

Tatar, Maria. *Off with Their Heads! Fairy Tales and the Culture of Childhood.* Princeton, NJ: Princeton University Press, 1992.

Taylor, Brian. 'The Hand of St James'. *Berkshire Archaeological Journal* 75 (1994–97): 97–102.

Thomas, Keith. *Religion and the Decline of Magic.* London: Penguin, 1971.

Watt, Diane. *Secretaries of God: Women Prophets in Late Medieval and Early Modern England.* Woodbridge: D. S. Brewer, 1997.

Chapter 3
The Witch of Edmonton:
The Witch Next Door
or Faustian Anti-Heroine?

Pauline Ruberry-Blanc

As the penny-catching title page informs us, *The Witch of Edmonton* is a play based on a true crime story: the misdemeanours of Elizabeth Sawyer, alias the Witch of Edmonton, who was tried and condemned as a witch, and executed at Tyburn on 19 April 1621 – just a few months before the play took to the stage. Even though witch-hunting was not at its peak at this time, witchcraft was a popular – and lucrative – theme with writers of treatises, pamphlets and ballads. The play itself was performed at court (on 29 December 1621, during the Christmas revels), as well as in the popular theatre (according to the title page of the first edition in 1658, 'often at the Cock-Pit in *Drury-Lane*, once at Court, with singular Applause'[1]).

The gender-coded theme of witchcraft is now, of course, a popular one with literary critics. But with regard to this collaborative piece (co-authored by Thomas Dekker, John Ford and William Rowley[2]), criticism seems to have formed a nexus around two well-defined and contrasting approaches, to be discussed below. This may be in part because the text's referentiality and allusive range have been restricted by its immediate derivation, including verbal echoes and reiterations, from Henry Goodcole's account, *The wonderfull discouerie of Elizabeth Sawyer a witch, late of Edmonton*, which was published a few days after the execution.[3]

Goodcole was not only a regular minister to the condemned of Newgate prison but a semi-professional retailer of their edifying confessions.[4] He claims that his

---

[1]   The title page is reproduced in Thomas Dekker, John Ford and William Rowley, *The Witch of Edmonton*, ed. Arthur F. Kinney, *The New Mermaids* (London: A. and C. Black, 1998), xliii. Citations are taken throughout from this edition.

[2]   The title page adds '&c.', but no other author has ever been identified.

[3]   Henry Goodcole, *The wonderfull discouerie of Elizabeth Sawyer a witch, late of Edmonton, her conuiction and condemnation and death. Together with the relation of the Diuels accesse to her, and their conference together, etc.* (London: A. Mathewes for William Butler, 1621).

[4]   Cf. Marisha Caswell's discussion of the tension between edifying purpose and commercial interest in the published accounts of the 'ordinary' chaplains of Newgate in Chapter 6 of the present volume. Goodcole's approach and style may be gathered from the titles of his other publications, especially one that bears on the crime of infanticide, another concern of Caswell's essay: *Natures cruell step-dames: or, Matchlesse monsters of*

narrative constitutes an objective record of Mother Sawyer's life and crimes as related at her trial in the Old Bailey ('I meddle heare with nothing but matter of fact'⁵). He adds to this the confession that he obtained from her in Newgate – supposedly with great difficulty, because of her ignorance and obtuseness – which he induced her to confirm publicly at her execution, where she prayed for divine mercy. The questions and answers that figure in the account, written in dialogue form, effectively sketch a portrait of the typical garden-variety witch as found in so many of the pamphlets, while exposing the social tensions surrounding such a presence within a small rural community. The key questions include by what means she came to have acquaintance with the devil (he appeared when she was 'cursing, swearing and blaspheming');⁶ whether the devil forbade her to pray to Jesus Christ (yes, and ordered her to pray solely to the devil);⁷ how many 'Christians and Beastes' she had caused to die, and what her reasons were (she had killed many of both, out of 'malice and enuy', determined to revenge herself when they angered her in any way);⁸ whether she particularly 'witch[ed] to death' her neighbour Agnes Ratcliefe (Anne Ratcliffe in the play), the main reason for her condemnation (no, she did not);⁹ what the devil wanted from her (the promise of her soul and body, 'sealed' by giving him permission to suck her blood).¹⁰ One key question directly bearing on the play was in what shape the devil came to her, to which she replied, 'Always in the shape of a dogge and of two collars [i.e., colours], sometimes of blacke and sometimes of white'.¹¹

Critics of the play have generally taken one of two approaches to this raw material and its dramatic transformation. One, which draws on the considerable work of social historians of witchcraft, is to build on the hints in Goodcole's account, quite deliberately developed in the stage version, of the local tensions, prejudices and alliances involving class and gender that resulted in such witchcraft accusations and trials.¹² Other critics have insisted on the significance of the

---

the female sex; Elizabeth Barnes, and Anne Willis. Who were executed the 26. day of April, 1637. at Tyburne, for the unnaturall murthering of their owne children. Also, herein is contained their severall confessions, an the courts just proceedings against other notorious malefactors, with their severall offences this sessions. Further, a relation of the wicked life and impenitent death of Iohn Flood, who raped his owne childe (London: E. Purslowe for Francis Coules, 1637).

⁵   Goodcole, *Discouerie*, sig. A3ʳ.

⁶   Goodcole, *Discouerie*, sig. Cʳ⁻ᵛ.

⁷   Goodcole, *Discouerie*, sig. C4ᵛ.

⁸   Goodcole, *Discouerie*, sig. C2ʳ. She held against her neighbours, amongst other things, the fact that they would not buy her brooms (sig. Bᵛ).

⁹   Goodcole, *Discouerie*, sig. C2ᵛ.

¹⁰   Goodcole, *Discouerie*, sig. C2ᵛ–3ʳ.

¹¹   Goodcole, *Discouerie*, sig. C2ᵛ.

¹²   With regard to the play itself, this approach is exemplified by Viviana Comensoli, *'Household Business': Domestic Plays of Early Modern England* (Toronto: University of Toronto Press, 1996), 110–30, and Anthony B. Dawson, 'Witchcraft/Bigamy: Cultural

belief in the demonic. Among the most recent and convincing of these is David Nicol, who, inspired by Stuart Clark's investigation of demonology, promotes a renegotiation between the play's representations of social and demonic causation.[13] This means accentuating, as Robert Hunter West had also done,[14] the influence of a second recognized source for at least one detail in the play, George Gifford's *A dialogue concerning witches and witchcraftes*, in which the power of witches is recognized but subordinated to that of their diabolic masters.[15] It also means resisting, in particular, the tendency of the social school to neglect the role of the dog, which, in keeping with Goodcole's account, incarnates the devil on stage. The character 'Dog', also known as Tom, is given a very prominent role as a maleficent spirit crossing the paths of several of the characters in the three interlaced plots. To undervalue the dog by appealing to notions of superstition, hallucination or symbolism, Nicol argues, is 'to misunderstand the ways in which skepticism about witchcraft was typically articulated in the period'.[16] I am in basic agreement with Nicol's approach. However, to my mind, the social and the demonic dimensions of the play are far from mutually exclusive but, on the contrary, profoundly inform each other. Nicol neglects further allusions and intertexts beyond Goodcole that arguably would have had resonance for the contemporary audience. These notably include elements bearing on the black dog.

Conflict in *The Witch of Edmonton*', *Renaissance Drama* 20 (1989): 77–98. Behind such readings lie the investigations of such social and anthropological historians as Keith Thomas, *Religion and the Decline of Magic*, 2nd ed. (Harmondsworth, Middlesex: Penguin, 1980); Alan Macfarlane, *Witchcraft in Tudor and Stuart England: A Regional and Comparative Study*, 2nd ed. (London: Routledge, 1999); J. A. Sharpe, *Instruments of Darkness: Witchcraft in Early Modern England* (Philadelphia: University of Pennsylvania Press, 1997); Robin Briggs, *Witches and Neighbours: The Social and Cultural Context of European Witchcraft* (London: HarperCollins, 1995); Annabel Gregory, 'Witchcraft, Politics and "Good Neighbourhood" in Early Seventeenth-Century Rye', *Past and Present* 133 (1991): 31–66; and Anne Reiber DeWindt, 'Witchcraft and Conflicting Visions of the Ideal Village Community', *Journal of British Studies* 34.4 (1993): 427–63.

[13]   David Nicol, 'Interrogating the Devil: Social and Demonic Pressure in *The Witch of Edmonton*', *Comparative Drama* 38.4 (2005): 425–46; Stuart Clark, *Thinking with Demons: The Idea of Witchcraft in Early Modern Europe* (Oxford: Clarendon Press, 1997). Other critical treatments of the play emphasizing the demonic include Robert Hunter West, *The Invisible World: A Study of Pneumatology in Elizabethan Drama* (Athens: University of Georgia Press, 1939), 144–54; Diane Purkiss, *The Witch in History: Early Modern and Twentieth-Century Representations* (London: Routledge, 1996), 231–49; and Nathan Johnstone, *The Devil and Demonism in Early Modern England*, Cambridge Studies in Early Modern British History (Cambridge: Cambridge University Press, 2006), 170–73.

[14]   West, *Invisible World*, 144–53.

[15]   George Gifford, *A dialogue concerning witches and witchcraftes. In which is laide open how craftely the Diuell deceiueth not onely the witches but many other and so leadeth them awrie into many great errours, etc.* (London: John Windet for Tobie Cooke and Mihil Hart, 1593).

[16]   Nichol, 'Interrogating the Devil', 425–26.

Despite their general fidelity to Goodcole's tract, the playwrights do not present the witch in a clear-cut way. At times, we do indeed find her fitting the contemporary stereotypical portrait of the witch – what I think of as the garden-variety witch, or the witch next door – as outlined by Goodcole and many precursors. And in adapting this material to produce an essentially sympathetic figure, a victim of her malicious and uncharitable neighbours, the playwrights might almost be (and perhaps were) applying the debunking account of Reginald Scot in his *The discouerie of witchcraft* (1584).[17] Scot, whose treatise was actually appropriated in some respects by Gifford (especially in the latter's 1587 *A discourse of the subtill practises of deuilles by witches and sorcerers*[18]), traces in detail the typical pattern by which a poor old woman, hostile and aggrieved, attracts accusations of being responsible for illnesses of children and cattle, as well as for other misfortunes; thereupon,

> being called before a Justice, by due examination of the circumstances [she] is driuen to see hir imprecations and desires, and hir neighbors harmes and losses to concurre, and as it were to take effect: and so confesseth that she (as a goddes) hath brought such things to passe.[19]

Scot has ample room in his portrait, then, for the witch's internalizing of the accusations against her, her development of a belief in her own 'goddes'-like power: 'they take vpon them; yea, and sometimes thinke, that they can doo such things as are beyond the abilitie of humane nature.'[20] This intersects with the fact that we sometimes seem to hear Elizabeth Sawyer claiming a different status for herself, something approaching that of the protagonist of Christopher Marlowe's great Christian tragedy. To the extent that Faustus's magical career is itself suggestive of witchcraft, the resemblance is hardly surprising: indeed, Paul Kocher made witches' 'vain imagination to be as gods' one of his criteria for putting Faustus in that category.[21] But this is only one aspect of Faustus, as Kocher agreed, and it is a different matter to propose that audiences of Dekker, Ford and Rowley's play might have registered echoes of the magician's spiritual and intellectual aspiration. My rereading stems not only from several remarkably poetic soliloquies delivered by Sawyer, but also from her interaction with Dog, which has been incompletely interpreted, even by Nicol.

---

[17] Reginald Scot, *The discouerie of witchcraft, etc.* (London: [Henry Denham for William Brome], 1584).

[18] George Gifford, *A discourse of the subtill practises of deuilles by witches and sorcerers, etc.* (London: T. Orwin for Toby Cooke, 1587).

[19] Scot, *Discouerie*, 8.

[20] Scot, *Discouerie*, 7.

[21] Paul H. Kocher, 'The Witchcraft Bias in Marlowe's *Faustus*', *Modern Philology* 38.1 (1940): 17, citing Thomas Cooper, *The mystery of witch-craft, etc.* (London: Nicholas Okes, 1617), 9.

Dog has no exact parallel in the extant drama of the period, but records of a lost play, or rather two, not only provide a substantial hint about staging but also suggest the dramatic appeal and currency of such diabolic representation. The playwrights of *The Witch of Edmonton* were not wholly original in this respect; indeed, they were reaching back to a theatrical practice of some 20 years previous. Philip Henslowe's invaluable *Diary* establishes that a play called *The Black Dog of Newgate*, written by John Day, Richard Hathaway, Wentworth Smith and another unnamed 'poet', was staged in 1602, with a second part following (presumably on account of the first's popularity) in 1603.[22] The *Diary* further makes it clear that the title role would have been played by an actor in a dog costume, since payments are recorded 'to by Lame skenes for the blacke dogge of newgate' and 'for a canves sewt & skenes for the black doge of newgate'.[23] It may well be, then, that the series of negative descriptions of the dog offered by Young Banks, the natural fool in *The Witch of Edmonton*, contains a theatrical in-joke:

> This is no Paris-garden bandog [mastiff] ... that keeps a bow-wow-wowing, to have butchers bring their curs thither, and when all comes to all, they run away like sheep. Neither is this the Black Dog of Newgate. (IV.i.248–51).

When his father comments, 'No, Goodman Son-fool, but the Dog of Hell-gate' (252), his allusion to the infernal Cerberus serves, in fact, to link the Black Dog of the play with that of Newgate.

We know nothing of the plot of the lost plays, but they almost certainly staged aspects of the well-established legend of a terrifying black hell-hound, known in at least one account by the name of Shagge,[24] which appeared before executions.[25] To procure the hanging of Elizabeth Sawyer is, after all, explicitly the object of the play's equivalent:

> *Dog.*   she has done killing now, but must be killed
> For what she has done. She's shortly to be hanged.
>
> *Young Banks.* Is she? In my conscience if she be, 'tis thou hast brought her to the gallows, Tom.
>
> *Dog.* Right. I served her to that purpose, 'twas part of my wages. (V.i.102–6)

---

[22]   See Philip Henslowe, *Henslowe's Diary*, ed. Walter W. Greg (London: A. H. Bullen, 1904), fols 118ᵛ–20ʳ, *passim*.

[23]   Henslowe, *Diary*, fol. 119ʳ.

[24]   Luke Hutton, *The discouery of a London monster called, the black dog of Newgate* (London: G. Eld for Robert Wilson, 1612), refers to 'his rugged Diuelship Mounsier Shagge the Black Dog of Newgate' (sig. A3ʳ).

[25]   See Peter Corbin and Douglas Sedge, eds, *The Witch of Edmonton*, by William Rowley, Thomas Dekker and John Ford, Revels Student Editions (Manchester: Manchester University Press, 1999), n. to IV.i.261–62.

The association between black dogs and devils is ancient and widespread in Christian folklore. Enriching and complicating the Christian content, moreover, is a widespread and potent folkloric prototype in Anglo-Saxon and Scandinavian legend, generally 'regarded as an augur of fatal disaster'.[26] Far from being limited to the role of 'familiar', or agent of a witch's evil power, the dog was often taken to be a shape assumed by the devil himself. This has been documented by Barbara Allen Woods, who has made a detailed study of legends in which the devil figures as a dog.[27] It is notable here that, while the term 'familiar' appears in the 'Actor's Names', within the play-text it figures only when Sawyer is thinking about becoming a witch (II.i.35, 101–4); when Dog actually appears, its diabolic essence is explicitly declared:

> *Dog.* Ho! Have I found thee cursing? Now thou art mine own.
>
> *Sawyer.* Thine? What art thou?
>
> *Dog.*   He thou hast so often importuned
> To appear to thee, the Devil. (II.i.120–23)

In the same frank manner, Mephistopheles identifies himself to Faustus, states his intention of damning him and links his apparition to transgressive language – blasphemy, in that case, rather than cursing (I.iii.43–51).[28] Yet the moment of apparition in response to a curse, illustrated in the title-page engraving of the first edition, equally conforms to the tradition of the diabolic summons, and what follows, as in *Faustus*, is the traditional pact: both elements, again, are widespread in devil-as-dog accounts.[29] So common does the association seem to have been that, around 1613, a young girl in Lancashire, Grace Sowerbutts, a child-informer of the kind common in witchcraft accusations, invented stories of being haunted and harassed by a witch 'in the likeness of a black dog with two legs' on several occasions.[30] All in all, it is reasonable to suppose that the effect of the black dog on

---

[26]   Alexandra Walsham, *Providence in Early Modern England* (Oxford: Oxford University Press, 1999), 189.

[27]   Barbara Allen Woods, *The Devil in Dog Form: A Partial Type-Index of Devil Legends*, Folklore Studies, 11 (Berkeley: University of California Press, 1959).

[28]   All references are to Christopher Marlowe, *Doctor Faustus B-Text*, in *Doctor Faustus and Other Plays*, ed. David Bevington and Eric Rasmussen, Oxford English Drama, Oxford World's Classics (Oxford: Oxford University Press, 1995).

[29]   See Woods, *Devil in Dog Form*, 55.

[30]   Thomas Potts, *The Wonderfull Discoverie of Witches in the Countie of Lancaster* (1613), ed. G. B. Harrison (1929), cited in *Elizabethan-Jacobean Drama: A New Mermaid Background Book*, ed. G. Blakemore Evans (London: A. and C. Black, 1989), 269. In this case, the justice in charge of the trial became sceptical and induced the girl and other witnesses to admit that their testimony was false, and that they had been suborned by a disgruntled Catholic priest.

stage might well have been electrifying and highly disturbing for the contemporary audience.

This is far from inconsistent with the likelihood that Dekker, Ford and Rowley were also tapping into a vein of contemporary journalism – one, moreover, that was already in theatrical circulation and that mirrored the superstitions and fears of the local populace in the country surrounding Edmonton in East Anglia. Indeed, that populace had recently been electrified rather literally during a thunderstorm so violent as to earn a place in the annals (several persons were struck dead or scorched) and the status of a sign of divine wrath, especially since it caused damage to two churches – those of Bungay (about 10 miles distant from Norwich) and nearby Blythburgh – during Sunday services. It seems perfectly reasonable to presume that a London audience of *The Witch of Edmonton* would have had its perception enhanced by a pamphlet documenting this impressive event and connecting it with the legend of the so-called Black Dog of Bungay, which remains to this day notorious in the area and commonly goes under the name of 'Shuck' (cf. 'Shagge', the Black Dog of Newgate).[31]

I am referring to what the 1577 account by Abraham Fleming refers to as the '*straunge and terrible wunder wrought very late in the the* [sic] *parish church of Bongay* [Bungay], *a town of no great distance from the citie of Norwich*' – or from Edmonton, for that matter.[32] According to the parish records (and Holinshed's *Chronicles*[33]), on a Sunday in August 1577, in the midst of a storm of unprecedented and terrifying violence, two men sitting in the belfry of St Mary's Church, Bungay, were struck dead by lightning. Another was seriously injured, and major damage was caused to the tower and clock. What Fleming adds – on the authority of eye-witnesses, as he claims – and moralizes as punishment for sin is the intervention of a 'mooste horrible similitude and likeness', 'a dog as they might discerne it, of a black colour', that 'moued such admiration in the mindes of the assemblie, that they thought doomes day was already come'.[34] The 'black dog, or the diuel in such a likenesse'[35] supposedly wrung the necks of two kneeling members of the congregation 'clene backward' and, gripping the back of a third, scorched him with such hot fire that he shrivelled up like a piece of leather or a purse 'drawen

---

[31]   The most complete discussion of the legend, including references to Fleming's pamphlet, Holinshed's *Chronicles* and local records is by David Waldron and Christopher Reeve, *Shock! The Black Dog of Bungay: A Case Study in Local Folklore* (Harpendon, Harts: Hidden Publishing, 2010). See also Walsham, *Providence*, 186–94.

[32]   Abraham Fleming, *A straunge and terrible wunder wrought very late in the the* [sic] *parish church of Bongay* [Bungay], *a town of no great distance from the citie of Norwich, namely the fourth of this August, in ye yeere of our Lord 1577, etc.* (London: [J. Allde?] for Francis Godly, 1577).

[33]   See Raphael Holinshed et al., *The first and second volumes of Chronicles, etc.*, 3 vols (London: [Henry Denham], 1587), vol. 3, 1270–71. It is noteworthy that Fleming himself probably wrote this brief account, which makes no mention of a diabolic black dog.

[34]   Fleming, *Wunder*, sig. A5[r–v].

[35]   Fleming, *Wunder*, sig. A5[v].

togither with a string'.[36] Fleming claims confirmation of his story on the basis of 'the marks as it were of his clawes or talans' still to be seen 'in the stones of the Church, and likewise in the Church dore which are maruelously renten & torne'.[37] He states that the dog did similar damage in nearby Blythburgh.[38]

Background to this story that may be pertinent to *The Witch of Edmonton* is the existence of socio-religious tensions in the parish of Bungay between Puritan and more conservative Anglican factions, which had recently led to the defacement of a 'Popish' rood-screen, followed by repression of the Puritans by the church hierarchy.[39] It would have been plausible, given the mentality of the age, to consider the appearance of the diabolic dog as divinely dispatched chastisement of the ecclesiastic authorities. That such readings were eminently reversible is shown by the diametrically opposed application of the story produced by the recusant Roland Jenkes, who published a French version of Fleming's pamphlet in Paris shortly after its appearance with the divine admonition redirected squarely against all those who had swerved from 'la saincte foy Catholique'.[40]

On the one hand, then, Fleming's account obviously conforms to an admonitory discourse of manifestations of divine displeasure at religious deviance, major or minor. Walsham cites another account, this one anonymous dating from 1613, of the intrusion of a shape resembling a 'broad eyd bul' into a church at Great Chart in Kent during a violent tempest, apparently to chastise chatterers who habitually discussed worldly affairs in the aisles rather than concentrating on the minister's edifying sermon.[41] On the other hand, the incident of the Black Dog of Bungay resonates with quite specific local folklore and demonology,[42] and one may suspect that it so resonated as well for another dramatist concerned with relations between the diabolic and the divine, Robert Greene.

---

[36]   Fleming, *Wunder*, sig. A5ᵛ–A6ʳ.

[37]   Fleming, *Wunder*, sig. A6ᵛ.

[38]   Fleming, *Wunder*, sig. A7ʳ.

[39]   Waldron and Reeve, *Black Dog*, 60–62; see also Walsham, *Providence*, 192–93.

[40]   Roland Jenkes, trans., *Extrait d'un petit livre anglois, escrit par Abraham Fleming, imprimé à Londres en Angleterre, chez François Godly, contenant la narration & rapport des choses estranges & merveilleuses advenues en leurs temples babiloniques des villes de Bengay, & Blybery, pres de Norwich en Angleterre*, published with *Histoire mervelleuse advenues par feu du Ciel en trois villes d'Angleterre, à l'encontre de douze juges heretiques, & de deux ministres qui voulloient persecuté les Catholiques* (Paris: Jean Poupy [c. 1577]), sig. b3ᵛ.

[41]   *The wonders of this windie winter* (London: [George Eld for] Joseph Hunt, 1613), sig. C2ᵛ; Walsham, *Providence*, 188.

[42]   It may be relevant that the medieval gargoyle dogs on St Mary's Church, Bungay, are especially prominent and hideous (see Figure 3.1), and that the North Porch is surmounted by a statue evoking a hellhound sitting on its hind-legs (see Figure 3.2).

Whichever of the two plays is precursor of the other (their relative dating cannot be established with certainty), Greene's romantic *Friar Bacon and Friar Bungay*[43] and Marlowe's tragic *Doctor Faustus* have long been recognized as standing in a close intertextual relation. Both are concerned, most centrally, with sorcerers who deal with the devil in return for supernatural knowledge and power, and who come to regret that dealing. Both derive from similar popular and episodic narratives of their magician protagonists – Marlowe's most immediately from the English *Faustbuch*, Greene's from *The famous history of Frier Bacon containing the wonderful things that he did in his life, also the manner of his death, with the lives and deaths of the two conjurers Bungey and Vandermast.*[44] It is suggestive, first, that Greene's title, in contrast with that of his source, gives equal billing to Friar Bungay, who is secondary in the story, as in magical ability and diabolic complicity. More significantly, Greene shifts the geographical location of the Bungay plot (essentially, the friar's attempt to marry the two lovers against the Prince's wishes) to the region surrounding the town of Bungay, whereas in the source it is vaguely located close to Oxford, and Bacon's magic mirror is explicitly restricted to a range of 50 miles. Greene was a native of Norwich, and his local knowledge is applied as well in designating the fair maid as Margaret of Fressingfield, and in having her lover, Lord Lacy, disguise himself as a farmer's son from Beccles. Fressingfield, Beccles and Bungay, as well as Framingham, where Margaret plans to enter the nunnery, are all in close proximity. The places involved are specified with considerable precision, and repeatedly. Bacon's magic must explicitly reach from Oxford to Sussex, though Prince Edward's dagger cannot (''Twere a long poniard, my lord, to reach between / Oxford and Fressingfield' [vi.131–32]), and not until then is Bungay transported to Oxford. He can thus witness the penitent aftermath of the climactic episode of the Brazen Head, while in the source he assists Bacon from the start in that project, which figures early in the narrative sequence.[45] All in all, it very much looks as if Greene is taking his cue from the mere name of Bungay in his source and encouraging his audience to apply an entire set of regional associations consistent with his theme of diabolic intervention in human affairs of the head and the heart.

At this point, it is useful to describe the role of Dog in the three intertwining plots of *The Witch of Edmonton*, which reveals more than the play's concern with representing Mother Sawyer as the garden-variety witch and the community's reaction to such marginal women. Besides the character's interaction with Mother Sawyer, Dog enters into essential contact with two other agents of human mischief,

---

[43]   Robert Greene, *Friar Bacon and Friar Bungay*, ed. J. A. Lavin, The New Mermaids (London: Ernest Benn, 1969). This edition is used for citations.

[44]   *The famous history of Frier Bacon containing the wonderful things that he did in his life, also the manner of his death, with the lives and deaths of the two conjurers Bungey and Vandermast* (London: M. Clark for T. Passenger, 1679). No edition contemporary with Greene's play survives; there is a 1627 printing, but it is incomplete.

[45]   *The famous history of Frier Bacon*, sig. B4ᵛ–C3ᵛ.

one serious – the bigamist murderer, Frank Thorney – one less so, the Clown Cuddy Banks.

Young Frank Thorney, under pressure from his father, an impoverished gentleman, commits bigamy when he makes a financially attractive match with Susan Carter after secretly marrying the penniless servant-girl Winifred, whom he loves but who has been impregnated by her villainous employer, Sir Arthur Clarington. Frank tries to run away with Winifred but is pursued by the unsuspecting Susan, whom he stabs to death in order to conceal the truth. He wounds himself, pretending to have been attacked by Warbeck, a former rival for Susan's hand, and his friend Somerton, but his treacherous behaviour is discovered, and Frank is sentenced to death. Dog is present, if invisible to Frank, to inspire and encourage his scheming throughout the scene of the murder; it also appears suggestively to herald the incriminating discovery of the fatal knife. These are manifestations of the ominous kind described by Woods, who documents folk legends that tell of the devil in the form of a black dog appearing when a killing is about to be perpetrated.[46] It is striking that Mother Sawyer has nothing to do with the Thorney plot, anymore than with Anne Ratcliffe's death – the two principal crimes for which she is condemned. The playwrights, in showing clearly to the audience the devil's role in abetting the criminal impulse of Frank, seem to be aligning themselves with Gifford by suggesting that witches could not reasonably be incriminated for bringing about *maleficia*. As far as the dog is concerned, we are well beyond the territory of the witch's familiar.

The comic underplot concerning Cuddy Banks has its own serious side. Cuddy becomes a sort of sorcerer's apprentice, like Wagner in *Doctor Faustus* and Miles in Greene's play, by gaining the services of Dog up to a point. For Mother Sawyer deceptively promises to help Cuddy gain his beloved, with the idea of partly displacing onto him her revenge against his father, her chief persecutor and the provoker of her devil-summoning curses. With respect to Cuddy, the independent power of the diabolic is extended and projected through a series of supernatural interventions, including the shape-changing of spirits, when, in a parodic reminiscence of Mephistopheles' fabrication of a false Helen for Faustus, Dog produces a likeness of Cuddy's unattainable Katherine. Dog also dumps Cuddy into the Edmonton swamp (III.i.94–98), as the Horse-Courser in *Doctor Faustus* is left magically adrift in a river on a bottle of hay (IV.v.35–41).

Dog's sabotage of the morris dance in which Cuddy is to play the key role of the hobby horse is presented as his own initiative and bears only an indirect, though a significant, relation to Sawyer's vindictiveness. This neatly makes the point that, even when the witch's will is performed, the devil is not her servant; she is his. Dog prevents the fiddler Sawgut from getting a sound out of his instrument, which becomes 'speechless' (III.iv.43), as Young Banks says. The inhibition of speech and other bodily functions is a standard mark of the devil's power, as

---

[46]   See Woods, *Devil in Dog Form*, 102–4.

Kocher points out with respect to Faustus ('O, he stays my tongue!' [V.ii.58]),[47] and it confirms the diabolic origin of Friar Bacon's magic in striking Friar Bungay dumb when the latter is about to marry the lovers.[48] When Dog actually takes over the fiddler's role, he enacts the traditional association between the devil and more-or-less rough music. Indeed, there is at least one account of the devil playing for a witches' sabbath in dog-form,[49] and one might see a parody of such a celebration in his effective hijacking of the morris, which is then broken up ('Away with jollity' [III.iv.52]) by the Constable arresting the innocent Warbeck and Somerton for Susan's murder. Dog was Frank's invisible accomplice in falsely accusing them; ironically, Frank at first claims that he cannot denounce the murderers because he has passed such an oath 'As pulls damnation up if it be broke' (III.iii.85), thereby eliciting Old Thorney's comment, 'Keep oath with murderers? That were a conscience / To hold the Devil in' (87–88). Thus Frank, in effect, unknowingly concludes a pact with the devil.

Morris dancing evokes, in this text, the potential of the social dynamic to cohere, to function harmoniously, but that dynamic contains the seeds of its own destruction. The devil visibly and audibly presides here over its symbolic implosion – the result of a tangle of greed and lust. And this becomes a reminder of the hatred and prejudice that produce Mother Sawyer as witch and scapegoat. For the morris dancers, too, accuse and taunt her early in the play, fearing her spoiling of their 'mirth' (II.i.87); she calls this being 'tortured' (98): it proves the last straw in making her resolve, ''Tis all one, / To be a witch as to be counted one' (117–18).

Cuddy Banks, the human hobby horse, is saved from diabolic harm by his asinine innocence (one meaning of 'Cuddy' is donkey, another is 'A stupid fellow, an "ass"'[50]), which leads him to accept a talking dog at face value. This may have evoked, for audiences, a further set of potentially disturbing spiritual resonances in parodic form. Marocco, the preternaturally intelligent dancing horse of one William Bankes, was a popular spectacle across England and abroad from the late 1580s until around 1608, and remained famous in memory. Dekker himself sardonically recalls one of the animal's notable accomplishments (climbing the stairs of St Paul's steeple) in *The Gul's Horne-booke* (1609), and exhorts his young gallant 'to believe verily that it was not a horse, but something else in the likeness of one'.[51] In fact, accusations of witchcraft came close to getting his clever trainer into serious trouble on several occasions, and Ben Jonson in 1610, in his poem

[47]   Kocher, 'Witchcraft', 31–32. Faustus's previous power to strike his adversaries dumb (IV.vi.104–12) thus ironically turns against him.

[48]   Greene, *Friar Bacon and Friar Bungay*, vi.149–62.

[49]   Harvey B. Gaul, 'Music and Devil-Worship', *Musical Quarterly* 11.2 (1925): 194.

[50]   See *OED*, s.v. Cuddy comments on his deception by Tom, after his ducking in the pond, that Mother Sawyer 'may call me Ass' (III.i.115).

[51]   Thomas Dekker, *The Gul's Horne-booke*, ed. R. B. McKerrow (London: De la More Press, 1904), 38.

'On the Famous Voyage', fancifully imagined both horse and man as having been condemned:

> Old *Bankes* the juggler, our *Pythagoras*,
> Grave tutor to the learned horse. Both which,
> Being, beyond sea, burned for one witch:
> Their spirits transmigrated to a cat.[52]

Erica Fudge cites this reference to point up Jonson's humorous evocation of 'the dangerous possibility of the transmigration of souls';[53] he does the same thing, then, in *Volpone*, where religious questions are actually toyed with.[54] In *The Witch of Edmonton*, too, the stakes are high. In recounting to Cuddy the devil's infinite ability to change shapes, and in particular to animate a variety of vicious human forms, Dog seems almost to be describing a diabolic metempsychosis. The latter hypothesis itself, of course, is antithetical to the Christian belief in a unique human soul which the devil may come to possess, as is clear from the tortured final longing of Faustus:

> O, Pythagoras' *metempsychosis*, were that true,
> This soul should fly from me and I be changed
> Into some brutish beast.
> All beasts are happy, for, when they die,
> Their souls are soon dissolved in elements;
> But mine must live still to be plagued in hell. (V.ii.169–74)

In the plot that centres on the identity of Mother Sawyer as a woman who traffics with the forces of evil, it is generally accepted by commentators that the playwrights undertake a remarkably sympathetic analysis of the processes by which her identity as witch is socially constructed. But the way in which Mother Sawyer is sympathetic acquires far deeper resonances when we take into account the association of Dog with the incarnation of the devil himself and the development of Mother Sawyer's discontent. For what might have been mere local rural grievances become a metaphysical quest reminiscent of the spiritual crisis of Faustus. The playwrights have taken this example of witchcraft of a commonplace, indeed trivial, kind and grafted onto it the trappings of the most significant metaphysical tragedy in the early modern English theatre.

They do this, first, by selecting material from Goodcole's account that would be calculated to evoke the career of Faustus for audiences steeped in that perennially

---

[52] Ben Jonson, 'CXXXIII. On the Famous Voyage', in *The Complete Poetry of Ben Jonson*, ed. William B. Hunter, The Norton Library (New York: W. W. Norton, 1968), lines 156–59.

[53] Erica Fudge, *Brutal Reasoning: Animals, Rationality, and Humanity in Early Modern England* (Ithaca, NY: Cornell University Press, 2006), 127.

[54] See the entertainment of Nano and Androgyno in Ben Jonson, *Volpone*, ed. R. Brian Parker, The Revels Plays (Manchester: Manchester University Press, 1983), I.ii.6–62.

popular Elizabethan precursor. Dog is empowered to set essentially the same terms for Elizabeth Sawyer's petty vindictive intentions as does Mephistopheles for the celestial aspirations of the German doctor. He requires that she cease praying to Christ and pray to the devil instead. He demands that she seal her pact with blood – here, ironically, not the blood that will not flow when Faustus tries to produce it to serve as ink, but the blood with which she will nourish him. What goes with the role of a mere familiar thereby resonates with overtones of the devil as dominator. And Dog's repeated threat to tear her body in pieces corresponds to the climactic sparagmos evoked by Marlowe. These elements are all obviously part of conventional witch-lore, but in the context of the dynamic interchange between Sawyer and Dog, they strike a tragic chord on a much higher plane than that of the village green.

When it comes to the witch's soliloquies, the playwrights are in the realm of pure invention, and here the calculated effect seems clear. The ugly old woman that Goodcole disdains as ignorant and stupid is from the start given highly dignified, if homely, verse in which to articulate her sense of injustice and thirst for revenge. Some of it, moreover, gestures, in parodic form, towards transcendental aspiration:

> Would some power good or bad
> Instruct me which way I might be revenged
> Upon this churl, I'd go out of myself,
> And give this fury leave to dwell within
> This ruined cottage, ready to fall with age. (II.i.106–10)

When Mother Sawyer declares herself prepared to

> Abjure all goodness. Be at hate with prayer,
> And study curses, imprecations,
> Blasphemous speeches, oaths, detested oaths,
> Or anything that's ill (111–14),

she shows herself ready to rise above (or descend below) her 'ignorant' (3) condition, and couples Faustus's more academically respectable self-injunction to 'settle' his 'studies' (I.i.1) with that to 'begin thine incantations, / And try if devils will obey thy hest' (I.iii.5–6). She, too, has hit upon what Mephistopheles calls 'the shortest cut for conjuring' – namely, 'to abjure all godliness / And pray devoutly to the prince of hell' (49–51). The parallel extends, with due irony, to the witch's charmed corruptions of learned language:

> *Contaminetur nomen tuum.* I'm an expert scholar;
> Speak Latin, or I know not well what language,
> As well as the best of 'em. (II.i.182–84)

It arguably extends, moreover, to the final despairing soliloquies of both protagonists. For Elizabeth Sawyer, too, time is up; the devil has turned against her, although she does not know it yet, and she seeks him throughout the elements, expressing herself in language whose exceptional grandeur calls attention to the doom awaiting her:

> If in the air thou hover'st, fall upon me
> In some dark cloud, and as I oft have seen
> Dragons and serpents in the elements,
> Appear thou now so to me. ...
> > ... let earth cleave,
> And break from hell, I care not. (V.i.13–20)

The desperate illusion of the witch would surely have resonated strongly for an audience weaned on the final elemental imaginings of Faustus, trapped between the opposed wraths of heaven and hell:

> O, I'll leap up to heaven! Who pulls me down? ...
> And see a threat'ning arm, an angry brow.
> Mountains and hells, come, come and fall on me,
> And hide me from the heavy wrath of heaven!
> No? Then will I headlong run into the earth.
> Gape, earth! O, no, it will not harbour me. (V.ii.144–53)

If any proof were needed that we are in the realm of deliberate parody, it suffices to add the similarity, which has been noticed, between Mephistopheles' declaration about the Old Man who calls on Faustus to repent and that of Dog about Old Banks, who most insistently identifies her as a witch.[55] To Faustus's twisted demand, 'Torment, sweet friend, that base and agèd man / That durst dissuade me from thy Lucifer' (V.i.78–79), Mephistopheles replies, 'His faith is great. I cannot touch his soul; / But what I may afflict his body with / I will attempt, which is but little worth' (81–83). With regard to her enemy, Banks – for her the 'old churl' (II.i.148), but for his son 'a kind of God-bless-us' (202–3) – Sawyer asks Dog to 'touch his life' (152), only to be told, in a virtually Mephistophelian explication of the limits of evil power,

> Though we have power, know, it is circumscribed,
> And tied in limits. Though he be cursed to thee,
> Yet of himself he is loving to the world,
> And charitable to the poor. Now men
> That, as he, love goodness, though in smallest measure,
> Live without compass of our reach. His cattle
> And corn I'll kill and mildew. But his life,
> (Until I take him as I late found thee,
> Cursing and swearing) I have no power to touch. (II.i.158–66)

---

[55]   See Corbin and Sedge, eds, *Witch*, n. to II.i.164.

A notable part of the parallel here lies in the implication of an underlying Calvinistic concept of grace and election.

It goes along with the addition of such metaphysical apparatus to a banal affair of corn-blighting and cattle-killing – and indeed, the kissing of a cow's arse, to which Old Banks claims her witchcraft has driven him (IV.i.55–61) – that the old woman's drive to revenge assumes in itself an existential dimension, projecting the inward upon the outward. From a crude impulse to eradicate her enemies, she progresses to the impulse to pursue them inwardly, on the level of subjectivity, imaginatively transferring to them her own injury: '*To scandal and disgrace pursue 'em / Et santabicetur nomen tuum*' (II.i.251–52). This is to appropriate the standard psychological mechanism of the early modern revenger, for whom by definition, as Elizabeth Sawyer states outright, 'Revenge ... is sweeter far than life' (V.i.7): by his vengeance he seeks not merely to destroy his enemies' bodies but to fill an emptiness marking his own experience of meaninglessness – in effect, the absence of a soul.[56] The standard language of witchcraft – of the possession of 'soul and body', as reiterated by Goodcole[57] – is effectively redeployed on a metaphysical level.

Given the multiple evocations of *Doctor Faustus*, the recasting of revenge thus enacted by the witch may be read back ironically into Marlowe's play. It is not common to reduce that grand tragedy to a mere sordid history of revenge, but that may be one possible reading of its protagonist's opening soliloquy, with its list of grievances, not against the insults and injuries of neighbours, but against intellectual competitors and, beyond them, the authors of textbooks, including the originator of the Book that pretends to deliver the ultimate Word: 'What doctrine call you this?' (I.i.47). He feels, in other words, that he is not just unduly confined but unjustly put down.

What makes a proud scholar into an overreacher on a cosmic scale may finally be little different from what makes a wretched old woman into the witch next door. When she challenges, at the outset, both a social and a religious structure that already brand her as a damnable criminal – 'And why on me? Why should the envious world / Throw all their scandalous malice upon me?' (II.i.1–2) – she, too, is asking, 'What doctrine call you this?' She presses the question home later in her persuasive moralistic insistence that witches of all sorts abound untouchable by the law because outwardly acceptable ('A witch? Who is not?' [IV.i.111]): lecherous temptresses, profligate wasters of hard-earned wealth, scolds, unscrupulous men of law, spoilers of virginity. The presence on stage of the Black Dog, the devil incarnate who appears at the call of forms of inner criminality already present, might have made it more difficult for the audience to respond with easy answers. Yet one wonders whether, given the temper of the times, their doubts would have extended to the doctrine of witchcraft itself.

---

[56]   See Richard Hillman, 'Meaning and Mortality in Some Renaissance Revenge Plays', *University of Toronto Quarterly* 49.1 (1979): 1–17.

[57]   Goodcole, *Discouerie*, sig. C3ᵛ.

Works Cited

Primary Sources

Cooper, Thomas. *The mystery of witch-craft. Discouering, the truth, nature, occasions, growth and power therof. Together with the detection and punishment of the same, etc.* London: Nicholas Okes, 1617. STC 5701.

Dekker, Thomas. *The Gul's Horne-booke.* Edited by R. B. McKerrow. London: De la More Press, 1904.

Dekker, Thomas, John Ford, and William Rowley. *The Witch of Edmonton.* Edited by Arthur F. Kinney. The New Mermaids. London: A. and C. Black, 1998.

The famous history of Frier Bacon containing the wonderful things that he did in his life, also the manner of his death, with the lives and deaths of the two conjurers Bungey and Vandermast. London: M. Clark for T. Passenger, 1679. Wing F373.

Fleming, Abraham. *A straunge and terrible wunder wrought very late in the the [sic] parish church of Bongay* [Bungay]*, a town of no great distance from the citie of Norwich, namely the fourth of this August, in ye yeere of our Lord 1577, etc.* London: [J. Allde?] for Francis Godly, 1577. STC 11050.

Gifford, George. *A dialogue concerning witches and witchcraftes. In which is laide open how craftely the Diuell deceiueth not onely the witches but many other and so leadeth them awrie into many great errours, etc.* London: John Windet for Tobie Cooke and Mihil Hart, 1593. STC 11850.

———. *A discourse of the subtill practises of deuilles by witches and sorcerers, etc.* London: T. Orwin for Toby Cooke, 1587. STC 11852.

Goodcole, Henry. *Natures cruell step-dames: or, Matchlesse monsters of the female sex; Elizabeth Barnes, and Anne Willis. Who were executed the 26. day of April, 1637. at Tyburne, for the unnaturall murthering of their owne children. Also, herein is contained their severall confessions, an the courts just proceedings against other notorious malefactors, with their severall offences this sessions. Further, a relation of the wicked life and impenitent death of Iohn Flood, who raped his owne childe.* London: E. Purslowe for Francis Coules, 1637. STC 12012.

———. *The wonderfull discouerie of Elizabeth Sawyer a witch, late of Edmonton, her conuiction and condemnation and death. Together with the relation of the Diuels accesse to her, and their conference together, etc.* London: A. Mathewes for William Butler, 1621. STC 12014.

Greene, Robert. *Friar Bacon and Friar Bungay.* Edited by J. A. Lavin. The New Mermaids. London: Ernest Benn, 1969.

Henslowe, Philip. *Henslowe's Diary.* Edited by Walter W. Greg. London: A. H. Bullen, 1904.

Holinshed, Raphael, et al. *The first and second volumes of Chronicles, etc.* 3 vols. London: [Henry Denham], 1587. STC 13569.

Hutton, Luke. *The discouery of a London monster called, the black dog of Newgate.* London: G. Eld for Robert Wilson, 1612. STC 14029.

Jenkes, Roland, trans. *Extrait d'un petit livre anglois, escrit par Abraham Fleming, imprimé à Londres en Angleterre, chez François Godly, contenant la narration & rapport des choses estranges & merveilleuses advenues en leurs temples babiloniques des villes de Bengay, & Blybery, pres de Norwich en Angleterre.* Published with *Histoire mervelleuse advenues par feu du Ciel en trois villes d'Angleterre, à l'encontre de douze juges heretiques, & de deux ministres qui voulloient persecuté les Catholiques.* Paris: Jean Poupy [c. 1577].

Jonson, Ben. *The Complete Poetry of Ben Jonson.* Edited by William B. Hunter. The Norton Library. New York: W. W. Norton, 1968.

———. *Volpone.* Edited by R. Brian Parker. The Revels Plays. Manchester: Manchester University Press, 1983.

Marlowe, Christopher. *Doctor Faustus B-Text.* In *Doctor Faustus and Other Plays.* Edited by David Bevington and Eric Rasmussen. Oxford English Drama, Oxford World's Classics. Oxford: Oxford University Press, 1995.

Potts, Thomas. *The Wonderfull Discoverie of Witches in the Countie of Lancaster* (1613). Edited by G. B. Harrison (1929). In *Elizabethan-Jacobean Drama: A New Mermaid Background Book,* edited by G. Blakemore Evans. London: A. and C. Black, 1989. 269–71.

Scot, Reginald. *The discouerie of witchcraft, etc.* London: [Henry Denham for William Brome], 1584. STC 21864.

Secondary Sources

Briggs, Robin. *Witches and Neighbours: The Social and Cultural Context of European Witchcraft.* London: HarperCollins, 1995.

Clark, Stuart. *Thinking with Demons: The Idea of Witchcraft in Early Modern Europe.* Oxford: Clarendon Press, 1997.

Comensoli, Viviana. *'Household Business': Domestic Plays of Early Modern England.* Toronto: University of Toronto Press, 1996.

Corbin, Peter, and Douglas Sedge, eds. *The Witch of Edmonton,* by William Rowley, Thomas Dekker and John Ford. Revels Student Editions. Manchester: Manchester University Press, 1999.

Dawson, Anthony B. 'Witchcraft/Bigamy: Cultural Conflict in *The Witch of Edmonton*'. *Renaissance Drama* 20 (1989): 77–98.

DeWindt, Anne Reiber. 'Witchcraft and Conflicting Visions of the Ideal Village Community'. *Journal of British Studies* 34.4 (1993): 427–63.

Fudge, Erica. *Brutal Reasoning: Animals, Rationality, and Humanity in Early Modern England.* Ithaca, NY: Cornell University Press, 2006.

Gaul, Harvey B. 'Music and Devil-Worship'. *Musical Quarterly* 11.2 (1925): 192–95.

Gregory, Annabel. 'Witchcraft, Politics and "Good Neighbourhood" in Early Seventeenth-Century Rye'. *Past and Present* 133 (1991): 31–66.

Hillman, Richard. 'Meaning and Mortality in Some Renaissance Revenge Plays'. *University of Toronto Quarterly* 49.1 (1979): 1–17.

Johnstone, Nathan. *The Devil and Demonism in Early Modern England.* Cambridge Studies in Early Modern British History. Cambridge: Cambridge University Press, 2006.

Kocher, Paul H. 'The Witchcraft Bias in Marlowe's *Faustus*'. *Modern Philology* 38.1 (1940): 9–36.

Macfarlane, Alan. *Witchcraft in Tudor and Stuart England: A Regional and Comparative Study.* 2nd ed. London: Routledge, 1999.

Nicol, David. 'Interrogating the Devil: Social and Demonic Pressure in *The Witch of Edmonton*'. *Comparative Drama* 38.4 (2005): 425–46.

Purkiss, Diane. *The Witch in History: Early Modern and Twentieth-Century Representations.* London: Routledge, 1996.

Sharpe, J. A. *Instruments of Darkness: Witchcraft in Early Modern England.* Philadelphia: University of Pennsylvania Press, 1997.

Thomas, Keith. *Religion and the Decline of Magic.* 2nd ed. Harmondsworth, Middlesex: Penguin, 1980.

Waldron, David, and Christopher Reeve. *Shock! The Black Dog of Bungay: A Case Study in Local Folklore.* Harpendon, Harts: Hidden Publishing, 2010.

Walsham, Alexandra. *Providence in Early Modern England.* Oxford: Oxford University Press, 1999.

West, Robert Hunter. *The Invisible World: A Study of Pneumatology in Elizabethan Drama.* Athens: University of Georgia Press, 1939.

Woods, Barbara Allen. *The Devil in Dog Form: A Partial Type-Index of Devil Legends.* Folklore Studies, 11. Berkeley: University of California Press, 1959.

Fig. 3.1   Fifteenth-century gargoyle dog on North Wall of St Mary's Church, Bungay, Suffolk (Photograph by P. Ruberry-Blanc, 2010)

Fig. 3.2   Statue of sitting dog above North Porch, St Mary's Church, Bungay, Suffolk (Photograph by P. Ruberry-Blanc, 2010)

Chapter 4
Fact versus Fiction:
The Construction of the Figure of the
Prostitute in Early Modern England, Official
and Popular Discourses

Frédérique Fouassier-Tate

If you were able to step back in time and have a stroll through the streets of early modern London, you would no doubt bump into a punk, a strumpet, a cockatrix, or, in other – and more contemporary – words, a prostitute. Prostitution was particularly developed in early modern London, and the numerous, and not always clandestine, brothels of the capital and its suburbs were peopled by thousands of women who catered to the needs of men from all ages and social classes.[1] It is, of course, very difficult to provide a precise overall description of the historical conditions of prostitution in early modern England, given the scarcity of surviving documents and the numerous facets of the subject, be they legal, religious, political, economic or social. What remains certain, though, is that prostitution was greatly developed, as Hugh Latimer complained in a sermon before Edward VI's court in 1549. The preacher laments that Henry VIII's decision to close the licensed brothels in Southwark in 1546 had been to no avail: 'My Lords, you have put down the stews: but I pray you what is the matter amended? ... Ye have but changed the place, and not taken the whoredom away. ... I here say there is now more whoredom in London than ever there was on the Bank.'[2]

One must distinguish between London and the rest of England. As J. A. Sharpe indicates in *Crime in Early Modern England*, towards the middle of the sixteenth

---

[1]   For a more thorough description of the extent and conditions of prostitution in early modern London, see E. J. Burford, *Bawds and Lodgings: A History of the London Bankside Brothels c. 100–1675* (London: Peter Owen 1976); J. A. Sharpe, *Crime in Early Modern England 1550–1750* (London: Longman, 1984); Wallace Shugg, 'Prostitution in Shakespeare's London', *Shakespeare Studies* 10 (1977): 291–313; Faramerz Dabhoiwala, 'The Pattern of Sexual Immorality in Seventeenth- and Eighteenth-Century London', in *Londinopolis: Essays in the Cultural and Social History of Early Modern London*, ed. Paul Griffiths and Mark S. R. Jenner (Manchester: Manchester University Press, 2000), 86–106; as well as my unpublished PhD thesis: 'Représentations de la transgression sexuelle féminine dans le théâtre anglais de la Renaissance', 3 vols (Université François-Rabelais de Tours, 2005), esp. vol. 1.

[2]   Quoted in Shugg, 'Prostitution', 264.

century, the effects of great demographic growth were felt.[3] Inflation as well as the pressure on food resources and on land created a mass of proletarianized poor.[4] As Sharpe explains, there is little evidence of more than casual prostitution in rural areas, contrary to London, where brothels and professional prostitution had long been established,[5] mainly through Henry II's ordinance of 1161, which gave birth to the first officially licensed brothels in England (although the king was essentially legalizing some ecclesiastically owned operations that had been in existence for at least 30 years).[6] Yet, as Sharpe notes, although there were in London well-equipped brothels catering for a variety of tastes, court records suggest the existence of an underclass of what he calls 'unimpressive' and possibly part-time prostitutes, who seemed to have worked most typically on an amateur and opportunistic basis.[7] Prostitutes were often independently operating women whose involvement in prostitution was very temporary.[8] Given the harsh economic circumstances, many women had no other choice than to turn to prostitution, so that streetwalkers were swarming in early modern London, as many contemporary statements suggest.[9]

Given the ubiquity of prostitution, it is not surprising that the figure of the prostitute recurs in discourse, both in official texts like laws and edicts and in popular literature such as drama and pamphlets. Her figure is very carefully and deliberately constructed in a negative way. This chapter proposes to study the paradox at the heart of the discursive creation of the figure of the prostitute in early modern England and its consequences for real-life prostitutes. Indeed, with all her carefully built negativity, the prostitute actually constitutes a cohesive medium for the moralists, preachers, judges and members of municipal and civil authorities, or, in other words, the representatives of official discourses. Although they define her as an abominable Other who should remain outside respectable society, she is in fact at the very heart of the system and crucial to its existence. This essential paradox brings us back, among other things, to the theories of the carnivalesque, as defined by Bakhtin, and to the normative function of transgression, as explained by Peter Stallybrass and Allon White.[10] These critics, of course, base themselves on Foucault, who explained that marginal figures, like the repressed criminal, madman or sexual transgressor, give their central position to those occupying the centre. All those who will not conform to the norm are seen as threats to the status quo by official discourses, which treat them as pariahs. Abnormal creatures are thus beaten and punished till they conform to the norm. This paradox may also be

---

3   The number of inhabitants of England doubled between 1500 and 1630.

4   Sharpe, *Crime*, 16.

5   Sharpe, *Crime*, 114.

6   Burford, *Bawds and Lodgings*, 9.

7   Sharpe, *Crime*, 116; Dabhoiwala, 'Sexual Immorality', 94.

8   Sharpe, *Crime*, 213.

9   Burford, *Bawds and Lodgings*, 145.

10   Peter Stallybrass and Allon White, *The Politics and Poetics of Transgression* (Ithaca, NY: Cornell University Press, 1986).

found in popular literature, where it is sometimes endorsed (mainly in pamphlets and plays for the public theatre), but sometimes also called into question. Thus, the prostitute's subversive potential becomes doubtful: is her image entirely controlled by official discourses, or does she constitute an actual threat for the established society?

I shall first analyze the devices used by official discourses to construct the prostitute as Other. Chief among these devices were negative definitions, a phenomenon facilitated by the fact that early modern society was obsessed with categories and types. I shall then argue that, given the extent of her negative dimension, the prostitute naturally emerges as a convenient scapegoat. Her symbolic exclusion gives the illusion that problems have been solved and exonerates spokesmen for official discourses from having to acknowledge their own share of responsibility. So that, to draw an analogy with Greek literature and mythology, the *pharmakos* is also a *katharmos*, a purifying agent, without which it is impossible to uphold order. The common assimilation of prostitution to other crimes and the centrality of sexuality to female identity make the turning of the prostitute into a scapegoat all the easier. These phenomena are echoed in popular discourse, mainly drama and pamphlets. The prostitute often appears as a source of laughter in plays, but if laughter excludes, it is also potentially subversive, and playwrights were far from always endorsing the values of official discourses, as I shall show in the last part of my analysis.

I

As the psycho-sociologist Sander L. Gilman argues, it is when a group feels it loses control over the external world that it creates stereotypes. He explains that the complacent image which the spokesmen of the dominant discourse have of themselves is shaped by the creation of a repelling Other enabling them to legitimize their own culture, even their own existence. The Other is labelled as such by a group sharing the same values and/or interests (which brings us back to Foucault's theories, alluded to above). The way roles are constituted in a given society thus does not reflect absolute values, but depends on the needs and judgements of the community. Identity is thus a historical product, and stereotypes constitute a way to make sense of a disordered universe, to impose order, to define oneself and to give an identifiable shape to one's fears. The Other is given all the qualities of 'good' or 'evil', the 'evil' Other embodying everything we fear to become, while the 'good' Other represents the ideal we cannot reach.[11] For Gilman, stereotypes are formed according to the three basic, often overlapping, categories of race, disease and sexuality.[12] What matters for official discourses is the mere fact that the Other differs from the norm, much more than the particular

---

[11]   Sander L. Gilman, *Difference and Pathology: Stereotypes of Sexuality, Race, and Madness* (Ithaca, NY: Cornell University Press, 1985), 20.

[12]   Gilman, *Difference and Pathology*, 23.

features which make him or her different. In the Middle Ages, for example, Jews, lepers and prostitutes were submitted to the same laws in London: access to the city was forbidden to them.

As Barbara A. Babcock demonstrates, paradoxically enough, what is socially peripheral very often coincides with what is symbolically central.[13] The prostitute's otherness is indeed far from blatant. If she must be constructed as different, it is precisely because she is dangerously similar. The abhorred Other is indispensable to the dominant discourse – that is, official discourses as they are shaped, transformed and represented by the actions and words of many representatives – because it confers the power of self-definition. If all systems of stereotypical signifiers are essentially bipolar, this was particularly true in the early modern period, which inherited from the Middle Ages a dialectical system of thought, and which was consequently predisposed to see things in terms of binary oppositions: without a negative pole, the positive and legitimate pole of the dominant discourse cannot exist. In this perspective, the prostitute's negativity is far from threatening: it is a tool serving to reinforce the prevailing social structures.

The representatives of official discourses were ill at ease with prostitutes precisely because they seemed to embody what these men repressed and tried to ignore. Because she lives by her body and for men's bodies, the prostitute seems to represent everything which does not belong to the field of reason. But the representatives of official discourses have a body as well, a body they try to control. As the image of the sexualized woman par excellence, the prostitute represents the anarchic potential the dominant discourse bears within itself. At the same time, her apparent sexual freedom tends to inspire castration anxiety in a patriarchal society based on narrow ideas of masculine sexuality.

As the prostitute could not fit into usual categories, she was defined by what she was not, so that the resort to what was reassuringly known and familiar was still possible. A brief Shakespearean reference will illustrate this point. The following dialogue involving the Duke, Mariana and Lucio in Shakespeare's *Measure for Measure* (1604) perfectly shows the fundamental problem of the categorization of the prostitute:

> *Duke.* What, are you married?
>
> *Mariana.* No, my lord.
>
> *Duke.* Are you a maid?
>
> *Mariana.* No, my lord.
>
> *Duke.* A widow, then?
>
> *Mariana.* Neither, my lord.

---

[13] Barbara A. Babcock, introduction to *The Reversible World: Symbolic Inversion in Art and Society*, ed. Barbara A. Babcock (Ithaca, NY: Cornell University Press, 1978), 32.

Duke. Why, you are nothing then. Neither maid, widow, nor wife?

Lucio. My lord, she may be a punk. For many of them are neither maid, widow nor wife.[14]

Women are systematically put into categories, because each role has economic, social and moral implications, which contribute to maintaining order within society. But the insistence on order betrays the unease of the dominant discourse towards a much more porous and blurry reality.

The relentless effort to define the prostitute corresponds to the will both to contain and to keep out what is impossible to grasp. This was first realized in terms of space. One witnesses in the history of London a constant desire to keep prostitution outside the city walls. Prostitutes were recurrently referred to as belonging to the suburban space. The suburbs were thought to gather the scum of society and imagined as a running sore always on the brink of contaminating the body of London. The district of Southwark was first a no man's land in Roman times. It then became a 'liberty', a zone beyond the mayor of London's jurisdiction. As the historians of London prostitution, E. J. Burford and Wallace Shugg, explain, legal prostitution in London was limited to a few licensed brothels on the Bankside, in Southwark. This state of things was officially fixed by Henry II's ordinance of 1161, which legalized and officially authorized a series of brothels in Southwark ('the Stews'), and prevailed till its abolition by Henry VIII in 1546. The ordinance reflects concerns about public health, religion, law and order, and exploitation. The area was under the supervision of the Bishop of Winchester, and (to take up the imagery used notably by Aquinas and St Augustine), the brothels in this zone played the role of sewers serving to absorb the filth of the city. Around 1240, another 'assigned' place for prostitution was recognized: Cock's Lane in Smithfield. The desire to keep pollution outside the city walls can be seen as early as the London enactment of 1393, which strictly forbade prostitutes to wander in any other district than Southwark and Cock's Lane.[15] In Burford's view, the creation and legalization of a red-light district may have constituted an attempt at prophylaxis, at creating a *cordon sanitaire* by which venereal diseases could be checked.[16] As Shugg indicates, there were nevertheless serious attempts to close brothels in the early sixteenth century, the first notable one in 1506. Yet, the main effect of this (only temporary) closing was to scatter prostitutes across London.[17] In 1546, crime and disorder in the brothel districts had grown to such proportions that Henry VIII issued a proclamation stating that all brothels should be closed definitively.

---

14 William Shakespeare, *Measure for Measure*, in *The Riverside Shakespeare*, ed. G. Blakemore Evans, J. J. M. Tobin et al., 2nd ed. (Boston: Houghton Mifflin, 1997), V.i.171–80.

15 Shugg, *Prostitution*, 292.

16 Burford, *Bawds and Lodgings*, 52.

17 Shugg, *Prostitution*, 293.

Southwark nevertheless remained an important centre for prostitution. Besides, the trade was not, and had never been, confined to the few authorized brothels. All the zones surrounding the walls were concerned. Kent Street and High Street, which were the main routes between the north and the south, were famous for prostitution and the haunting places of many freelance prostitutes. Courtesans, the highest class of prostitutes, operated in Westminster near the circles of power and the Court. Smithfield, just outside the north-west wall of the city, was also a notorious district for prostitution, mainly because its horse and cattle fair attracted thousands of potential clients for prostitutes. The 1393 law specified that Cock's Lane was the only street north of the Thames where brothels could operate, but prostitution soon spread to the entire district, Turnbull Street in Clerkenwell being the most notorious venue for prostitutes.[18] In the north-east of London, Shoreditch had a very bad reputation. Prostitutes there found their clients in playhouses, taverns and inns. Whitefriars, between Fleet Street and the Thames, was close to the city walls and enjoyed a privilege of sanctuary; it operated as a stronghold for outlaws, debtors and prostitutes openly defying the law, and these last found their clients among the residents of the nearby Inns of Court.[19]

Yet prostitution also existed within the city walls, and was mainly rooted near the waterfront because of the proximity to the river, which conveyed a great many travellers every day. This explains its association with Lucas Lane, Stew Lane and Cold Harbour. At the beginning of the seventeenth century, prostitution developed a great deal and spread throughout the city because of the rise in the number of coaches, which made prostitutes more mobile and less dependent on procurers. This change particularly affected the East End. As Shugg specifies, until the proclamation of 1546 closing all brothels and stating that prostitutes and bawds must go back where they came from, authorities had been able to confine prostitution largely to the licensed districts. Thereafter, prostitutes scattered about London, which made supervising them more difficult.[20] Besides, as Dabhoiwala indicates, it was often very difficult to distinguish between prostitution and other kinds of acts of sexual immorality, such as fornication and adultery, as well as between prostitution and more personal relationships, like those involving kept mistresses or cohabitation outside of marriage.[21] By Henry VIII's time, brothels had sprung up like weeds in surrounding areas, despite all the fulminations and injunctions against them. The Bankside cockpits, bear-baiting rings and taverns attracted thousands of unattached men daily. By the end of the sixteenth century, the opening of the playhouses brought thousands more. The number of brothels in the other peripheral areas of the city also increased mightily.[22]

---

[18]   Shugg, *Prostitution*, 296–98.

[19]   Shugg, *Prostitution*, 298.

[20]   Shugg, *Prostitution*, 306.

[21]   Dabhoiwala, 'Sexual Immorality', 87, 90.

[22]   Shugg, *Prostitution*, 306.

On top of the laws which were passed to keep prostitution outside the walls, numerous acts also aimed at controlling the prostitutes' clothing, which enabled the authorities to identify them, punish them and drive them out on the spot. A reproach commonly made against the suburbs was that they sheltered a large number of foreigners. Prostitutes were often identified as foreign, for it was very convenient to stamp vice as coming from elsewhere, in order to avoid questions about its real origins. Everything concerning prostitutes was seen as coming from abroad, especially syphilis, 'the French disease'. It is a fact that immigration fuelled the development of the suburban areas in the sixteenth century. Foreigners represented 4% to 5% of the population of the metropolis. As Burford states, it was during Elizabeth's reign that the political and economic complexion of Southwark changed substantially. Industry was taking root, and with it, a steady working-class element reinforced by large numbers of Protestant refugees from Spanish and French oppression.

Burford further explains that these changes brought about major property development on the Bankside, which started around 1570, hit its stride at the turn of the century and turned into a gold rush between 1600 and 1660.[23] By 1580, there were more than a thousand Dutch families in Southwark, which were mainly composed of artisans, craftsmen and traders, as well as some highly trained bawds and prostitutes. By the turn of the century, they settled in the area of Paris Garden.[24] The Flemish implantation dated back to William the Conqueror and the mercenaries who came with him. Dutch immigrants came later, with the religious troubles in their country. Ton Hoenselaars explains, in an article on the representation of the Dutch in early modern literature, that Hollandophobia developed in the early modern period because of the economic competition between English and Dutch craftsmen, but also because the Low Countries had become a republic, and a republic which was becoming more and more powerful, both politically and economically.[25]

Foreign prostitutes and procurers were thus actually common in early modern London. Flemish and Dutch brothels were an institution in England. Italian and French women were also commonly regarded as prostitutes, although there is no evidence of French and Italian prostitution in early modern London. But despite the objective presence of foreign prostitution in London, most of these women were English, practised prostitution occasionally and were driven to the trade by necessity. It is thus striking that edicts, decrees and laws as early as Henry II's ordinance insist on foreign prostitution and that stage prostitutes are also often portrayed as foreign. As Jean E. Howard argues, by labelling prostitutes as foreign,

---

[23]   Burford, *Bawds and Lodgings*, 146.

[24]   Burford, *Bawds and Lodgings*, 145.

[25]   Ton Hoenselaars, 'The Topography of Fear: The Dutch in Early Modern Literature', in *The Elizabethan Theatre XV: Papers Given at the International Conferences on Elizabethan Theatre Held at the University of Waterloo, Ontario, in the 1990s*, ed. C. E. McGee and A. L. Magnusson (Toronto: P. D. Meany, 2002), 237–38.

official discourses deny any responsibility for the prostitutes' delinquency.[26] She explains further that one of the main problems linked with prostitutes, and especially with foreign prostitutes, is that they threaten national integrity by erasing the differences between men and nations, since their clients are interchangeable.[27]

The prostitute's otherness also operated on the level of religion. She was designated as non-Protestant, an essential fact in a newly reformed country. The figure of the prostitute enabled the authorities to attack the Catholic Church so as to reinforce the legitimacy of the Protestant dogma. Before the Reformation, the Catholic clergy were recurrently criticized for their supposedly debauched mores, and the Catholic religion was commonly regarded as venal and salacious. One might also note in passing that on the Continent, the Catholic Church was more tolerant towards prostitution than its Protestant counterparts, partly because of the celibacy of priests, partly because of the financial gains prostitution represented. The vocabulary of prostitution, and above all the image of the Catholic Church as the Whore of Babylon taken from the book of Revelation (17–18), were also commonly used to attack the Catholic clergy and the religious threat the Catholic faith constituted. The result was that the imagery of prostitution and that of Roman Catholicism were tightly linked in people's minds.

When they were not assimilated to Catholicism, prostitutes and their environment were often referred to as Jewish. These two groups' all too blatant otherness made them impossible to assimilate for the dominant discourse: they shared the function of scapegoat. Although Jews were seen as a deicidal people, anti-Semitism also had more down-to-earth causes. As Lionel Ifrah explains, in an age when patriotism mattered so much, a landless people was bound to be seen as threatening. Jews were officially absent from England in the early modern period, since they had been expelled by Edward I in 1290. Yet some had stayed, and the 200 or so Jews who remained in Tudor England led a clandestine life.[28] Many of them had become involved in the business of prostitution, which was finally better than begging. Jews also often practised usury, one of the few trades which was not forbidden them, but an activity which was frowned upon. Thus, the figure of the Jew was written so as to take on the qualities deemed unacceptable in Europeans, a characteristic shared by the prostitute. Sometimes, these two groups actually collided: in Roman times already, numerous prostitutes were Jewish slaves brought back from Palestine.[29] It is therefore not surprising that prostitutes

---

[26]   Jean E. Howard, 'Prostitutes, Shopkeepers and the Staging of Urban Subjects in *The Honest Whore*', in *The Elizabethan Theatre XV: Papers Given at the International Conferences on Elizabethan Theatre Held at the University of Waterloo, Ontario, in the 1990s*, ed. C. E. McGee and A. L. Magnusson (Toronto: P. D. Meany, 2002), 170.

[27]   Howard, 'Prostitutes', 170.

[28]   Lionel Ifrah, *De Shylock à Samson. Juifs et judaïsme en Angleterre au temps de Shakespeare et Milton* (Paris: H. Champion, 1999), 9.

[29]   Burford, *Bawds and Lodgings*, 70.

are often referred to as Jews, as for example in Dekker's *First Part of The Honest Whore* (1604), when Pioratto calls the prostitute Bellafront 'sweet Jew'.[30]

Another way to ostracize prostitutes was to refer to them as being of low social status, as can be seen through the obsessive recurrence of the word 'common' to allude to them. The word carries an interesting polysemy. In early modern England, it designated all persons without a title, in other words, the great majority of the English people. But 'common' also evokes the very definition of what a prostitute is – namely, that she is not the woman of one single man, that she is shared by many. In a society where the social structure based on land and birth inherited from the Middle Ages was being shaken by the ascending middle class, it was essential that prostitutes be referred to as 'common' so as to anchor even more firmly the idea that these women did not interact with respectable society. As Dabhoiwala indicates, categorizing prostitution as a separate type of behaviour, engaged in by 'common' whores who were cut off from respectable society, made it possible to stamp them as necessarily poor and sexually indiscriminate.[31] In this perspective, prostitution appears much more as a social than as a sexual problem. If prostitutes stayed aloof, the established order of property, that is to say the transmission of property based on the legitimacy of heirs, would be kept intact. In these conditions, as Burford notes, men could slake their sexual desires without incurring obligations.[32] Authorities tended to rely on sumptuary laws to keep 'common women', whether prostitutes or not, at a safe distance. To preclude any ambiguity, special attention was given to clothes, as they reflected social status. Already in 1351, a London ordinance specified that prostitutes and common women (thus putting them on the same level) had to wear striped hoods, so that they could be more easily recognized.[33] The recurrence of such laws only indicates that they were constantly transgressed, and shows that when property and capital are concerned, what really matters is not so much to distinguish prostitutes from other women in order to be able to exclude them, as to distinguish common women from upper-class women. This goes with the fact that poverty became increasingly criminalized in early modern England.

As Sharpe explains, hard economic circumstances, combined with demographic growth, in the sixteenth century prompted a growth of the 'law and order consciousness', which took the form, among other things, of steady pressure against petty crime. The criminal code hardened, and one observed a fundamental concern about social order.[34] The heightened preoccupation with order was fuelled by the numerous social changes that were taking place, as well as the fears of the elites, who had been unsettled by events such as the 1549 popular

---

[30] Thomas Dekker, *The Honest Whore. In Two Parts*, in *Thomas Dekker*, ed. Ernest Rhys, Mermaid Series (London: Ernest Benn, 1949), II.i.224.

[31] Dabhoiwala, 'Sexual Immorality', 92.

[32] Burford, *Bawds and Lodgings*, 53.

[33] Burford, *Bawds and Lodgings*, 73.

[34] Sharpe, *Crime*, 16–17.

rebellions.[35] Sharpe insists on the fact that in early modern England, behaviour classed as criminal came to be regarded as the prerogative of the poor.[36] Crime seems to have been committed by the poor as a class, who often were the victims of circumstances. For instance, prostitutes were often young servant girls who had been thrown out of service for pregnancy.[37] These people were not criminals at heart: for them, crime was a means of survival. Official reports of crime in early modern London testify to the gentry's involvement in acts of violence.[38] But the latter were much less stigmatized for crime than the poor.

II

The prostitute, as an obvious and recurring sinner, was the ideal culprit on whom to blame a great variety of problems. Official discourses unloaded the responsibility for all the evils of the time onto the prostitute, notably through the figure of Eve, the original sinner, who constituted an ideal archetype by means of which to denounce these women as guilty of all sorts of plagues. Not only was the prostitute conveniently vested with qualities the various representatives of official discourses did not accept in themselves, but her punishment and eviction gave to the man in the street the impression that order was restored, and prevented any questioning regarding the possible responsibility of the representatives of official discourses. It was, then, essential to punish the prostitute, to exclude her symbolically, so as to keep the illusion that problems had been solved.

The word 'scapegoat' finds its origin in a Hebrew ritual of expiation described in Leviticus (16:20–22). In his *Anatomy of Criticism*, Northrop Frye dwells on the notion of *pharmakos*, which has its roots in ancient Athens. He insists on the fact that the *pharmakos* had to be inside in the first place so as to be able to be led outside. The ceremony of the scapegoat is thus played out on the boundary between the inside and the outside, and retraces this boundary.[39] Thus the scapegoat is a fundamentally ambiguous figure, both a being of abjection and a cathartic element which, once expelled, allows the city to be liberated from pollution.[40]

Over the course of the sixteenth century, civil authorities in Europe became increasingly involved in the repression of prostitution, which in general coincided with the Reformation. In July 1519, Henry VIII ordered Cardinal Wolsey to purge London and Southwark of vagrants and loose women.[41] On the Continent, a

---

[35] Ian Archer, *The Pursuit of Stability: Social Relations in Elizabethan London* (Cambridge: Cambridge University Press, 1991), 100–103.

[36] Sharpe, *Crime*, 91.

[37] Sharpe, *Crime*, 100, 103.

[38] Sharpe, *Crime*, 98–99.

[39] Northrop Frye, *Anatomy of Criticism* (London: Penguin Books, 1957), 41.

[40] Frye, *Anatomy*, 43.

[41] Burford, *Bawds and Lodgings*, 120.

general campaign began in 1520, carried on by leaders of the Reformation.[42] This movement led to Henry VIII's proclamation decreeing the final closing of brothels in 1546. But repression could be observed throughout Europe, even in Catholic countries. Repression hardened as Protestantism gained force from the 1570s on. Even the prostitutes' clients started to be punished. As the sixteenth century wore on, the movement to suppress prostitution grew in strength and complexity. The main concern of authorities was the preservation of order, and brothels were seen as places gathering people who were a threat for the community. Health was also a major concern, and the heightened repression of prostitution coincides with the havoc wreaked by the epidemic of syphilis in the sixteenth century. The syphilis epidemic made authorities tighten up sanitary regulations.[43] The number of trials for sexual crimes such as fornication, prostitution and adultery increased significantly. The law was actually more severe with bawds than with prostitutes.[44] The authorities were also fighting back against the increase in vice, crime and disease which accompanied the rise in prostitution. England did indeed experience a rise in crime from the early years of Elizabeth's reign onwards. It reached crisis proportions in many areas at some point between the late 1590s and 1630.[45] Southwark prostitutes had more to fear once the district had passed under the authority of the city in 1550. The King's first Charter of 1550 granted the Lord Mayor and the sheriffs of the city the power to 'farm' the borough of Southwark. The City gained extension of its juridical powers, but the king had excepted the Liberties of the Clink and Old Paris Garden.[46] The authorities' efforts were often undermined by the corruption and inefficiency of officers and the sheer size of the problem.[47] This movement led to James I's proclamation of 16 September 1603, which called for the pulling down of the houses in the suburbs, which were seen as the haunt of dissolute people.[48] One can see an echo of this decision at the beginning of *Measure for Measure*, when Mistress Overdone and her bawd Pompey find themselves homeless.

One must add that the Reformation brought a heightened sense of sin. In the 1580s, a Puritan campaign for moral reform developed. Moralists like Philip Stubbes and Donald Lupton called for stricter measures (including the death penalty) against prostitution. New, much more severe courts were given the power to punish crimes of fornication. Until Elizabeth's accession, the sexual offences committed by lay people fell under ecclesiastical jurisdiction. They were judged by the archdeacon's court, or 'bawdy court', a system which lent itself to much bribery and extortion. Elizabeth created the Court of High Commission, having concurrent

---

[42]   Shugg, *Prostitution*, 293.

[43]   Burford, *Bawds and Lodgings*, 118.

[44]   For more details on this aspect, see Fouassier, 'Représentations', 254–75.

[45]   Sharpe, *Crime*, 70.

[46]   Sharpe, *Crime*, 130–31.

[47]   Shugg, *Prostitution*, 301.

[48]   Shugg, *Prostitution*, 303.

yet superior jurisdiction over moral offences. But civil authorities were probably neither more efficient nor less corruptible. The court was abolished in 1640 for its corruption and inefficiency.[49] Judgements and trials were also complicated because there was a threefold administrative division of metropolitan crime, between the courts of Westminster, the city of London and Middlesex, and the Surrey assizes, which exercised jurisdiction over serious crime in Southwark.[50] Offenders were now submitted to the combined forces of civil and religious authorities, which collaborated to apply a more efficient system of moral control. All forms of female disorder, be it prostitution, fornication, adultery or the domination of the husband, were criminalized in the seventeenth century and became an affair of state.[51]

The punishment of the prostitute gave, however fleetingly, the illusion of a return to order that the community which accused her could relish. It was essential that punishment be public, so that both the culprit and the agent of redemption would be clearly identified by the community and people might feel part of the healing process.[52] The punishments enforced were the shaving of the head, whipping at the cart half-naked, standing in the pillory or in a cage, ducking in stinking water, and incarceration in the Clink or Bridewell.[53] The sentence imposed in 1597 on one of the most notorious bawds, Bess Holland, can be regarded as typical:

> she shalbe put into a carte at Newgate and be carted with a paper on her hed showing her offence, from thence to Smythfeilde, from thence to her howse, from thence to Cornehill, from thence to the Standerd in Cheepe, from thence to Bridewell, and all the waye [barbers'] basons to be runge before her, at Bridewell to be punished [by flogging], and from thence to be broughte to Newgate, there to remaine untill she have payed a fine of xl and put in sewerties for the same, and to be bounde to her good behaviour.[54]

The 'rough music' of the crowd while accompanying the cart recalls ancient practices of the eviction of the scapegoat or carnivalesque charivaris. John Stow explains in his *Survey of London* (the first extensive topographical description of early modern London) that there were stocks and pillories in every ward.[55] In Thomas Dekker's *The Second Part of The Honest Whore* (1630), one learns that whipping was meant to 'let forth [the prostitutes'] wanton blood, / Making them calm', and carting 'to calm their pride' (V.ii.507–8). Branding, which was the

---

[49]   Shugg, *Prostitution*, 304.

[50]   Sharpe, *Crime*, 56.

[51]   This previously mostly affected the lower classes. Authorities tended to turn a blind eye to the aristocracy's much more dissolute sexual mores.

[52]   See Terence Eagleton, *Shakespeare and Society* (London: Chatto and Windus, 1967), 67.

[53]   Burford, *Bawds and Lodgings*, 132.

[54]   *Middlesex Sessions Rolls*, quoted in Shugg, *Prostitution*, 303–4.

[55]   John Stow, *A Survey of London*, ed. Charles Lethbridge Kingsford, 2 vols (Oxford: Clarendon Press, 1908), vol. 2, 176.

most common punishment before the early modern period, was gradually being abandoned, although the most extreme Puritans, such as Philip Stubbes, wanted it to be applied again. It was mainly enforced for prostitutes who kept penetrating the city walls.[56] Penitent prostitutes had to don special clothes (most often, a blue dress) to show their penitence. Ostracism, marking difference and making it visible to all, is the common point of all these measures.

Prostitutes were often sent to Bridewell. The building was given by Edward VI to the city in order to set the poor and the idle to work. It soon became a house of correction for scolds, vagrants, loose women and disorderly people. Its creation marks a significant step in the criminalization of poverty. With Bridewell, the notion of discipline through work is added to the concept of imprisonment as a means of punishment and dissuasion. Puritan reformers believed in the efficiency of houses of correction to eradicate the evil of prostitution thanks to physical castigation, hard work and humiliation. Bridewell's inmates had to beat chalk and hemp, work mills and make and spread sand, gravel and lime. At the time, prisons were mainly seen as a waste of money for the community, and so setting vagrants and criminals to work was a way to make them useful to society. Bridewell soon became an essential landmark for the moral and geographical control of the poor. For example, from 1618 on, people deported to Virginia set out from Bridewell.[57]

Banishment was a very popular measure, too, because it was much cheaper and easier to implement than imprisonment. Although Scotland was more prone to practise banishment than England (one of the reasons being to prevent the propagation of syphilis), recurrent offenders in England were sometimes banished to Virginia.[58] Again, the idea was to remove the supposed source of evil, so that the community could feel safe, but the larger problem remained unsolved.

All punishments were not institutionalized, and the population sometimes decided to punish offenders themselves. For instance, as early as 1383, the citizens of Southwark imprisoned women guilty of fornication or adultery, showed them to the crowd, shaved their heads and drove them through the city to the sound of trumpets and pipes (treatment which, again, recalls ancient practices). In doing so, they wanted to purge the city from filthiness out of fear of God's vengeance.[59] Burford explains that 'whorebashing' was one of the earliest and most enduring sports on the Bankside. People shot stones at prostitutes from the river with a bow, which could of course prove lethal. There is no recorded punishment for the people who did so.[60] On Shrove Tuesday, apprentices pulled down brothels and

---

[56]   See Fouassier, 'Représentations', 259.

[57]   See Fouassier, 'Représentations', 268.

[58]   Linda Mahood, *The Magdalenes: Prostitution in the Nineteenth Century* (London: Routledge, 1990), 19–28, esp. 20–24. One can find an example of banishment in Philip Massinger's 1632 comedy, *The City Madam*, ed. Cyrus Hoy, Regents Renaissance Drama Series (Lincoln: University of Nebraska Press, 1964), V.i.

[59]   Stow, *Survey*, vol. 1, 189.

[60]   Burford, *Bawds and Lodgings*, 124.

playhouses. Their violence also targeted foreigners – in other words, people and activities that stood on the margins of the community. Apprentices signified their belonging to the dominant culture by means of such violence, although they were regular patrons of playhouses and brothels the rest of the year. This 'collective expiation' is a fixed and recurring time of licence, which plays the part of a safety valve, and recalls the functioning of carnival: giving way to licence once a year allows order to be kept more easily the rest of the time. Hence, authorities often condoned such targeted violence, as it was a guarantee of order.

The figure of the prostitute thus stands out as a hypocritical social construction. She is at one and the same time, and ambivalently, an object of desire, a source of fear and socially useful. The same tensions can be traced in popular discourse.

III

Writers often function as the unconscious vehicles of feelings too obvious even to be noticed by themselves or by their contemporaries. In showing stereotypes, plays and pamphlets took part in the shaping of the representation of reality for audiences and readers. In this perspective, criminal pamphlets (a genre destined for citizens which depicts criminals' lives in a sensational way) built up the concept of an underworld, thus constructing types of criminals easy to identify. As Sharpe explains, court records give a very different impression of London criminals from that found in these didactic pamphlets dealing with spectacular cases.[61] The central purpose of ballads and pamphlets, he argues, is to act as a warning to readers. Execution is thus central to them, and forms what the historian calls 'a theatre of punishment'.[62] A set piece of these texts is the dying confession, which is marked by the acceptance of justice and of the deservedness of the sentence, as well as a warning to those present to avoid a similar fate.[63] But of course, as Sharpe insists, this literature's representation of the underworld is mainly fictional and normative.[64] Its aim is to reinforce the values of 'straight' society, and it is therefore highly stereotyped.[65] But what is even more important, according to Sharpe, is that by constructing the concept of an underworld, this literature gave crime an identity which made it comprehensible. If it is restricted to certain groups, Sharpe argues, 'crime' can emerge as a clearly defined 'problem' for which 'solutions' can be proposed. The main effect is to simplify a very complex phenomenon, and to allow contemporaries the luxury of reacting to crime with a stock response rather than thinking too deeply about the issues involved.[66]

---

[61]   Sharpe, *Crime*, 116.
[62]   Sharpe, *Crime*, 161.
[63]   Sharpe, *Crime*, 162.
[64]   Sharpe, *Crime*, 165.
[65]   Sharpe, *Crime*, 165.
[66]   Sharpe, *Crime*, 165.

The prostitute is particularly at home in city comedies, a genre that flourished at the turn of the seventeenth century. These plays dissect the tensions between the social classes at a time of economic change and expose the cupidity rampant in the urban society that was emerging. In city comedy, the prostitute is kept aloof, thanks to the double means of dramatic inflation and comic deflation. Theodore B. Leinwand explains that city comedies staged the way Londoners 'typified' each other by representing, exaggerating and parodying set types, either approving them or calling them into question.[67] The characters of city comedies are shaped by the city and crystallize, in turn, the attitudes of city-dwellers for a city-dwelling audience. These plays are peopled with pure and innocent virgins and threatening prostitutes, whose names are often symbolic. The presence of the one necessarily entails that of the other. This dialectic takes up the hackneyed polar opposition between Eve and Mary.

The tendency towards the polarization of female roles in city comedies is particularly well illustrated by the opposition between the virtuous Beatrice (a name evoking, thanks to Dante, the ideal lover in the tradition of courtly love) and the Machiavellian prostitute Franceschina in *The Dutch Courtesan* by John Marston (1605).[68] The play demonstrates that the stereotypes of women as either goddess or whore are inseparable, and one finds in it the constant threat that a Beatrice may become a Franceschina. Yet *The Dutch Courtesan* obsessively tries to separate and oppose the wife and the prostitute. Women and sexual pleasure are alluded to in derogatory terms, and this type of pleasure is seen as belonging to the sphere of prostitutes. Beatrice stands as the quasi-saintly embodiment of the female virtues of silence, humility and innocence. The two women are diametrically opposed: whereas Beatrice represents constancy and contentment, advocates moderation and proves incredibly patient, Franceschina is portrayed as the image of an avenging fury, who knows no limits, swears, rants and plots. Though the two characters live in different worlds (Beatrice dwells in a world of purity and romance, whereas Franceschina inhabits a contradictory world of comedy and ridicule, on the one hand, and of realism and revenge, on the other), they are nevertheless two sides of the same stereotypical coin.

The stage prostitute often shares with her real-life sisters the function of scapegoat. Laughter is not devoid of consequences, and it can play a conservative role. As Keith Thomas argues, laughter has an important social function, which, among other things, allows the reader or the viewer to welcome or exclude a given social group.[69] When you laugh at someone, you exclude him or her and ally yourself with those with whom you laugh; you assert what values you share

---

[67] See Theodore B. Leinwand, *The City Staged: Jacobean Comedy, 1603–1613* (Madison: University of Wisconsin Press, 1986), 7.

[68] John Marston, *The Dutch Courtesan*, in *The Plays of John Marston*, ed. Harvey Wood, 2 vols (London: Oliver and Boyd, 1938), vol. 1.

[69] Keith Thomas, 'The Place of Laughter in Tudor and Stuart England', *Times Literary Supplement* 21 (January 1977): 77–81.

with the dominant group. One must add to this the cathartic dimension of laughter. The prostitute is first cathartic through her link with sexuality. Not only are lewd jokes a guarantee of a comic effect, but they also allow for ritual liberation from the constraints of everyday life. Laughter acts in a cathartic way with respect to everything one cannot prevent, such as death and illness, but it also mitigates disorders with more social consequences, such as adultery. Because she is a source of laughter about venereal diseases, and also about the production of illegitimate heirs – a real subject of anxiety in a society which saw traditional relationships of power upset – the stage prostitute had a cathartic function. Like the pamphlet criminal, she allowed the community to put a name and a face on what they feared and to make it symbolically controllable.

Theatre made it possible to channel the prostitute's threatening potential and at the same time to divert it to the advantage of the dominant discourse. However, staging this threat also enabled the audience to take part in the licence the prostitute represents within the limits of the play, hence in a controlled, safe way. In this perspective, the theatre can be viewed as an islet of freedom for the women in the audience. 'Common' London women, who, in their everyday life, had to submit themselves to the restrictions imposed by the patriarchal order, could see onstage women who spoke up, women who went out of their homes when they wished, in a word, women who had at least a warped form of the freedom they were more or less deprived of. Yet this freedom is all relative, and prostitutes are ostracized for it.

But laughter can also have a subversive value. If it can act as a support for social conventions, it can also undermine them. Laughter bears within itself an attack on hierarchy, and the triumph of non-official values over official ones. As Frye argues, the scapegoat is an essential figure of the type of ironic comedy practised by Ben Jonson, thus of city comedy.[70] Comedy usually ends with a return to order (often symbolized by marriage), which permits the creation of a new, purified society. The return to order is carried out, among other means, through the eviction of the scapegoat.[71] But city comedy underlines the absurdity of the attempt to define the enemy of society as coming from the outside. The figure of the *pharmakos* draws the audience's attention to its own artificiality and to the fact that it may only be a symptom of the vice of the society ostracizing him or her. Thus the social revenge enacted against an individual tends to make him seem less guilty, and society much more so. One observes in this kind of play a tendency to ridicule and scold the audience, who are supposed to be asking for the triumph of normative moral values. Sometimes dramatists (especially Jonson and Thomas Middleton) go so far as to show the scapegoat as worthier than the society which despises her.[72] If the crooks of Jonson's *Alchemist* (1610) and *Bartholomew Fair*

---

[70]   For more details on this point, see also Brian Gibbons, *Jacobean City Comedy* (London: Rupert Hart-Davis, 1968).

[71]   Frye, *Anatomy*, 286.

[72]   Frye, *Anatomy*, 41, 45, 48.

(1614) do not ultimately profit from their tricks, the citizens and representatives of justice surrounding them are exposed as foolish and deserving to be duped. In the same perspective, the courtesan of Middleton's *A Trick to Catch the Old One* (1608) is shown as clever and deserving a better life, contrary to the stupid, greedy characters surrounding her.[73]

One is thus led to wonder whether the figure of the prostitute, as created both by official and by popular discourses, has a real subversive potential. In his article, 'Shakespeare Understudies: The Sodomite, the Prostitute, the Transvestite and their Critics', Jonathan Dollimore doubts it very much. According to him, the prostitute is, along with the thief, an authorized type, onto whom it is very easy to project the immorality which the dominant discourse represses in itself and through whom the repressed can be safely controlled. The prostitute is thus used as a visible source of disorder within the family and the community. In assigning to prostitutes all the characteristics public opinion reproves, the norms of society can be upheld. Since guilt must be assigned to someone, the ideal culprit is the female prostitute, standing as a lecherous and insatiable temptress, rather than her tempted male client. To Dollimore, nothing is more predictable, in a falsely respectable society, than the exploitation of a controlled underworld which is kept at a safe distance.[74] Yet it might be supposed that the prostitute constituted a real threat, and did not merely loom as an imaginary one, for established society. After all, when he cheated on his wife, a married man gave up his patriarchal role in his home. Prostitution took money and goods normally destined for the home and thus unsettled domestic economy. The prostitute also appropriated a man's time, and sometimes affection, elements he should have dedicated to his family. Finally, the economically independent prostitute stood outside patriarchal norms. Therefore, ambiguity remains the prostitute's key characteristic, as she stands out both as a cohesive instrument and as an unsettling element for the dominant discourse. And it is precisely this characteristic which makes her so interesting.

Works Cited

Primary Sources

Dekker, Thomas, *The Honest Whore. In Two Parts*. In *Thomas Dekker*. Edited by Ernest Rhys. Mermaid Series. London: Ernest Benn, 1949.

---

[73] Ben Jonson, *The Alchemist*, ed. Douglas Brown, The New Mermaids (London: Ernest Benn, 1966); *Bartholomew Fair*, ed. E. A. Horsman, The Revels Plays (Manchester: Manchester University Press, 1960); Thomas Middleton, *A Trick to Catch the Old One*, ed. G. J. Watson, The New Mermaids (London: Ernest Benn, 1968).

[74] Jonathan Dollimore, 'Shakespeare Understudies: The Sodomite, the Prostitute, the Transvestite and Their Critics', in *Political Shakespeare: New Essays in Cultural Materialism*, ed. Jonathan Dollimore and Alan Sinfield (Manchester: Manchester University Press, 1985), 136.

Jonson, Ben. *The Alchemist*. Edited by Douglas Brown. The New Mermaids. London: Ernest Benn, 1966.

———. *Bartholomew Fair*. Edited by E. A. Horsman. The Revels Plays. Manchester: Manchester University Press, 1960.

Marston, John. *The Dutch Courtesan*. In *The Plays of John Marston*. Edited by Harvey Wood. 2 vols. London: Oliver and Boyd, 1938. Vol. 1.

Massinger, Philip. *The City Madam*. Edited by Cyrus Hoy. Regents Renaissance Drama Series. Lincoln: University of Nebraska Press, 1964.

Middleton, Thomas. *A Trick to Catch the Old One*. Edited by G. J. Watson. The New Mermaids. London: Ernest Benn, 1968.

Shakespeare, William. *Measure for Measure*. In *The Riverside Shakespeare*. Edited by G. Blakemore Evans, J. J. M. Tobin et al. 2nd ed. Boston: Houghton Mifflin, 1997.

Stow, John. *A Survey of London*. Edited by Charles Lethbridge Kingsford. 2 vols. Oxford: Clarendon Press, 1908.

Secondary Sources

Archer, Ian. *The Pursuit of Stability: Social Relations in Elizabethan London*. Cambridge: Cambridge University Press, 1991.

Babcock, Barbara A. Introduction to *The Reversible World: Symbolic Inversion in Art and Society*. Edited by Barbara A. Babcock. Ithaca, NY: Cornell University Press, 1978. 13–36.

Burford, E. J. *Bawds and Lodgings: A History of the London Bankside Brothels c. 100–1675*. London: Peter Owen, 1976.

Dabhoiwala, Faramerz. 'The Pattern of Sexual Immorality in Seventeenth- and Eighteenth-Century London'. In *Londinopolis: Essays in the Cultural and Social History of Early Modern London*. Edited by Paul Griffiths and Mark S. R. Jenner. Manchester: Manchester University Press, 2000. 86–106.

Dollimore, Jonathan. 'Shakespeare Understudies: The Sodomite, the Prostitute, the Transvestite and Their Critics'. In *Political Shakespeare: New Essays in Cultural Materialism*. Edited by Jonathan Dollimore and Alan Sinfield. Manchester: Manchester University Press, 1985. 129–52.

Eagleton, Terence. *Shakespeare and Society*. London: Chatto and Windus, 1967.

Fouassier, Frédérique. 'Représentations de la transgression sexuelle féminine dans le théâtre anglais de la Renaissance'. 3 vols. PhD thesis, Université François-Rabelais de Tours, 2005.

Frye, Northrop. *Anatomy of Criticism*. London: Penguin Books, 1957.

Gibbons, Brian. *Jacobean City Comedy*. London: Rupert Hart-Davis, 1968.

Gilman, Sander L. *Difference and Pathology: Stereotypes of Sexuality, Race, and Madness*. Ithaca, NY: Cornell University Press, 1985.

Hoenselaars, Ton. 'The Topography of Fear: The Dutch in Early Modern Literature'. In *The Elizabethan Theatre XV: Papers Given at the International Conferences on Elizabethan Theatre Held at the University of Waterloo,*

Ontario, in the 1990s. Edited by C. E. McGee and A. L. Magnusson. Toronto: P. D. Meany, 2002. 221–40.

Howard, Jean E. 'Prostitutes, Shopkeepers and the Staging of Urban Subjects in *The Honest Whore*'. In *The Elizabethan Theatre XV: Papers Given at the International Conferences on Elizabethan Theatre Held at the University of Waterloo, Ontario, in the 1990s*. Edited by C. E. McGee and A. L. Magnusson. Toronto: P. D. Meany, 2002. 161–79.

Ifrah, Lionel. *De Shylock à Samson. Juifs et judaïsme en Angleterre au temps de Shakespeare et Milton*. Paris: H. Champion, 1999.

Leinwand, Theodore B. *The City Staged: Jacobean Comedy, 1603–1613*. Madison: University of Wisconsin Press, 1986.

Mahood, Linda. *The Magdalenes: Prostitution in the Nineteenth Century*. London: Routledge, 1990.

Sharpe, J. A. *Crime in Early Modern England 1550–1750*. London: Longman, 1984.

Shugg, Wallace. 'Prostitution in Shakespeare's London'. *Shakespeare Studies* 10 (1977): 291–313.

Stallybrass, Peter, and Allon White. *The Politics and Poetics of Transgression*. Ithaca, NY: Cornell University Press, 1986.

Thomas, Keith. 'The Place of Laughter in Tudor and Stuart England'. *Times Literary Supplement* 21 (January 1977): 77–81.

Chapter 5
Appropriating a Famous Female Offender: Mary Frith (1584?–1659), alias Moll Cutpurse

Pascale Drouet

Mary Frith (1584?–1659) was better known by her underworld nickname: Moll Cutpurse. Although closely associated with her notoriety as a female offender, the sobriquet inadequately conveys the full range of her eccentric attitudes and illegal practices. Frith was accused and, at times, convicted of thieving, but also of receiving stolen goods, prostitution and procuring, drinking and swearing, cross-dressing and performing – at least as a musician – on a stage then forbidden to actresses.[1] In *Society and Politics in the Plays of Thomas Middleton*, Swapan Chakravorty observes that Moll Cutpurse was also considered as guilty of 'deviant mirth' – and masterlessness.[2] It then comes as no surprise that 'Moll and her crew [were] associated with every slander brought against players – theft, prostitution, sodomy, vagrancy, levity, shape-shifting, cross-dressing'.[3]

Mary Frith's dramatic confession of her offences against convention, her consequent imprisonment in Bridewell, London's ill-famed house of correction, but also her denial of being a bawd, were recorded in *The Consistory of London Correction Book* as early as January 1611. The very same year, Thomas Middleton and Thomas Dekker's city comedy, *The Roaring Girl, or Moll Cut-Purse*, was performed at the Fortune Theatre by the Prince's Men, catapulting Frith and her persona into popular mythology and memorializing her for posterity. The

---

[1] This is what the 27 January 1611 record of *The Consistory of London Correction Book* suggests with Frith's confession: '[she] also sat there [at the Fortune Theatre] upon the stage in the public view of all the people there present in mans apparel and played upon her lute and sang a song' (quoted in Elizabeth Cook, introduction to *The Roaring Girl*, by Thomas Middleton and Thomas Dekker, 2nd ed., The New Mermaids [London: A. and C. Black, 1997], xviii).

[2] Swapan Chakravorty, *Society and Politics in the Plays of Thomas Middleton* (Oxford: Clarendon Press, 1996), 90. As regards masterlessness, see A. L. Beier, *Masterless Men: The Vagrancy Problem in England, 1560–1640* (London: Methuen, 1987). In Moll's case, masterlessness particularly refers to her being unmarried. 'Not immured within a domestic role within the house', Jean E. Howard notes, 'she retains her freedom to move about' (Jean E. Howard, *The Stage and Social Struggle in Early Modern England* [London: Routledge, 1994], 122).

[3] Chakravorty, *Society and Politics*, 94.

process continued in 1662, three years after her death, when her misdemeanours were revived in an anonymous work purporting to offer both biography and autobiography: *The Life and Death of Mistress Mary Frith, alias Moll Cutpurse*, incorporating *Moll Cutpurse's Diary*.[4]

This essay will consider how Frith was represented, romanticized, appropriated and capitalized upon in the Jacobean play and the Restoration publication, both of which stray from the historical data, however scanty the latter may be. The paucity of legal documents registering Frith's colourful offences may be due to her own success in avoiding prosecution, but also to the fact that, regardless of her cross-dressing, she was, after all, a woman. Martin Ingram notes,

> Studies of female criminal activity have also revealed marked gender differences. Then, as now, far fewer women came before the courts than men. Females were under-represented most markedly in crimes involving physical violence, major larcenies or, more generally, activities that required a high degree of initiative and self-assertion. When they were in trouble for criminal behaviour it was more likely to be as perpetrators of petty theft in households, workshop or market and of offences involving verbal rather than physical abuse, or as mere aiders and abettors of more serious crimes.[5]

By contrast, the play and the biography present Moll Cutpurse as central, self-assertive, larger than life. Did Frith stand apart? Could she be regarded as the exception which proved the rule? Did she actually acquire the stature of a male deviant, or was she merely magnified by topical performances and writings?

Two elements are striking in the aforementioned subjective sources: the deterrent aspect of punishing and shaming practices is played down, and the offender turns out to be a dispenser of justice – even, in the play by Middleton and Dekker, an epitome of honesty, as is underlined by Marie-Thérèse Jones-Davies.[6] This essay will first concentrate on the references to chastisement in both *The Roaring Girl* and *The Life and Death of Mistress Mary Frith*, in order to show to what extent they are positively biased: watered down, displaced, subverted or appropriated; in so doing, it will address the relationship between punishment and performance, exposing the implicit ideologies of the playwrights, authors and editors. The focus will then be put on the various reversal strategies involved –

---

[4]   *The Life and Death of Mrs Mary Frith, Commonly Called Moll Cutpurse*, in *The Renaissance Imagination, Important Literary Texts and Theatrical Texts from the Late Middle Ages through the Seventeenth Century*, ed. Stephen Orgel (New York: Garland Publishing, 1993).

[5]   Martin Ingram, '"Scolding Women Cucked or Washed": A Crisis in Gender Relations in Early Modern England?', in *Women, Crime and the Courts in Early Modern England*, ed. Jenny Kermode and Garthine Walker (London: UCL Press, 1994), 49.

[6]   See Marie-Thérèse Jones-Davies, *Un peintre de la vie londonienne: Thomas Dekker (circa 1572–1632)*, 2 vols (Paris: Didier, 1958), vol. 1, 130: 'Si, dans la capitale, Moll ne jouit pas d'une réputation sans tache, Middleton et Dekker font de l'extraordinaire "rugisseuse" un exemple d'honnêteté.'

the presentation of Moll as a mediator between the city and its underworld, as a protector of the oppressed, as a castigator of male crimes, as a warrior-woman, even as a conservative agent of social order. This will raise the question of whether the original criminal figure, Protean and elusive, has not ultimately given way to a sort of popular mythical construct, stereotyped and easy to appropriate.

I

In the January 1611 confessions recorded in *The Consistory of London Correction Book*, Frith mentions having been punished in Bridewell for her offences. Gustav Ungerer surmises that there, 'like all the inmates, she must have undergone the regular punitive regime of reform consisting of corporal punishment and hard work, a process that used to last two or three months for non-recalcitrant inmates'.[7] He reminds us that Frith was caught again trespassing against public morality around Christmas 1611 and sent back to the house of correction. Given the destruction of the volume of the Bridewell Court Books covering the years 1611 to 1616, we cannot be sure of much concerning Frith's imprisonment. It can be gathered, as Ungerer suggests, that the reformatory policy failed, although he does not document his more interesting suggestion that Frith's 'dramatic talents saved her from a prolonged detention in Bridewell'.[8] There is no mention of Bridewell either in *The Roaring Girl* or in *The Life and Death of Mistress Mary Frith*, and the emphasis is put on performance rather than on punishment.[9]

The heroine of Middleton and Dekker's play is presented in a favourable light; the play offers, as Clare McManus puts it, 'a sanitized version of her life'.[10] What remains of the offender is just 'a black ill name' connected with her past in the underworld and the 'ill things' (V.i.326) she knew then, and a plea: 'Good my Lord, let not my name condemn me to you or to the world' (337–38).[11] It is as if Moll had severed all connections with her past – except for her role as a useful mediator between 'respectable' citizens and rogues. It is normal, then, that punishment should apparently not occur: there is nothing to reproach Moll with any more. The butt of the satire is not Moll but, as can be expected in a city comedy, the citizens, particularly those who think themselves above the law. Dekker had already made

---

[7]   Gustav Ungerer, 'Mary Frith, Alias Moll Cutpurse, in Life and Literature', *Shakespeare Studies* 28 (2000): 66.

[8]   Ungerer, 'Mary Frith', 67.

[9]   Bridewell is, in fact, mentioned in the *Diary* but kept at a distance from Moll herself: 'I resolved to run no longer the desperate hazard of these courses (which I see so many of my comrades monthly expiate with their lives, &c., at least by whipping and the satisfaction of Bridewell workhouse)' (*Life*, 26).

[10]   Clare McManus, '*The Roaring Girl* and the London Underworld', in *Early Modern English Drama: A Critical Companion*, ed. Garrett A. Sullivan, Patrick Cheney and Andrew Hadfield (Oxford: Oxford University Press, 2006), 215.

[11]   Thomas Middleton and Thomas Dekker, *The Roaring Girl*, ed. Elizabeth Cook, 2nd ed., The New Mermaids (London: A. and C. Black, 1997); this edition is cited throughout.

the most of Bridewell as a dramatic subject, with a harsh criticism of the house of correction, in *The Honest Whore, Part 2*, which was performed by the same company of actors in 1604. In Act V of that play, Bridewell is bleakly presented as 'the brick-house of castigation' where one can see 'men carved up for anatomy', loose and/or criminal women punished with hard labour, such as 'breaking chalk, grinding in mills, raising sand and gravel and making of lime', and whipped if they prove refractory to 'let forth their wanton blood'.[12] So going back to Bridewell in *The Roaring Girl* might have been redundant and served little purpose.

Although the house of correction is not mentioned in Middleton and Dekker's play, two punishments are clearly evoked: hanging and cucking. As opposed to Shakespeare's *Henry IV, Part 1*, in which Falstaff wonders whether there will be gallows when Prince Hal is king,[13] the one obsessed with hanging in *The Roaring Girl* is not the cutpurse, but the one who sides with the law and wants to see her hanged, Sir Alexander; the obsession has been comically displaced. Sir Alexander's fantasy of punishment, which surprises even his unscrupulous henchman Trapdoor by its excessive subjectivity and violence, debunks the menace of the gallows and the anxiety and terror usually associated with it, but it nevertheless reminds the audience of the fate supposedly awaiting rogues and cutpurses. 'Supposedly' because the gallows may rather, in practice, have had the function of a scarecrow for petty thieves. Garthine Walker offers the following analysis:

> Characterised by secrecy, deception and violation of the person's physical boundaries, one might expect cutpurses and pickpockets to have high conviction and execution ranges. Certainly, the perceived seriousness of their crime made it one of the first offences to be removed from benefit of clergy in the sixteenth century. Yet despite the distinguishing features, most sixteenth- and seventeenth-century defendants, male and female, charged with these crimes, did not end their lives on the gallows. ... Pickpockets and cutpurses were infrequently prosecuted. Compared to other categories of offender, they might not have appeared to the courts as threatening the fabric of social order.[14]

When Moll defies Sir Alexander at the end of the play, she shows that she knows much more than he does in terms of female-oriented punishments:

---

[12]   Thomas Dekker, *The Honest Whore, Part the Second*, in *Thomas Dekker*, ed. Ernest Rhys, Mermaid Series (London: T. Fisher Unwin, [1894]), V.ii.268, 272, 269, n. 2, 285.

[13]   See I.ii, particularly 56–60: 'But I prithee, sweet wag, shall there be gallows standing in England when thou art king? and resolution thus fubbed as it is with the rusty curb of old father Antic the law? Do not thou when thou art king hang a thief' (William Shakespeare, *King Henry IV, Part 1*, ed. A. R. Humphreys, The Arden Shakespeare, 2nd ser. [London: Routledge, 1992]). The theme of the gallows, as John Dover Wilson puts it, 'recurs with damnable iteration in this scene' (John Dover Wilson, *The Fortunes of Falstaff* [Cambridge: Cambridge University Press, 1943]), 40.

[14]   Garthine Walker, *Crime, Gender and Social Order in Early Modern England*, Cambridge Studies in Early Modern British History (Cambridge: Cambridge University Press, 2003), 186.

> I pursue no pity:
> Follow the law: and you can cuck me, spare not:
> Hang up my viol by me, and I care not. (V.ii.253–55)

To 'cuck' meant 'to punish by setting in the cucking-stool', which was 'an instrument of punishment formerly in use for scolds or disorderly women, fraudulent trades people etc., consisting of a chair (sometimes in the form of a close-stool), in which the offender was fastened and exposed to the jeers of the bystanders, or conveyed to a pond or river and ducked'.[15] Ingram's definition of a scold as 'a turbulent, chiding, brawling person'[16] evokes one type of 'roaring girl' depicted in the prologue by Middleton and Dekker, but one which actually serves as a foil to their heroine:

> she
> That roars at midnight in deep tavern bowls,
> That beats the watch, and constable controls. (Prol.16–18)

Ingram's extended description adds the information that 'alleged scolds were simultaneously accused of one or more mundane neighbourhood offences of breaches of personal morality: petty theft; hedgebreaking; sexual immorality; swearing and blaspheming; drunkenness; unlicensed ale-selling; or, more generally, "lewd", "wicked" or "evil" behaviour'.[17] This is in keeping with Frith's confession and the boasting tone of the cony-catching-like biography, but is at odds with the dramatic character, whose rough edges have been smoothed out. Coming from Frith, the reference to cucking might not have been so surprising, but when Moll refers to it in the city comedy as possibly applying to her own case, it does sound incongruous. Although the reference to cucking may pass unnoticed at the end of the comedy, when all is well that ends (and not hangs) well, it is telling in several ways. It exposes the gap between the criminal and the character,

---

[15] *OED*, s.v. 'cuck', *v*2, and 'cucking-stool'. See also Ingram, '"Scolding Women"', 58–59:

> Modern research into early history of the cucking-stool has revealed that, in fact, there was a great variety of usage in different manors, boroughs and cities. In some places the aim was primarily to exhibit the offenders to public ridicule, which might be achieved either by placing them in a fixed position in some prominent place or by carrying them about the town. Elsewhere the emphasis was on the ducking of the culprits, the effect of which might be simply to soak them or, more brutally, to defile them with mud or filth. These objects were achieved by means of a wide variety of engines and contraptions, not always chair-like in form, their precise nature depending on local tradition and available resources. To add to the confusion, up to the early sixteenth century, these multifarious penalties had been applied not only to scolds – instead of or as an alternative to fines – but to bakers, brewers and other tradespeople who sold underweight or adulterated goods, and to other offenders such as bawds, prostitutes, cheats and cozeners.

[16] Ingram, '"Scolding Women"', 67.
[17] Ingram, '"Scolding Women"', 67.

between reality and dramatic appropriation. It indicates that the playwrights were familiar with this female-oriented punishment and interested in the subject of scolds and disorderly women as dramatic material but also as they figured in Jacobean society. It further suggests that they intended to create a jarring note and have the audience associate cucking with inappropriateness, that is, understand that cucking was an unsuitable punishment in this particular case, and maybe in other cases. It may ultimately reveal reservations about such means of castigation, which could explain why Moll's defiant reference to cucking is ironically turned into a means of self-assertion, whereas the shaming practice was supposed to sap female assertiveness.[18]

Subverting punitive measures, that is, transforming shaming practices into self-assertive or entertaining ones and appropriating them to alter the interpretation of both sentence and crime, was something the real Frith seemed to be expert in. The most famous example is her histrionic public penance at St Paul's Cross, as reported by the court writer Sir John Chamberlain in a letter addressed to Sir Dudley Carleton and dated 12 February 1612:

> this last Sonday Mall Cut-Purse a notorious baggage (that used to go in mans apparell and challenged the field of divers gallants) was brought to [St Paul's Cross], where she wept bitterly and seemed very penitent, but yt is since doubted she was maudlin druncke, beeing discovered to have tippled of three quarts of sacke before she came to her penaunce: she had the daintiest preacher or ghostly father that ever I saw in pulpit, one Ratcliffe of Brazen Nose in Oxford ... but the best is he did extreem badly, and so wearied the audience that the best part went away, and the rest tarried rather to heare Mall Cutpurse then him.[19]

Elizabeth Cook interprets the event as 'a knowing contribution to the street theatre which the occasion provided';[20] Ungerer regards Frith as 'a Tarltonesque entertainer'.[21] *Mutatis mutandis*, the episode brings to mind Michel Foucault's analysis of public executions and their possible appropriation by criminals: 'In these executions, which ought to show only the terrorizing power of the prince, there was a whole aspect of carnival, in which rules were inverted, authority mocked and criminals transformed into heroes.'[22]

In *Moll Cutpurse's Diary*, the episode of the mock penance is presented from a subjective viewpoint, supposedly that of the heroine herself, and becomes redolent of picaresque novels: she says that she follows 'the laudable example of others who

---

[18]   Ingram, '"Scolding Women"', 59.

[19]   John Chamberlain, *The Letters of John Chamberlain*, ed. Norman Egbert McClure, 2 vols (Philadelphia: American Philosophical Society, 1939), vol. 1, 334.

[20]   Elizabeth Cook, introduction to *The Roaring Girl*, xx.

[21]   Ungerer, 'Mary Frith', 46.

[22]   Michel Foucault, *Discipline and Punish: The Birth of the Prison*, trans. Alan Sheridan (New York: Vintage Books, 1995), 61.

have in part preceded me, as Senor Guzman and the Spanish tribe of cheaters'.[23] It is also redolent of Robert Greene's 1592 cony-catching pamphlets, in which ruse thumbs its nose at order and authority, insofar as it is 'a book of comic anecdotes revealing the secrets of cozenage and theft, and proclaiming Frith's own expertise at these arts'.[24] The men of the Church are even more ridiculed in the *Diary* version, since Moll's friends avenge her by 'cutting of part of their cloaks and gowns and sending them home as naked behind as an ape's tail'.[25] In *The Life and Death of Mistress Mary Frith* – as in *The Roaring Girl* – Moll is never presented as an offender submissively undergoing a sentence; she is the one who gives punishing agents and instruments a rough ride. Embedded anecdotes about other offenders being hanged and old Moll's illness – the dropsy, which is presented as a sort of poetic justice – utterly fail to counterbalance the heroine's lifetime of illicit feats and read as an unconvincing strategy of moral containment.[26] What clearly emerges from both the play and the biography is a figure able to divert punishment into performance, to alter the course of the law not only for herself but also – if not chiefly – for others, thus manipulating patriarchal imperatives and prejudices. The difference between the play and the narrative lies in the fact that, in *The Roaring Girl*, the character is a decriminalized version of the real Frith (Moll makes it a point to be honest, cleansed of her dubious past), whereas in the *Life*, Frith's persona asserts herself as an outlaw, although a benign and a merry one (the tone is that of a wit and a trickster – playfully boasting, humorous and provocative).

Moll's fame is due both to her self-assertiveness and appropriating abilities, and to her interfering and compromising qualities. To take up Stephen Orgel's phrasing, 'she sees herself less as a transgressor than as a mediator between the illicit and the licit'.[27] Not only does she play the arbitrator among thieves in the underworld but, as a fence, she also ensures a (lucrative) link between offenders and victims. This is also due to her social and gender ambivalence: because she epitomizes 'the paradox of the man-woman and the honest cutpurse', because she 'combines the contrary traits of prince and prostitute',[28] Moll stands out as the perfect go-between. In 'her' diary, she presents the receiving of stolen goods as

---

[23] *Life*, 21. The reference is to Matheo Aleman's *The Rogue, or, The Life of Guzman de Alfarache*. Written in Spanish in 1599 (first part) and 1604 (second part), it was translated into English by James Mabbe in 1623.

[24] Stephen Orgel, *Impersonations: The Performance of Gender in Shakespeare's England* (Cambridge: Cambridge University Press, 1996), 141.

[25] *Life*, 44.

[26] Embedded anecdotes about other offenders being hanged include, for example, the case of Mrs Pike, a fence, who was hanged at Tyburn (*Life*, 70–71), and that of Walker, a notable pickpocket and recidivist, to the point where, Frith tells us, 'the court would no means spare him but the next sessions delivered him to Gregory, who showed him a sleight worth twenty of his and sent him swinging in the other world' (82).

[27] Orgel, *Impersonations*, 144.

[28] Chakravorky, *Society and Politics*, 87.

both a clever form of racketeering and an inestimable service profitable to each party:

> In my house, I should have told you, I set up a kind of brokery or a distinct factory of jewels, rings and watches which had been pinched or stolen any manner of way, at never so great distances from any person; I might properly enough call it the 'insurance office' for such merchandise, for the losers were sure upon composition to recover their goods again, and the pirates were as sure to have a good ransom, and I so much in the gross for brokerage without any more danger, the hue and cry being always directed to me for the discovery of the goods, not the takers.[29]

The absence of danger incurred by Moll is no fiction. Walker reminds us that 'there was no effective statute against receiving stolen goods until 1691, and it remained an offence that was notoriously difficult to prosecute'.[30] Ungerer adds: 'given the fact that there was neither effective statute against receiving stolen goods nor a professional police force, the local authorities, in the interest of crime control, welcomed women as paralegal intermediaries in the return and custody of stolen goods.'[31] When in 'her' diary Moll writes that her 'lawless vocation' is 'more advantageous by far to the injured than the courts of justice and benefits of the law',[32] she implicitly refers to the Crown's custom, in the event of a conviction, of confiscating the stolen goods.[33] Fencing was considered as more a paralegal than an illegal practice.

In *The Roaring Girl*, the emphasis is hardly put on the receiving of stolen goods, but Moll is still associated with paralegality rather than crime. As Jodi Mikalachki analyzes her behaviour, 'contravening and enforcing the law at different moments, she [Moll] engages throughout in what I shall call the paralegal activities of identifying rogues, explicating their language and behaviour, and mediating between them and an elite audience'.[34] Middleton and Dekker's Moll has nothing of the frightening offender about her. Instead, she appears as an innocuous underworld guide, part of an economy of entertainment. And yet her function, as we shall see, is far from being limited to dramatic paralegal mediation.

Moll is, in fact, more an interfering than a mediating figure. In the *Life*, she is presented as the *doyenne* of the London underworld, and her authority over her band of thieves is hyperbolically depicted as 'an absolute incontrollable power,

---

[29]   *Life*, 29.

[30]   Garthine Walker, 'Women, Theft and the World of Stolen Goods', in *Women, Crime and the Courts in Early Modern England*, ed. Jenny Kermode and Garthine Walker (London: UCL Press, 1994), 91.

[31]   Ungerer, 'Mary Frith', 55.

[32]   *Life*, 29.

[33]   Ungerer, 'Mary Frith', 64.

[34]   Jodi Mikalachki, 'Gender, Cant, and Cross-talking in *The Roaring Girl*', *Renaissance Drama* 25 (1994): 124.

more than ever the law or justice had over that Mercurial tribe, they being entirely at her beck and command, submitting themselves and their stolen purchases to her only order, will and pleasure'.[35] Such power includes compassionate acts to better the lot of those taken prisoner or to save others from the hangman.[36] In *The Roaring Girl*, she intervenes to help Davy Dapper escape from Sergeant Curtilax, and she teaches a lesson to the impudent Laxton, whom she threatens, in the guise of legal action, with quasi-legal capital punishment: 'Draw, or I'll serve an execution on thee' (III.i.68). She meddles with the law both verbally and physically, serving as a vehicle of satire in acting as a dispenser of justice. She especially denounces the tricks of lawyers and the abuses of power perpetrated by authoritarian men cunning enough to use the law to achieve their own ends. (Sir Alexander is one of them, resolved as he is to 'find law to hang her up' [I.ii.234].) This is made more explicit in the *Diary*:

> For I always hated cruelty and oppression, but of all people I affected not a lawyer. I had tasted of their covetousness and dilatoriness so much that I never advised any person upon any misusing whatsoever to have recourse to them for remedy or redress. I knew their quirks and quillets and how they could and did wrest the law to anything for their own advantage.[37]

Both in the play and the biography, the satire is justice-oriented and gender-oriented: Moll's satirical comments target men of law and men *tout court*. Orgel observes: 'Moll is surrounded by men who are less than men; the play is full of references to impotence, castration, false phalluses, countertenors.'[38] The playwrights may have followed in the wake of the Long Meg of Westminster stories, in which 'the butts of the jokes were decidedly the braggarts, corrupt legal officials, cowardly gentlemen and other dastardly fellow whom Meg resisted or "corrected" with her combative skill and wit'.[39] Moll is turned into the champion of poor, oppressed women, into the voice of embryonic feminism, as part of her answer to Laxton exemplifies:

> In thee I defy all men, their worst hates,
> And their best flatteries, all their golden witchcrafts,
> With which they entangle the poor spirits of fools.
> Distressed needlewomen and trade-fallen wives,
> Fish that must needs bite or themselves be bitten,
> Such hungry things as these may soon be took
> With a worm fastened on a golden hook:
> Those are the lecher's food, his prey, he watches
> For quarrelling wedlocks, and poor shifting sisters,

---

35 *Life*, 19.

36 See *Life*, 58, 27.

37 *Life*, 62.

38 Orgel, *Impersonations*, 152.

39 Walker, *Crime, Gender and Social Order*, 87.

'Tis the best fish he takes: but why, good fisherman,
Am I thought meat for you, that never yet
Had angling rod cast towards me? 'Cause, you'll say,
I'm given to sport, I'm often merry, jest:
Had mirth no kindred in the world but lust?
Oh shame take all her friends then: but howe'er
Thou and the baser world censure my life,
I'll send 'em word by thee, and write so much
Upon thy breast, 'cause thou shalt bear't in mind:
Tell them 'twere base to yield, where I have conquered. (III.i.91–109)

A sword-fight follows, and Moll gains the upper hand. Here she can but evoke the warrior-woman, one of the scant positive models of feminine force in early modern England, which was associated with the mythological Penthesilea, Queen of Amazons, and incorporated into Queen Elizabeth I's iconography. 'The warrior-woman', Walker notes, 'was an emblem of social and political order'.[40] As Walker explains,

> this virtuous warrior-woman fought an individual battle against oppressive and unjust violence. As men normally occupied the positions that enabled oppression or unjust treatment of others, her targets were invariably male. Yet far from subverting order, the warrior-woman upheld and reinforced it.[41]

Indeed, the historical Frith was supposedly a royalist and strongly conservative, an image that goes counter to the belief about criminality that 'in every sentence there was a *crimen majestatis* and in the least criminal a potential regicide'.[42] In the *Diary*, she clearly portrays herself as an enthusiastic supporter of Charles I, supplying a conduit with wine in Fleet Street to celebrate his return from Scotland, 'after that unnatural and detestable rebellion of the Scots in 1638',[43] and shaking hands with him: 'And as the king passed by me, I put out my hand and caught him by his, and grasped it very hard, saying, "Welcome home Charles!".'[44] Although the anecdote seems too fantastic to be true, the text presents her as benefiting from her welcoming gesture, and she is rehabilitated as a loyal, if not lawful, subject; as she supposedly puts it herself: 'it was no more Moll Cutpurse but Mistress Mary Frith, my neighbours using me with new respect and civility.'[45]

This supposed royal encounter could not have taken place in the reign of James I. Leah S. Marcus gives the character of the warrior-woman a topical reverberation and an ideological function:

---

[40]   Walker, *Crime, Gender and Social Order*, 87.

[41]   Walker, *Crime, Gender and Social Order*, 86.

[42]   Foucault, *Discipline and Punish*, 53–54.

[43]   *Life*, 56.

[44]   *Life*, 57.

[45]   *Life*, 58.

As reformers harked back to the glorious reign of Elizabeth in their impatience with the autocracy and ineptitude of her successor, James I, so Dekker and Middleton seem deliberately to have constructed an ambivalent, low-life variant upon the once-threatening Amazonian image, a self-sufficient yet isolated virgin figure whose virtue shows up the corruption of the times.[46]

In 1611, Frith was still single, and the dramatic Moll asserts, 'I have no humour to marry, I love to lie o'both sides o'th'bed myself, and again o'th'other side; a wife you know ought to be obedient, but I fear me I am too headstrong to obey, therefore I'll ne'er go about it' (II.ii.36–39). But historical evidence shows that Frith married Lewknor Markham in 1614.[47] Tellingly enough, the marriage is never mentioned in the biography, whose title, *The Life and Death of Mistress Mary Frith*, already points to the omission. The warrior-woman with glorified feats emerges then as a fictional construct – shadowing the original criminal whose offences ought to be condemned – or as 'a mythic construct made up of invented facts and conditioned by absences and displacements'.[48]

Middleton and Dekker's 1611 dramatic representation of Moll Cutpurse, however clearly wandering from the historical figure in its sanitizing, romanticizing and early mythologizing process, retains some originality, insofar as it shows a genuine concern for women. What also makes it stand apart is the possibility that Frith herself may have been associated, in some way or other, with the show, as may be suggested in the epilogue:

> if what both [the writers and the actors] have done
> Cannot full pay your expectation,
> The Roaring Girl herself, some few days hence,
> Shall on this stage give larger recompense. (Epil.32–35)

In the *Life*, published 51 years later, the appropriation appears less original, more mechanical, especially in the light of Ungerer's analysis:

> the main strategy the author(s) pursued was to integrate scanty historical records into the pre-existing parameters of criminal biography as they had been evolved for male criminals and, if needs be, to transcend or invert the pattern. As the result of this transmutation, Mary Frith suffered the same fate at the hands of her anonymous pseudo-biographers as did Hind and the like.[49]

The appropriation and transformation of the real Frith into an entertaining cross-dressed figure, retaining more or less subversive features, did not stop there; the diachronic perspective was to be extended with further writings. In 1665, partly plagiarizing Elizabethan and Jacobean roguery pamphlets, Richard Head

---

[46] Leah S. Marcus, *Puzzling Shakespeare: Local Reading and Its Discontents* (Berkeley: University of California Press, 1988), 104.

[47] Ungerer, 'Mary Frith', 68.

[48] Ungerer, 'Mary Frith', 45.

[49] Ungerer, 'Mary Frith', 45.

and Francis Kirkman wrote *The English Rogue described in the life of Meriton Latroon, a witty extravagant: Being a Complete History of the Most Eminent Cheats of Both Sexes*. The chapter in which the hero, on the road, meets 'a woman robber in man's apparel' can read as a veiled reference to Moll Cutpurse.[50] In 1719, Mary Frith's story was included in Alexander Smith's *History of the Lives of the Most Notorious High-way Men, Foot-Pads, and Other Thieves*. In 1722, Daniel Defoe's eponymous heroine, Moll Flanders, claimed to be a follower of Moll Cutpurse.[51] The sensational quality of the story – almost eclipsing the character herself – was revived and capitalized upon in the wake of the fashionable and lucrative (sub)genres constituted by cony-catching pamphlets, chapbooks, picaresque novels and criminal biographies. The mythic construct was tightly connected with commercial stakes and the expectations of readers. What mattered was clearly the sensational aspect of the story and its capacity to give pleasure, rather than any reflection it might inspire on issues of marginality and gender, although something equivocal could probably still be traced. As Foucault reminds us,

> the effect, like the use, of this literature [accounts of crimes and infamous lives] was equivocal. The condemned man found himself transformed into a hero by the sheer extent of his widely advertised crimes, and sometimes the affirmation of his belated repentance. Against the law, against the rich, the powerful, the magistrates, the constabulary or the watch, against taxes and their collectors, he appeared to have waged a struggle with which one all too easily identified. The proclamation of these crimes blew up to epic proportions the tiny struggle that passed unperceived in everyday life.[52]

Middleton and Dekker's play was not put on again before 1951 – at least, there is no record of theatrical production – and its revival in the 1970s coincided with the growth of the feminist movement and the interest in gender studies. But more fundamentally, in a way that transcends times and fashions, the Moll Cutpurse who was given a dramatic life by Middleton and Dekker may deserve attention, as McManus puts it, as 'the glamorous figure of the rebel, outlaw or rogue whose energies revitalize conformist society'.[53]

---

[50]   Richard Head and Francis Kirkman, *The English Rogue described in the life of Meriton Latroon, a witty extravagant: Being a Complete History of the Most Eminent Cheats of Both Sexes* (London: G. Routledge and Sons, 1928). See part 1, ch. 33 (152–54), entitled: 'From his farmer's house he rides he cared not whither: on the road he is strangely surprised by a woman robber in man's apparel: he discovers it by unbuttoning her breeches to search for private pockets within: they two conclude a perpetual friendship.'

[51]   'I grew as impudent a Thief, and as dexterous as ever *Moll Cutpurse* was, tho' if Fame does not belie her, not half so handsome' (Daniel Defoe, *Moll Flanders*, ed. G. A. Starr [Oxford: Oxford University Press, 1971], 201).

[52]   Foucault, *Discipline and Punish*, 67.

[53]   McManus, '*The Roaring Girl*', 219.

Works Cited

Primary Sources

Chamberlain, John. *The Letters of John Chamberlain*. Edited by Norman Egbert McClure. 2 vols. Philadelphia: American Philosophical Society, 1939.

Defoe, Daniel. *Moll Flanders*. Edited by G. A. Starr. Oxford: Oxford University Press, 1971.

Dekker, Thomas. *The Honest Whore, Part the Second*. In *Thomas Dekker*. Edited by Ernest Rhys. Mermaid Series. London: T. Fisher Unwin, [1894].

Head, Richard, and Francis Kirkman. *The English Rogue described in the life of Meriton Latroon, a witty extravagant. Being a Complete History of the Most Eminent Cheats of Both Sexes*. London: G. Routledge and Sons, 1928.

The Life and Death of Mrs Mary Frith, Commonly Called Moll Cutpurse. In *The Renaissance Imagination, Important Literary Texts and Theatrical Texts from the Late Middle Ages through the Seventeenth Century*. Edited by Stephen Orgel. New York: Garland Publishing, 1993.

Middleton, Thomas, and Thomas Dekker. *The Roaring Girl*. Edited by Elizabeth Cook. 2nd ed. The New Mermaids. London: A. and C. Black, 1997.

Shakespeare, William. *King Henry IV, Part 1*. Edited by A. R. Humphreys. The Arden Shakespeare, 2nd ser. London: Routledge, 1992.

Secondary Sources

Beier, A. L. *Masterless Men: The Vagrancy Problem in England, 1560–1640*. London: Methuen, 1987.

Chakravorty, Swapan. *Society and Politics in the Plays of Thomas Middleton*. Oxford: Clarendon Press, 1996.

Foucault, Michel. *Discipline and Punish: The Birth of the Prison*. Translated by Alan Sheridan. New York: Vintage Books, 1977.

Gowing, Laura. 'Language, Power, and the Law: Women's Slander Litigation in Early Modern London'. In *Women, Crime and the Courts in Early Modern England*. Edited by Jenny Kermode and Garthine Walker. London: UCL Press, 1994. 26–47.

Howard, Jean E. *The Stage and Social Struggle in Early Modern England*. London: Routledge, 1994.

Ingram, Martin. '"Scolding Women Cucked or Washed": A Crisis in Gender Relations in Early Modern England?'. In *Women, Crime and the Courts in Early Modern England*. Edited by Jenny Kermode and Garthine Walker. London: UCL Press, 1994. 48–80.

Jones-Davies, Marie-Thérèse. *Un peintre de la vie londonienne: Thomas Dekker (circa 1572–1632)*. 2 vols. Paris: Didier, 1958.

McManus, Clare. '*The Roaring Girl* and the London Underworld'. In *Early Modern English Drama: A Critical Companion*. Edited by Garrett A. Sullivan,

Patrick Cheney and Andrew Hadfield. Oxford: Oxford University Press, 2006. 213–24.

Marcus, Leah S. *Puzzling Shakespeare: Local Reading and Its Discontents.* Berkeley: University of California Press, 1988.

Mikalachki, Jodi. 'Gender, Cant, and Cross-talking in *The Roaring Girl*'. *Renaissance Drama* 25 (1994): 119–43.

Orgel, Stephen. *Impersonations. The Performance of Gender in Shakespeare's England.* Cambridge: Cambridge University Press, 1996.

Ungerer, Gustav. 'Mary Frith, Alias Moll Cutpurse, in Life and Literature'. *Shakespeare Studies* 28 (2000): 42–84.

Walker, Garthine. *Crime, Gender and Social Order in Early Modern England.* Cambridge Studies in Early Modern British History. Cambridge: Cambridge University Press, 2003.

———. 'Women, Theft and the World of Stolen Goods'. In *Women, Crime and the Courts in Early Modern England.* Edited by Jenny Kermode and Garthine Walker. London: UCL Press, 1994. 81–105.

Wilson, John Dover. *The Fortunes of Falstaff.* Cambridge: Cambridge University Press, 1943.

PART II
Reading (into) the Social Picture

Chapter 6
Mothers, Wives and Killers: Marital Status and Homicide in London, 1674–1790

Marisha Caswell

Homicide is commonly regarded as one of the most horrific crimes. In most circumstances, taking a life is a serious offence that goes against moral and religious teachings. At the same time, not all forms of homicide are considered equally grave. This is apparent, for example, from the differentiation between first- and second-degree murder in today's Anglo-American legal system. The seventeenth- and eighteenth-century English criminal justice system drew distinctions of its own, some of which centred on the relationship between victim and killer, as is evident in the two distinctive offences of petty treason and infanticide. Both were forms of homicide with highly specific definitions, which meant that the treatment of the accused depended not just on whether or not they had killed a person but also on their marital status. Marriage excused a woman's actions in cases of infanticide, yet exacerbated them when it came to petty treason. Moreover, the experiences of the women accused of these crimes were shaped and informed by expectations of behaviour consistent with their marital status. Using trials for infanticide and petty treason in London between 1674 and 1790, this essay examines the role that marital status played in homicide trials, a place where coverture was not supposed to apply, but one where the legal consequences of marriage mattered nonetheless.

Marital status figured into the very definition of these two types of homicide. Infanticide can simply refer to the killing of any newborn, but after the passage of the remarkable 'Act to Prevent the Murthering of Bastard Children' in 1624 (21 Jac. 1, c. 27), the term becomes associated with the murder of newborn illegitimate children following a concealed pregnancy.[1] Under this statute, an unmarried woman who had concealed her pregnancy and whose child was found dead was assumed to have murdered her child unless she could prove otherwise. This unique reversal of the burden of proof remained in force until the statute's repeal in 1803.[2]

---

[1]   Contemporaries did not explicitly refer to this crime as infanticide, although the word is used here as a convenient shorthand, in accordance with common scholarly practice. For the purposes of this chapter, cases which referred to the murder of a 'bastard child' or referenced the 1624 statute have been classified as infanticide.

[2]   Martin Ingram, 'Infanticide in Late Medieval and Early Modern England', in *Childhood and Violence in the Western Tradition*, ed. Laurence Brockliss and Heather Montgomery (Oxford: Oxbow Books, 2010), 73.

According to the 1351 statute (25 Edw. 3 St. 5, c. 2), petty treason was a lesser form of treason and an aggravated form of murder, in which a servant killed his or her master or mistress, a cleric his superior, or a wife her husband. Although men could commit petty treason, its most common form involved a wife killing her husband. Petty treason remained an aggravated form of murder until 1828, when it was reclassified simply as murder.[3]

Both petty treason and infanticide were gender-related crimes. The infanticide statute's focus on single women meant that the offence was, as J. R. Dickinson and J. A. Sharpe argue, a more sex-specific crime than witchcraft, which is traditionally associated with women.[4] Petty treason was gender-related because its predominant form was a wife's murder of her husband and because of its unique punishment in such cases. While men convicted of high or petty treason received different punishments, women convicted of high or petty treason received the same punishment: death by burning. As Frances Dolan and Ruth Campbell argue, this punishment of death by burning for both forms of treason equated the husband with the monarch and provided a strong symbol of female subjection, designed to maintain a woman's subordinate place within marriage.[5] This symbolism changed in 1790, when the punishment for women convicted of petty treason became the same as the punishment of other murderers: death by hanging, followed by dissection.

Despite the shared gendered nature of these offences, historians tend to examine petty treason and infanticide in isolation from one another.[6] This is not surprising, since the definitions of the offences, as well as the treatment of the

---

[3]   Ruth Campbell, 'Sentence of Death by Burning for Women', *Journal of Legal History* 5 (1984): 44.

[4]   J. R. Dickinson and J. A. Sharpe, 'Infanticide in Early Modern England: The Court of Great Sessions at Chester, 1650–1800', in *Infanticide: Historical Perspectives on Child Murder and Concealment, 1550–2000*, ed. Mark Jackson (Aldershot: Ashgate, 2002): 35–36.

[5]   Frances Dolan, 'Home-Rebels and House-Traitors: Murderous Wives in Early Modern England', *Yale Journal of Law and the Humanities* 4.1 (1992): 4; Campbell, 'Sentence of Death by Burning'. For further discussion of the cultural significance of the punishment of death by burning, see Pompa Banerjee, *Burning Women: Widows, Witches, and Early Modern European Travelers in India* (Basingstoke: Palgrave Macmillan, 2003).

[6]   See, in particular, Peter C. Hoffer and N. E. H. Hull, *Murdering Mothers: Infanticide in England and New England, 1558–1803* (New York: New York University Press, 1981); Mark Jackson, *New-Born Child Murder: Women, Illegitimacy and the Courts in Eighteenth-Century England* (Manchester: Manchester University Press, 1997); Allyson May, '"She at first denied it": Infanticide Trials at the Old Bailey', in *Women and History: Voices in Early Modern England*, ed. Valerie Frith (Toronto: Coach House Press, 1995): 19–35; Laura Gowing, 'Secret Births and Infanticide in Seventeenth-Century England', *Past and Present* 156 (1997): 87–115; Mark Jackson, ed., *Infanticide: Historical Perspectives on Child Murder and Concealment, 1550–2000* (Aldershot: Ashgate, 2000); and Frances Dolan, *Dangerous Familiars: Representations of Domestic Crime in England, 1550–1800* (Ithaca, NY: Cornell University Press, 1994).

offenders, were quite different. But at the same time, these were both gendered crimes related directly to a woman's marital status. As such, reasons exist to consider the crimes in conjunction and to compare the treatment of the women accused of these killings. The overwhelming majority of women accused at the Old Bailey of killing their infants were unmarried. Juries acquitted the majority of these single women, but the acquittal rate for the few married women also accused of infanticide under the 1624 statute stands at a striking 100% (see Table 6.1). These 18 women,[7] whether guilty or innocent of killing the infants in question, went free precisely because they were married – a technicality in one sense, but a revealing one. When it came to the 25[8] married women accused of petty treason in the same period, juries convicted 8 (32%), acquitted 9 (38%), convicted another 7 (28%) of lesser offences, including both murder and manslaughter, and delivered a special verdict in one trial. In comparison, only 19% of married women charged with murder were found guilty, with a further 17.5% convicted on partial verdicts and a full 63% acquitted. Of all the different forms of homicide, married women faced the highest conviction rate for petty treason and the highest acquittal rate for infanticide during this period.

Table 6.1   Verdicts for married women accused of homicide in London, 1674–1790[9]

	Guilty	Not Guilty	Partial Verdict	Other	Total
Infanticide	0	18 (100%)	0	0	18 (100%)
Petty Treason	8 (32%)	9 (36%)	7 (28%)	1 (4%)	25 (100%)
Murder	11 (19.3%)	36 (63.2%)	10 (17.5%)	0	57 (100%)
Killing, Other	1 (25%)	3 (75%)	0	0	4 (100%)
Total	20 (19.2%)	66 (63.5%)	17 (16.3%)	1 (1%)	104 (100%)

Source: Old Bailey Online (www.oldbaileyonline.org).

---

[7]   This number includes those women who were identified as married or whose record indicates they were married at the time of conception, as well as two women who were accused of aiding and abetting an unmarried woman accused of infanticide. The Old Bailey Online also contains an additional 12 cases that clearly identify the victim as an infant, some of which the compilers and digitizers of the Old Bailey Online have classified as infanticide. However, I have not done so because the record indicates the murder of a child/infant, not the murder of a bastard child. Since contemporaries did not use the category of infanticide, it is necessary to look for the inclusion of 'bastard' or reference to the 1624 statute to determine whether a specific offence is classified as murder, or as infanticide according to the 1624 statute. If there is no reference to 'bastard child' or the 1624 statute, I have classified the case as murder. See above, note 1.

[8]   This number includes all women who were accused of killing their husbands.

[9]   In order to determine the marital status of the accused, I used the custom search function in the Old Bailey Online, looking for 'killing>all subcategories' and limiting the offender's gender to 'female'. After this, I read through all of the trials to determine the marital status of the accused. If an offender or witness indicated the accused was married, I classified them as 'married' unless evidence appeared to indicate otherwise.

These statistics demonstrate that marriage excused a woman's actions in one crime, but exacerbated them in another, drawing attention to the importance of marital status as a legal category of difference.[10] Upon marriage, all women, with the exception of the queen regnant, became subject to the common law doctrine of coverture.[11] That is, for many legal purposes, a wife's identity was 'covered' by her husband's. The most significant consequence of coverture was a married woman's almost complete loss of property rights.[12] Beyond the formal legal consequences, ideas shaped by coverture and marital status also indirectly influenced other aspects of women's lives – what I refer to as the subtext of coverture. This subtext had important consequences in women's lives, shaping their experiences outside property law. The subtext of coverture did not dictate women's lives, but it influenced them in different ways, depending on the context.

This influence is particularly evident in the criminal law, where coverture was not directly applicable. In certain circumstances, a married woman's civil subjection could translate into limited criminal liability through the defence of marital coercion, which held that if a married woman committed certain offences either with or in the presence of her husband, she was assumed to be acting under his coercion and was therefore not liable for her actions.[13] This defence did not apply to murder or treason, however. But, as the cases of petty treason and infanticide indicate, marital status still played an important role in determining criminal liability, even outside the confines of the coercion defence. A woman's marital status could exacerbate or excuse her actions in specific forms of homicide, demonstrating how the legal consequences of marriage were not limited solely to a woman's property rights, or lack thereof.

---

[10] Amy Froide, 'Marital Status as a Category of Difference: Singlewomen and Widows in Early Modern England', in *Singlewomen in the European Past*, ed. Judith Bennett and Amy Froide (Philadelphia: University of Pennsylvania Press, 1999), 236–69.

[11] Maeve E. Doggett, *Marriage, Wife-Beating and the Law in Victorian England* (Columbia: University of South Carolina Press, 1993), 34. On coverture, see also Chapter 10 in the present volume, by Krista Kesselring.

[12] The historiography of coverture focuses primarily on how women negotiated coverture's property restrictions. Some key studies include Amy Louise Erickson, *Women and Property in Early Modern England* (London: Routledge, 1995); Hendrik Hartog, *Man and Wife in America: A History* (Cambridge, MA: Harvard University Press, 2000); Susan Staves, *Married Women's Separate Property in England, 1660–1833* (Cambridge, MA: Harvard University Press, 1990); and Tim Stretton, *Women Waging Law in Elizabethan England* (Cambridge: Cambridge University Press, 1998).

[13] Deirdre Palk, *Gender, Crime and Judicial Discretion, 1780–1830* (London: Boydell Press, 2006), 21–24; Janelle Greenberg, 'The Legal Status of the English Woman in Early Eighteenth-Century Common Law and Equity', *Studies in Eighteenth-Century Culture* 4 (1975): 174.

The main sources for this essay are the *Old Bailey Papers* (hereafter *OBP*)[14] and *The Ordinary of Newgate's Accounts* (hereafter *Ordinary's Accounts*). The *OBP* were a recorded and compressed version of the trials heard at the Old Bailey, which were sold after each session. The *Ordinary's Accounts* were its sister publication that recounted the attempts of the Ordinary of Newgate – the prison chaplain – to minister to the condemned. They gave a detailed narrative of the life of the offenders and how their actions had brought them to the gallows. Both these sources offer particular insight into how the criminal justice system functioned and how people perceived particular crimes and alleged offenders. True, their commercial nature makes them somewhat problematic sources, with publishers attempting to reconcile the competing demands of affordability, accuracy, instruction and entertainment.[15] Yet, while neither the *OBP* nor the *Ordinary's Accounts* are perfect sources, they provide particular insight into the perceptions, treatment and experiences of the women accused of petty treason and infanticide in seventeenth- and eighteenth-century London.

Married Women and Infanticide under the 1624 Statute

In 1704, Mary Tudor was accused of murdering her female infant by throwing it into a privy where the baby choked and suffocated. The jury acquitted Mary not because they thought her innocent of the baby's death, but because the 'Child was no Bastard'.[16] Tudor's case was not an exception; the *OBP* contain 18 cases of married women accused of infanticide under the 1624 statute between 1674 and

---

[14]   In order to differentiate between the proceedings available online and the manuscript sessions papers, I have followed the lead of the creators of the Old Bailey Online and used *Old Bailey Papers* instead of *Old Bailey Sessions Papers*. See Robert B. Shoemaker, 'The Old Bailey Proceedings and Representations of Crime and Criminal Justice in Eighteenth-Century London', *Journal of British Studies* 47.3 (2008): 559.

[15]   For a discussion of the problems and potentials of these sources, see in particular Shoemaker, 'Old Bailey Proceedings', 559–80; John Langbein, 'Shaping the Eighteenth-Century Criminal Trial: A View from the Ryder Sources', *University of Chicago Law Review* 50.1 (1983): 1–136; Michael Harris, 'Trials and Criminal Biographies: A Case Study in Distribution', in *The Sale and Distribution of Books from 1700*, ed. Robin Myers and Michael Harris (Oxford: Oxford Polytechnic Press, 1982): 1–35; Simon Devereaux, 'From Sessions to Newspaper? Criminal Trial Reporting, the Nature of Crime, and the London Press, 1770–1800', *London Journal* 32.1 (2007): 1–27; Andrea McKenzie, 'Making Crime Pay: Motives, Marketing Strategies and the Printed Literature of Crime in England, 1670–1770', in *Criminal Justice in the Old World and the New*, ed. Greg T. Smith, Allyson N. May and Simon Devereaux (Toronto: University of Toronto Press, 1998), 235–69; Andrea McKenzie, *Tyburn's Martyrs: Execution in England, 1675–1775* (London: Hambledon Continuum, 2007); and Philip Rawlings, *Drunks, Whores and Idle Apprentices: Criminal Biographies of the Eighteenth Century* (New York: Routledge, 1992).

[16]   *Old Bailey Proceedings Online* (www.oldbaileyonline.org, version 6.0 (accessed 17 April 2011), March 1704, trial of Mary Tudor (t17040308-30).

1790, all of whom were acquitted. The 100% acquittal rate is striking in itself, but what is more interesting is that juries acquitted all of these women solely because they were married.

In some of these cases, juries seemed to respond both to a belief that the woman had not killed the infant and to the simple fact that if she was married, she could not be found guilty under the terms of the 1624 Act. In 1693, for example, Alice, the wife of Thomas Sawbridge, was accused of murdering her male infant child. Some workmen had found the child's body in a clay-pit full of water, and at her trial, Alice 'would not give any account why she so disposed of the Child'. Regardless of the circumstances, the jury acquitted Alice because 'there was no proof against her that she murthered the Child, which the Law provides should be made to appear; and the Child was no Bastard'.[17]

In most cases, juries focused solely on the marital status of the accused to the exclusion of other forms of evidence. Such was the case in 1718 when Mary Bristow was accused of murdering her bastard child. Responding to the charges, Bristow proved that she was a married woman whose husband had gone to the East Indies. As a result, the *OBP* explain, 'that it not being a Bastard Child, the Evidence, if true, could not support the Indictment'. Bristow's marital status ensured that her actions were not encompassed under the statute and the jury had no choice but to acquit her.[18] Similarly, in her 1723 trial for killing her male bastard infant by 'smothering it in a Cloth', Ann Leak called a number of witnesses to prove that she was married and that the child was thus no bastard. This evidence of marriage exempted 'her from the Statute on which the Indictment was founded', and she was also acquitted.[19]

Contemporaries knew that the statute applied only to unmarried women and relied on this technicality when accused of infanticide. In 1683, Margaret Benson and Joseph Axly were tried for killing their bastard child. In her defence, Margaret claimed that the child had been stillborn and that she was married to Axly in order 'to avoid the Penalty of the Act of the 13 of King James'. She called on Axly to confirm the marriage and 'brought a Fellow to witness they were Married [in] an Tavern'. The *OBP* indicated that the jury acquitted Margaret and Joseph because of this proof of marriage, not because of the claim that the child was stillborn.

The 1624 statute and the people who enforced it were concerned solely with unmarried mothers and bastard children.[20] As a result, women who were married at the time of the child's conception did not qualify under the statute and benefitted

---

[17] *OBP*, July 1693, Alice Sawbridge (t16930713-11). See also *OBP*, February 1684, Elizabeth Stafford (t16840227-18); *OBP*, December 1696, Mary Ingerley (t16961209-83).

[18] *OBP*, January 1718, Mary Bristow, Mary Rut, Ann Douglass, Jane Whitfield (t17180110-62).

[19] *OBP*, January 1723, Ann Leak (t17230116-37).

[20] Angus McLaren, *Reproductive Rituals: The Perception of Fertility in England from the Sixteenth to the Nineteenth Century* (London: Methuen, 1984), 131, and Ingram, 'Infanticide in Late Medieval and Early Modern England', 73.

from the technicality inherent in marital status. One such woman was Frances Deacon, who in 1733 was accused of drowning her female bastard infant in a pond. At her trial, William Pickersgill explained that he had come to the pond around seven in the morning, whereupon Deacon 'told [him] and others, that she had dropt her Child in'. Similarly, Mary Jones testified that when she searched Deacon for signs of her having given birth, she 'found [Deacon] had had a Child, and she own'd it and that she had drop't it in a Pond'. In her defence, Deacon told the jury that she was very sick and weak, and when she went by the pond, she 'was taken with a Fit, and took hold of the Post, and the Child dropt from [her]'. Deacon also claimed that her husband had died six weeks prior to the child's death, a fact which made her child legitimate. The witnesses in the trial all seemed to indicate that this was an accidental death, but the *OBP* were also careful to specify that since the child was not a bastard its death did not qualify as infanticide according to the 1624 statute.[21]

In each of these cases, the legitimacy of the infant in question essentially determined the verdict. Marriage was such an effective defence in infanticide cases that some single women attempted to use it in order to escape the gallows. One such woman was Ann Hasle, who in 1717 was accused of drowning her male bastard child in a 'copper'. After Hasle's master and neighbours had grown suspicious of her, they searched her lodgings and eventually found the child's body in a tub filled with water and clothing. The *OBP* explain that after hearing evidence from a number of people, including a midwife and a surgeon, the 1624 statute was read in court to provide 'better Information' for the jury. In order to 'put her self out of the Reach of this Act, [Hasle] alledged, that she was a Married Woman at the time of her Conception', although her husband Edward Wingate had died while she was still pregnant. Hasle called on a number of witnesses to prove her marriage. However, Wingate's sister deposed that Hasle and her brother had never been married, and Hasle 'was deemed not to be affected by the Statute'. As a single woman, she thus stood liable to be convicted. The jury ultimately acquitted Hasle, but did so because they lacked 'sufficient Proof that she had either murthered the Infant, or that it was born alive'.[22]

Marriage provided an effective way to secure an acquittal in cases of alleged infanticide, but juries required sufficient proof to accept it as a legitimate defence. Ann Hasle had not been able to provide the proof, but she was fortunate in that she could rely on other defences; other women were not as lucky. In response to an accusation of murdering her bastard child in 1683, Elenor Adams asserted that she had a husband at sea. The jury, however, was suspicious of this claim, and since there was no other proof of her marriage 'than her saying so, the Statute was Read'

[21] *OBP*, October 1733, Frances Deacon (t17331010-5).

[22] *OBP*, July 1717, Ann Hasle (t17170717-18). See also *OBP*, October 1746, Mary Hope (t17461015-23).

and she was convicted and sentenced to death.[23] In her 1691 trial for murdering her female infant bastard, Margaret Deane explained 'That her Husband was gone to Sea' but since nothing 'materially to her advantage' appeared, the jury convicted her.[24] Juries did not accept promises of marriage as proof of marriage, and Deane qualified as an offender under the 1624 statute.

Marriage was an effective defence because married women could not be found guilty of infanticide if charged under the terms of the 1624 Act. This was, of course, an important technicality, but it was also connected to the belief that single women had a reason to commit the crime and were far more likely to do so than their married counterparts. According to Mark Jackson, the infanticide statute was 'shaped by beliefs that single women (rather than married women) were concealing their pregnancies and murdering their children in order to evade the shame and punishment associated with mothering an illegitimate child'.[25] Since they did not face the shame of an illegitimate child, married women ostensibly had no motive for killing their infant children. This understanding of motive was an important point of differentiation between the treatment and perceptions of married and unmarried women accused of infanticide under the 1624 statute. As Dana Rabin explains, it meant that 'Infanticide by married women was considered so shocking and so unlikely that the only motive assigned to it was insanity'.[26] The assumption that married women had no motive for committing infanticide connected directly to their marital status. Unlike unmarried mothers, married mothers did not have to face the shame associated with illegitimate children, and their experiences as mothers differed.[27]

The shaping and enforcement of the 1624 statute grew from expectations about female behaviour and codes of conduct, which differed according to a woman's marital status. The 1624 statute focused largely on the sexual morality

---

[23]   *OBP*, December 1683, Elenor Adams (t16831212-2). See also *OBP*, January 1685, Jane Langworth (t16850116-5).

[24]   *OBP*, May 1691, Margaret Deane (t16910527-17); *Old Bailey Proceedings Online* (www.oldbaileyonline.org, version 6.0, accessed 17 April 2011), *Ordinary of Newgate's Account*, 3 June 1691 (OA16910603).

[25]   Mark Jackson, 'The Trial of Harriet Vooght: Continuity and Change in the History of Infanticide', in *Infanticide: Historical Perspectives on Child Murder and Concealment, 1550–2000*, ed. Mark Jackson (Aldershot: Ashgate, 2002), 6.

[26]   Dana Rabin, 'Bodies of Evidence, States of Mind: Infanticide, Emotion and Sensibility in Eighteenth-Century England', in *Infanticide: Historical Perspectives on Child Murder and Concealment, 1550–2000*, ed. Mark Jackson (Aldershot: Ashgate, 2002), 76.

[27]   For problems associated with illegitimacy and lone motherhood, see Linda A. Pollock, 'Childbearing and Female Bonding in Early Modern England', *Social History* 22.3 (1997): 301–4; Tanya Evans, *'Unfortunate Objects': Lone Mothers in Eighteenth-Century London* (Basingstoke: Palgrave Macmillan, 2005); and David Postles, 'Surviving Lone Motherhood in Early-Modern England', *Seventeenth Century* 21.1 (2006): 160–83.

of unmarried women. According to the preamble of the statute, it was designed to combat the problems of the

> many lewd Women that have been delivered of Bastard Children, to avoid their shame, and to escape punishment, do secretly bury or conceal the death of their Children, and after if the Child be found dead, the said Women do alledge, That the said Child was born dead; whereas it falleth out sometimes (although hardly it is to be proved) that the said Child or Children were murthered by the said Women, their lewd Mothers, or by their assent or procurement.[28]

This is not to say that people in the seventeenth and eighteenth centuries were unconcerned about the death of infants.[29] However, the emphasis on the 'lewd women' in the preamble, or at least on the consequences of extramarital sex, lay at the heart of the statute and its enforcement throughout the period.

The sexual morality central to the interpretation of the 1624 statute comes across in the emphasis many women accused of infanticide placed on the shame they felt from bearing a bastard child. In 1717, Elizabeth Arthur was charged with murdering her male bastard infant by 'drowning it in a House of Office'. Upon questioning, Arthur told the constable that she had hidden her child's body in order to 'conceal her Shame, and that by so doing she had brought her self to more, and was now heartily sorry for it'.[30] In her 1727 trial, Jane Lod affirmed 'that she flattered herself with concealing her Shame, by carrying it [her pregnancy] off with so much privacy'.[31] Responding to charges that she had thrown her bastard infant into a privy in 1746, Sarah Hayes explained, 'I was a Servant, and would not disgrace myself: I was making Preparations for it: I did it to hide Shame, and to be sure I got more'.[32] These three women were all acquitted, but the discussion of their shame reveals that one of the main emphases of the statute, as well as people's interpretation of it, was the sexual morality of the accused women, and this sexual morality was directly connected to their status as unmarried women.

Sexual morality remained a central component in infanticide trials, but over the course of the period, attitudes towards infanticidal mothers changed and doubts about the statute increased.[33] As a result, the enforcement and interpretation of

---

[28]   *The Statutes at Large, from Magna Charta, to the end of the session of Parliament, March 14 1704*, vol. 2 (London, 1706), 1086.

[29]   Despite high mortality rates for children, there was no sense that parents did not care for children, or that they did not grieve for their deaths, even as infants, in the premodern period. See in particular, Hugh Cunningham, *Children and Childhood in Western Society since 1500* (London: Longman, 1995), 52, 107, and Sara M. Butler, 'A Case of Indifference? Child Murder in Later Medieval England', *Journal of Women's History* 19.4 (2007): 59–82.

[30]   *OBP*, September 1717, Elizabeth Arthur (t17170911-50).

[31]   *OBP*, July 1727, Jane Lod (t17270705-10).

[32]   *OBP*, April 1746, Sarah Hayes (t17460409-47).

[33]   Marilyn Francus, 'Monstrous Mothers, Monstrous Societies: Infanticide and the Rule of Law in Restoration and Eighteenth-Century England', *Eighteenth-Century Life* 21.2 (1997): 133–34; Ingram, 'Infanticide in Late Medieval and Early Modern England', 73.

the statute changed. The seventeenth and early eighteenth century saw a strict enforcement and a high conviction rate. After 1715, the conviction rate dropped significantly, leading to the pattern Robert Malcolmson notes whereby the infanticide statute remained rigorous in theory, while juries seldom enforced it in practice.[34]

This pattern suggests that the prosecution rather than the conviction of the offenders was the key factor in cases of infanticide throughout the eighteenth century. The emphasis on prosecution, I would argue, indicates that the trial itself was a shaming process intended to discipline the sexually illicit woman and expose her sin. Juries did not need to convict every unmarried woman accused of infanticide under the 1624 statute; instead, they could rely on the trials to reveal the sexual transgressions these women had attempted to hide. Juries reserved their guilty verdicts for extreme cases of transgression: the women Marilyn Francus refers to as 'rebellious infanticidal mothers' – women who barbarously killed their newborn infants or who did not appear penitent in court.[35]

The 18 married women accused under the 1624 statute were acquitted because of their marital status, but also because they did not fit into this model. Even if they did kill their infants – and there is no way to determine if they did – their behaviour was not subject to the same scrutiny, since there was no shame attached to their pregnancies. Pregnancy within marriage was acceptable and generally something to be celebrated, whereas extramarital pregnancy was shameful, sinful and often hidden. Both married and unmarried women were subject to rigid ideas about sexual morality, but only unmarried women faced censure for bearing an illegitimate child. That marital status could remove certain women from the 'reach of the Act' was directly connected to these larger ideas about the expectations and experiences of married and unmarried women.

Petty Treason

In 1726, the Ordinary of Newgate, James Guthrie, explained that a wife's killing of her husband constituted a more serious crime than the reverse because the 'Laws of God and Man' made the husband a 'superiour Person in Power and Honour' to the woman he married. As a result, 'the Laws of this Kingdom have wisely declar'd it to be a greater Crime, and affix'd a severer Punishment upon a Wife's murdering her Husband, than upon other Murderers'.[36] Guthrie offered a

---

[34]   Robert Malcomson, 'Infanticide in the Eighteenth Century', in *Crime in England, 1550–1800*, ed. J. S. Cockburn (Princeton, NJ: Princeton University Press, 1977), 197.

[35]   Francus, 'Monstrous Mothers', 134.

[36]   *OBP, Ordinary's Accounts*, 5 May 1726 (OA17260509). For a discussion of contemporary perceptions of husbands killing their wives, see Jennine Hurl-Eamon, '"I Will Forgive You if the World Will": Wife Murder and Limits on Patriarchal Violence in London, 1690–1750', in *Violence, Politics and Gender in Early Modern England*, ed. Joseph P. Ward (Basingstoke: Palgrave Macmillan, 2008), 223–47.

subtle variation on these ideas in 1737 when he told Ann Mudd that 'her Crime was greater than that of other Murtherers, as having been committed in one sense upon her self, the Man and Wife being in Scripture considered as one Flesh'.[37] An analysis of the petty treason trials at the Old Bailey between 1674 and 1790 reveals that while the circumstances of each particular case were important, marriage influenced how contemporaries judged the woman's alleged behaviour.

The central role that marriage played in defining the crime is particularly evident in the 1725 case of Elizabeth Roberts. Elizabeth was accused of killing her husband Richard Bostock by stabbing him in the ribs during a particularly heated quarrel. Despite Elizabeth's claims that Richard had stabbed himself to 'terri[f]y' her, all of the witnesses seemed to indicate that Elizabeth was responsible for Richard's death. What is interesting about the trial, however, is that the witnesses also indicated they did not believe Richard and Elizabeth were actually married. Thomas Ball testified that he 'never suspected' Richard and Elizabeth were married, since 'they lived an abominable Life together'. The watchman Swarton explained that he had been at Elizabeth and Richard's house earlier, where he chastised Richard for beating his wife so severely. In response to this rebuke, Richard claimed, 'My Wife! ... D— her, a Bitch, she's none of my Wife, and I'll turn her a-drift to-morrow'. Elizabeth, for her part, also maintained that she had never been married to Richard. After hearing all of the evidence, the jury acquitted Elizabeth of petty treason, but convicted her of murder: she was sentenced to death, but death by hanging rather than the more fearsome flames that awaited those convicted of petty treason.[38] The evidence seemed to indicate that Elizabeth had killed Richard, which was likely why the jury convicted her of murder; however, without the marital relationship, her actions could not be considered a form of petty treason.

Although the outcome varied, other women also maintained that they were not actually married to their alleged victims. In 1744, Lydia Adler raised questions about whether or not she was married when she alleged that her husband 'had got 2 wives besides me'.[39] Sometimes the claims were more specific. At her 1747 trial for stabbing her husband Thomas, Anne Williams explained, 'This Mr Williams that I lived with. I never was married to him, I have had four Children by him'.[40] Adler and Williams were both convicted of manslaughter, although it is impossible to determine whether the juries reached these lesser verdicts because of the women's denials that they were married or because of the specific circumstances of the cases. Claims of being unmarried were not always an effective defence. In response to allegations that she had stabbed her husband Robert in 1773, Elizabeth Herring expostulated, 'they say he is my husband, but he is not; I lived with him

---

[37]   *OBP, Ordinary's Accounts*, 29 June 1737 (OA17370629).

[38]   *OBP*, June 1725, Elizabeth Roberts (t17250630-6).

[39]   *OBP*, July 1744, Lydia Adler (t17440728-23).

[40]   *OBP*, September 1747, Anne Williams (t17470909-21).

eleven years, but never was his wife'. Disbelieving her assertion, the jury convicted Elizabeth of petty treason.[41]

In contrast to the infanticide trials previously examined, a woman's marital status could not excuse her actions completely. Elizabeth Roberts was still convicted of murder, Anne Williams and Lydia Adler were convicted of manslaughter, and Elizabeth Herring was convicted of petty treason. Here it is important to note that marriage aggravated an existing offence; its presence was not necessary for the underlying crime of murder to exist, merely to transform murder into petty treason. It is therefore probable that the claim these women made to be unmarried was not a defence or an attempt to escape punishment, but rather an attempt to avoid the punishment of death by burning. While still liable to be convicted of murder or manslaughter, if they could prove they were not married to their victims, these women evaded the 'severer Punishment' that Guthrie referred to at the beginning of this section.

Juries focused largely on the circumstances of the case when determining their verdicts in petty treason trials. It was in the punishment of the offence that people saw how marital status exacerbated a woman's alleged actions. However, marital status played a role in the narratives and construction of the behaviour of the women accused. In petty treason trials, understandings of the order and hierarchy that were central to contemporary understandings of marriage shaped the experiences, perception and treatment of the accused women. The women accused and convicted of petty treason transgressed the behavioural expectations for married women, just as the unmarried women accused and convicted of infanticide under the 1624 statute did not conform to the ideal characteristics of a chaste single woman. Marital status helped determine what contemporaries believed was ideal, or at least acceptable, behaviour.

Marriage in the seventeenth and eighteenth centuries created a hierarchical relationship. The maintenance of order within the household mattered, since the household stood as a metaphor for the larger social world.[42] Unity, or at least harmony, constituted the primary characteristic of the ideal household. Conduct writers advised numerous ways to maintain this harmony, one of the most important of which was wifely obedience. As Wetenhall Wilkes explained in 1740, 'the duties of a wife to her husband in every degree and state of life, can be no less than fidelity, and obedience to all his lawful desires and prudent counsels'.[43]

---

[41]   *OBP*, September 1773, Elizabeth Herring (t17730908-6).

[42]   For a discussion of the household, see Susan Dwyer Amussen, *An Ordered Society: Gender and Class in Early Modern England* (New York: Columbia University Press, 1988), and Keith Wrightson, *Earthly Necessities: Economic Lives in Early Modern Britain* (New Haven, CT: Yale University Press, 2003).

[43]   Wetenhall Wilkes, 'A Letter of Genteel and Moral Advice to a Young Lady, 1740 (8th ed., 1766)', in *Women in the Eighteenth Century: Constructions of Femininity*, ed. Vivien Jones (London: Routledge, 1990), 35.

Discussions of women convicted of petty treason in the *OBP* and *Ordinary's Accounts* reflected the concern people had with maintaining the marital hierarchy and emphasized the disorderly nature of the accused women. Take, for example, the 1739 trial of Susannah Broom. By all accounts, Susannah and her husband, John, had a tumultuous marriage. William Allen, who lived in a room adjoining the Brooms' lodging, testified that Susannah 'was an obstinate Woman, and used to quarrel with [her husband]'. Allen further explained that he had 'saved [John] from her a great many Times'. Other neighbours had similar stories. Mary Matthias testified that Susannah 'has beat [John] out of Doors divers and divers (of) Times'. Mary Coombes explained to the court that when Susannah 'and her Husband quarrel'd, she used to beat him with a Poker, and say she would win the Horse, or loose the Saddle. I have often taken her Husband's Part, and then she would call me his Whore'. These witnesses were horrified, but not surprised, that one of these quarrels ended with Susannah killing John by stabbing him in the leg.[44] The *Ordinary's Accounts* echoed these sentiments in explaining that witnesses during the trial 'swore, that [John] was a peaceable, good natured Man, but that she was a most passionate, furious Woman, and constantly abused her Husband'.[45]

In a 1735 issue of *The Gentleman's Magazine*, a contributor wrote that 'Man claims superiority over the fairer sex: and the woman that will contest that point, lays a foundation for future misery in the married state'.[46] This sentence seems to encapsulate the key problems with the Brooms' marriage. Susannah did not conform to the model of wifely obedience and regularly usurped her husband's position of authority. Her refusal to submit meekly, combined with her abuse of her husband and usurpation of authority within the marriage, made this an unhappy marriage, at least according to the standards of the period. Readers of the *OBP* and *Ordinary's Accounts*, along with the members of the jury, understood that Susannah's disorderly nature led to John's death. This case also demonstrates how the narrative surrounding petty treason trials was directly connected to larger understandings of marriage and a wife's proper behaviour. Susannah was both a murderer and a bad wife.

Violence played a significant and symbolic role in almost all of the 25 petty treason trials.[47] In a 1714 case, for example, Joyce Hodgkis was accused of killing her husband John. At the trial, a witness explained how she had heard a great

---

44   *OBP*, December 1739, Susannah Broom (t17391205-2).

45   *OBP*, *Ordinary's Account*, 21 December 1739 (OA17391221).

46   *The Gentleman's Magazine* 5 (January 1735): 15.

47   Despite the emphasis in the sixteenth and seventeenth centuries on the danger of wives murdering their husbands through poison, violent deaths were the most common in the *OBP*. Only two women were accused of poisoning their husbands and they were both acquitted. See *OBP*, May 1762, Jane Sibson (t17620526-8), and *OBP*, April 1776, Mary Owen (t17760417-58). For a discussion of poison in relation to petty treason, see Pompa Banerjee, 'Hard to Swallow: Women, Poison, and Hindu Widowburning, 1500–1700', *Continuity and Change* 15.2 (2000): 187–207.

deal of noise in Joyce and John's lodging, at which point she went downstairs, where she saw Joyce 'run at [John] with a Knife, and immediately saw Blood run out at his Breeches'. Joyce claimed that John 'did it himself', but the violent nature of John's death seems to have offered sufficient evidence for the jury to convict her of petty treason.[48] The 1773 trial of Elizabeth Herring, the woman who unsuccessfully attempted to claim she was not actually married to her victim, conveys a similarly violent nature. John Boyle testified that he was with Elizabeth and her husband Robert at the Thistle and Crown, where Elizabeth demanded some bread from Robert to go with her meat. When Robert refused, Boyle explained that

> she had a knife in her hand picking a bone; in the space of two or three minutes, she went up to her husband; I thought she was going to give him a lick with her hand; instead of which she struck the knife into his throat; the blood immediately spouted as if a butcher had killed a pig.

John died of the wound five minutes later, and Elizabeth was convicted of petty treason.[49]

The violent nature of women such as Joyce Hodgkis and Elizabeth Herring stands in contrast to the passive nature of the infanticide cases previously examined. Throughout most of the eighteenth century, infanticide cases that resulted in convictions typically involved the violent death of the infant in question. Infant mortality, especially in the first 36 hours after birth, was high, and it was difficult to prove that an infant had died an unnatural death unless there were signs of violence on the body. The murder of husbands, on the other hand, was largely committed by violent means, making it easy to determine how a death had taken place. Feminine violence, moreover, was a demonstration of female authority and agency, which stood in direct contrast to a woman's subordinate position within the marital hierarchy.[50] Such violence, even in self-defence, upset the gender order. The violence in petty treason trials was an extreme example of this situation, since it went against a husband's direct authority and higher status within marriage.[51]

It is important to note that husbands did not have unlimited authority, and contemporaries showed great concern about husbands who abused their power

---

[48] *OBP*, September 1714, Joyce Hodgkis (t17140908-35).

[49] *OBP*, September 1773, Elizabeth Herring (t17730908-6).

[50] Garthine Walker, *Crime, Gender and the Social Order in Early Modern England* (Cambridge: Cambridge University Press, 2003), 40. For further discussions of violence, see Susan Dwyer Amussen, '"Being stirred to much unquietness": Violence and Domestic Violence in Early Modern England', *Journal of Women's History* 6.2 (1994): 70–89; Jennine Hurl-Eamon, *Gender and Petty Violence in London* (Columbus: Ohio State University Press, 2005); Laura Gowing, *Domestic Dangers: Women, Words and Sex in Early Modern London* (Oxford: Oxford University Press, 1996); and Frances Dolan, 'Battered Women, Petty Traitors, and the Legacy of Coverture', *Feminist Studies* 29.2 (2003): 229–77.

[51] Dolan, 'Home-Rebels and House-Traitors', 49.

within marriage.[52] The fear of abusive husbands increased when it appeared that the abuse led to a wife murdering her husband. In 1726, Katharine Hayes, who was accused of killing her husband John with the assistance of Thomas Billings and Thomas Wood, attempted to explain her actions by stating that 'John Hays was none of the best of Husbands, for I have been half starved ever since I was married'.[53] Katharine's crime seemed premeditated, since she used her husband's abuse to enlist Billings's and Wood's help in killing John. As Billings explained in the *Ordinary's Accounts*, he had been 'mov'd to murder Mr. Hayes' because 'he was so cruel and barbarous in beating and abusing his Wife'.[54] While people saw a husband's abuse of authority as problematic, they were even more troubled by a wife's usurpation of authority, especially if that usurpation ended in the murder of her husband.

At the same time, juries sometimes convicted women of the lesser offence of manslaughter in cases of an abusive husband.[55] Such was the case in the 1727 trial of Catherine Lewis. At her trial, Sarah Hartly told the court that Richard 'was very barbarous to the Prisoner', and used to beat her with the iron end of a yoke used to carry milk pails. A number of other witnesses also testified that Catherine 'went in danger of her Life from the Deceased [her husband Richard] on every trivial Occasion'. On the night of Richard's death, he and Catherine had been fighting, and when Richard was on top of Catherine, she 'put her Hand behind her and took up a Chopping Knife, with which she hit him on the Back'. This wound did not kill Richard, who continued to kick Catherine. At this point, according to George Anderson, Catherine took 'the Chopping Knife ... from under her Back and he ran against it'. In doing so, Richard received a wound in his stomach from which he died.[56]

The deciding factor in these two cases seems to rest on the motive of the accused, not the abuse. Both Katharine Hayes and Catherine Lewis seem to have been abused, but Hayes's actions were premeditated, whereas Lewis's appear accidental. Lewis was not a murderous wife usurping her husband's authority, but rather a docile wife caught up in unfortunate circumstances. These two cases demonstrate that verdicts depended not only upon the circumstances of the case but also on understandings of proper behaviour that were connected to larger ideas

---

[52] For a discussion of spousal abuse, see Hurl-Eamon, '"I Will Forgive You if the World Will"', 223–47; Margaret Hunt, 'Wife-Beating, Domesticity and Women's Independence in Eighteenth-Century London', *Gender and History* 4.1 (1992): 10–33; and Elizabeth Foyster, *Marital Violence: An English Family History, 1660–1857* (Cambridge: Cambridge University Press, 2005).

[53] *OBP*, April 1726, Katharine Hayes (t17260420-42).

[54] *OBP*, *Ordinary's Account*, 9 May 1726 (OA17260509).

[55] For a discussion of how provocation developed into a mitigating factor in petty treason trials, see Matthew Lockwood, 'From Treason to Homicide: Changing Conceptions of the Law of Petty Treason in Early Modern England', *Journal of Legal History* 34.1 (2013): 40–42, 47.

[56] *OBP*, February 1727, Catherine Lewis (t17270222-11).

about marriage. Ideal behaviour depended on gender and marital status, and the woman who transgressed the acceptable boundaries of how a wife was supposed to behave was more likely to be convicted than one who conformed to larger understandings of the ideal wife. The influence of marital status was present not only in the aggravated offence and the distinctive punishment for petty treason but also in the narratives of the trials themselves.

Conclusion

According to Maeve Doggett, 'there were situations ... in which a woman criminal was treated more harshly as a consequence of her status as a wife. Usually, however, it operated to her benefit'.[57] Petty treason and infanticide were gender-related forms of homicide that were also directly connected to a woman's marital status. A married woman could not commit infanticide according to the terms of the 1624 Act, and as a result all of the married women accused of infanticide between 1674 and 1790 were acquitted. In these cases, marriage acted as an effective defence. Yet, in the case of petty treason, marriage aggravated a woman's murderous act, and a woman convicted of petty treason received the same punishment as a woman convicted of high treason. Here, a woman's status as a wife clearly worked against her.

The differing treatment of these women was not connected to any sense of leniency or 'acceptable' murder victims, but rather to a woman's marital status. People conceptualized the actions of women accused of both crimes within the constraints of a society that shaped its understanding of women according to their marital status. The purposes of the statutes, the household structures of the period, the differing motives present in the cases, the methods of killing and the relationship between the victim and the accused all contributed to the differing treatments of married women accused of petty treason and infanticide. Each of these was in turn affected by understandings of the legal consequences of marriage.

The treatment of married women accused of infanticide and petty treason demonstrates that the legal consequences of marriage were not limited to property law. Coverture, that fundamental element of a married woman's legal experiences, was not supposed to apply in the criminal justice system, a legal realm where married women could be recognized as separate from their husbands. However, marital status still mattered, and it is in these trials that one can see how the subtext of coverture was never entirely absent from women's lives in the early modern period.

---

[57]   Doggett, *Marriage, Wife-Beating and the Law*, 51.

Works Cited

Primary Sources

The Gentleman's Magazine 5 (January 1735).
Old Bailey Proceedings Online. Version 6.0. www.oldbaileyonline.org (accessed 17 April 2011).
The Statutes at Large, from Magna Charta, to the end of the session of Parliament, March 14 1704. Vol. 2. London, 1706.
Wilkes, Wetenhall. [From] 'A Letter of Genteel and Moral Advice to a Young Lady, 1740 (8th ed., 1766)'. In *Women in the Eighteenth Century: Constructions of Femininity.* Edited by Vivien Jones. London: Routledge, 1990. 29–35.

Secondary Sources

Amussen, Susan Dwyer. '"Being stirred to much unquietness": Violence and Domestic Violence in Early Modern England'. *Journal of Women's History* 62 (1994): 70–89.
———. *An Ordered Society: Gender and Class in Early Modern England.* New York: Columbia University Press, 1988.
Banerjee, Pompa. *Burning Women: Widows, Witches, and Early Modern European Travelers in India.* Basingstoke: Palgrave Macmillan, 2003.
———. 'Hard to Swallow: Women, Poison, and Hindu Widowburning, 1500–1700'. *Continuity and Change* 15.2 (2000): 187–207.
Butler, Sara M. 'A Case of Indifference? Child Murder in Later Medieval England'. *Journal of Women's History* 19.4 (2007): 59–82.
Campbell, Ruth. 'Sentence of Death by Burning for Women'. *Journal of Legal History* 5 (1984): 44–59.
Cunningham, Hugh. *Children and Childhood in Western Society since 1500.* London: Longman, 1995.
Devereaux, Simon. 'From Sessions to Newspaper? Criminal Trial Reporting, the Nature of Crime, and the London Press, 1770–1800'. *London Journal* 32.1 (2007): 1–27.
Dickinson, J. R., and J. A. Sharpe. 'Infanticide in Early Modern England: The Court of Great Sessions at Chester, 1650–1800'. In *Infanticide: Historical Perspectives on Child Murder and Concealment, 1550–2000.* Edited by Mark Jackson. Aldershot: Ashgate, 2002. 35–51.
Doggett, Maeve E. *Marriage, Wife-Beating and the Law in Victorian England.* Columbia: University of South Carolina Press, 1993.
Dolan, Frances. 'Battered Women, Petty Traitors, and the Legacy of Coverture'. *Feminist Studies* 29.2 (2003): 249–77.
———. *Dangerous Familiars: Representations of Domestic Crime in England, 1550–1700.* Ithaca, NY: Cornell University Press, 1994.
———. 'Home-Rebels and House-Traitors: Murderous Wives in Early Modern England'. *Yale Journal of Law and the Humanities* 4.1 (1992): 1–31.

Erickson, Amy Louise. *Women and Property in Early Modern England*. London: Routledge, 1995.

Evans, Tanya. *'Unfortunate Objects': Lone Mothers in Eighteenth-Century London*. Basingstoke: Palgrave Macmillan, 2005.

Foyster, Elizabeth. *Marital Violence: An English Family History, 1660–1857*. Cambridge: Cambridge University Press, 2005.

Francus, Marilyn. 'Monstrous Mothers, Monstrous Societies: Infanticide and the Rule of Law in Restoration and Eighteenth-Century England'. *Eighteenth-Century Life* 21.2 (1997): 133–56.

Froide, Amy. 'Marital Status as a Category of Difference: Singlewomen and Widows in Early Modern England'. In *Singlewomen in the European Past*. Edited by Judith Bennett and Amy Froide. Philadelphia: University of Pennsylvania Press, 1999. 236–69.

Gowing, Laura. *Domestic Dangers: Women, Words and Sex in Early Modern London*. Oxford: Oxford University Press, 1996.

———. 'Secret Births and Infanticide in Seventeenth-Century England'. *Past and Present* 156 (1997): 87–115.

Greenberg, Janelle. 'The Legal Status of the English Woman in Early Eighteenth-Century Common Law and Equity'. *Studies in Eighteenth-Century Culture* 4 (1975): 171–81.

Harris, Michael. 'Trials and Criminal Biographies: A Case Study in Distribution'. In *The Sale and Distribution of Books from 1700*. Edited by Robin Myers and Michael Harris. Oxford: Oxford Polytechnic Press, 1982. 1–35.

Hartog, Hendrik. *Man and Wife in America: A History*. Cambridge, MA: Harvard University Press, 2000.

Hoffer, Peter C., and N. E. H. Hull. *Murdering Mothers: Infanticide in England and New England, 1558–1803*. New York: New York University Press, 1981.

Hunt, Margaret. 'Wife Beating, Domesticity and Women's Independence in Eighteenth-Century London'. *Gender and History* 4.1 (1992): 10–33.

Hurl-Eamon, Jennine. *Gender and Petty Violence in London, 1680–1720*. Columbus: Ohio State University Press, 2005.

———. '"I Will Forgive You if the World Will": Wife Murder and Limits on Patriarchal Violence in London, 1690–1750'. In *Violence, Politics and Gender in Early Modern England*. Edited by Joseph P. Ward. Basingstoke: Palgrave Macmillan, 2008. 223–47.

Ingram, Martin. 'Infanticide in Late Medieval and Early Modern England'. In *Childhood and Violence in the Western Tradition*. Edited by Laurence Brockliss and Heather Montgomery. Oxford: Oxbow Books, 2010. 67–74.

Jackson, Mark, ed. *Infanticide: Historical Perspectives on Child Murder and Concealment, 1550–2000*. Aldershot: Ashgate, 2000.

———. *New-Born Child Murder: Women, Illegitimacy and the Courts in Eighteenth-Century England*. Manchester: Manchester University Press, 1997.

———. 'The Trial of Harriet Vooght: Continuity and Change in the History of Infanticide'. In *Infanticide: Historical Perspectives on Child Murder and*

Concealment, 1550–2000. Edited by Mark Jackson. Aldershot: Ashgate, 2002. 1–17.

Langbein, John. 'Shaping the Eighteenth-Century Criminal Trial: A View from the Ryder Sources'. *University of Chicago Law Review* 50.1 (1983): 1–136.

Lockwood, Matthew. 'From Treason to Homicide: Changing Conceptions of the Law of Petty Treason in Early Modern England'. *Journal of Legal History* 34.1 (2013): 31–49.

McKenzie, Andrea. 'Making Crime Pay: Motives, Marketing Strategies and the Printed Literature of Crime in England, 1670–1770'. In *Criminal Justice in the Old World and the New*. Edited by Greg T. Smith, Allyson N. May and Simon Devereaux. Toronto: University of Toronto Press, 1998. 235–69.

———. *Tyburn's Martyrs: Execution in England, 1675–1775*. London: Hambledon Continuum, 2007.

McLaren, Angus. *Reproductive Rituals: The Perception of Fertility in England from the Sixteenth to the Nineteenth Century*. London: Methuen, 1984.

Malcolmson, Robert. 'Infanticide in the Eighteenth Century'. In *Crime in England, 1550–1800*. Edited by J. S. Cockburn. Princeton, NJ: Princeton University Press, 1977. 187–209.

May, Allyson. '"She at first denied it": Infanticide Trials at the Old Bailey'. In *Women and History: Voices in Early Modern England*. Edited by Valerie Frith. Toronto: Coach House Press, 1995. 19–35.

Palk, Deirdre. *Gender, Crime and Judicial Discretion, 1780–1830*. London: Boydell Press, 2006.

Pollock, Linda A. 'Childbearing and Female Bonding in Early Modern England'. *Social History* 22.3 (1997): 301–4.

Postles, David. 'Surviving Lone Motherhood in Early-Modern England'. *Seventeenth Century* 21.1 (2006): 160–83.

Rabin, Dana. 'Bodies of Evidence, States of Mind: Infanticide, Emotion and Sensibility in Eighteenth-century England'. In *Infanticide: Historical Perspectives on Child Murder and Concealment, 1550–2000*. Edited by Mark Jackson. Aldershot: Ashgate, 2002. 73–92.

Rawlings, Philip. *Drunks, Whores and Idle Apprentices: Criminal Biographies of the Eighteenth Century*. New York: Routledge, 1992.

Shoemaker, Robert B. 'The Old Bailey Proceedings and the Representation of Crime and Criminal Justice in Eighteenth-Century London'. *Journal of British Studies* 47.3 (2008): 559–80.

Staves, Susan. *Married Women's Separate Property in England, 1660–1833*. Cambridge, MA: Harvard University Press, 1990.

Stretton, Tim. *Women Waging Law in Elizabethan England*. Cambridge: Cambridge University Press, 1998.

Walker, Garthine. *Crime, Gender and the Social Order in Early Modern England*. Cambridge: Cambridge University Press, 2003.

Wrightson, Keith. *Earthly Necessities: Economic Lives in Early Modern Britain*. New Haven, CT: Yale University Press, 2003.

Chapter 7

Women and Violence in Seventeenth- and Eighteenth-Century England: Evidence from the Cheshire Court of Great Sessions

James Sharpe

This essay derives from a project aimed at studying the long-term history of violence in England. Its evidentiary base is drawn from materials amassed in the course of an Economic and Social Research Council-funded project on the history of violence, and in particular homicide, in the county of Cheshire between 1600 and 1800, and from subsequent research into Cheshire sources.[1] Cheshire was a palatinate county, which meant that though it applied English law and produced legal records to the same format as those found in other parts of the country, it possessed a court system which operated outside the normal English legal apparatus.[2] Most relevant for our purposes was the Cheshire equivalent of the assizes, the Court of Great Sessions, for which an almost unbroken series of gaol rolls survives between the fourteenth century and the 1830s. These rolls constitute the best extant source in England for studying the prosecution of serious crime over the *longue durée*. They contain numerous indictments, along with writs and other documents relevant to the running of the sessions of the court.[3] Depositions, our main concern here, survive irregularly in the rolls:[4] but enough survive to raise some intriguing questions about reactions to and perceptions of violence.[5]

---

[1]   ESRC Award Number L133251012, 'Violence in Early Modern England: A Regional Study'. This project formed part of the ESRC's Violence Research Programme, with Dr J. R. Dickinson as Research Fellow.

[2]   The Cheshire administrative system figures prominently in Steve Hindle, *The State and Social Change in Early Modern England, c. 1550–1640* (Basingstoke: Macmillan, 1999).

[3]   The rolls for the seventeenth and eighteenth centuries are held at the National Archives, London, The National Archives (TNA) CHES 24/127/1 to 24/179/5. They are supplemented by Crown Books, TNA CHES 21/4–7, and Cheshire and Chester Archives and Local Studies, Chester, CR 580.

[4]   There is also a collection of depositions in TNA CHES 38/41, 'Palatinate of Chester Miscellany'.

[5]   Depositions (also known as examinations and, where appropriate, confessions) were pretrial statements taken by justices of the peace in felony cases, normally followed by the committal of suspects to prison to await trial and the binding-over of accusers and witnesses to give evidence in court: for a discussion of the origins of this process, which occurred in

I shall be concentrating on what these depositions tell us about the involvement of women in homicides, not as victims or perpetrators, but rather as people who participated in other ways in violent events, if only as witnesses. This follows a line of approach suggested by various scholars attempting to study violence as a cultural entity. David Riches, editor of an important collection on the anthropology of violence, has stressed the importance of witnesses (in both the general and the technical senses of the word) in judging whether an act is violent or not, and hence in placing it in a social context.[6] William Miller, distinguished historian of the feud in medieval Iceland, has contended that 'the basic structure of violence involves a play of three perspectives: those of victim, victimizer, and observer', and comments further that,

> as a matter of social theory, the observer's position is the arbitral one, generally empowered to define the nature of the event at stake ... the observer's view is richly situated culturally, historically, and normatively. It brings to bear the relevant social norms and cultural competence by which the action will or will not be comprehended as violent.[7]

Another student of violence in medieval Iceland, Oren Falk, has broadened this approach, arguing from evidence relating to the Icelandic duel and feud the importance of not just the 'principals' in acts of violence but also what he terms 'auxiliaries' – 'a more motley category that may include seconds, surgeons, spectators, and other assorted sideliners', who might play a number of important roles: 'providing principals with moral or material support, negotiating an end to a fight or attending to casualties, giving testimony or seeking to enforce justice after the fact'.[8] Similarly, Thomas Gallant, discussing the sometimes highly ritualized knife-fights indulged in by nineteenth-century Greek villagers, notes the presence of onlookers who were 'to observe and evaluate performances, not become actors themselves'.[9] At the very least, and taking a cue from this last quotation, if we are to accept that violence was in some respect 'performative', we need to remember that a successful performance demands some sort of audience.

My findings are grouped into three sections, based in order of the declining strength of the relevant documentation. Firstly, I shall examine, via these Cheshire

---

Mary Tudor's reign, see John H. Langbein, *Prosecuting Law in the Renaissance: England, Germany, France* (Cambridge, MA: Harvard University Press, 1974).

[6]   David Riches, 'The Phenomenon of Violence', in *The Anthropology of Violence*, ed. David Riches (Oxford: Basil Blackwell, 1986), 3–4.

[7]   William Ian Miller, *Humiliation: And Other Essays on Honor, Social Discomfort, and Violence* (Ithaca, NY: Cornell University Press, 1993), 55, 59.

[8]   Oren Falk, 'Bystanders and Hearsayers First: Reassessing Participant Roles in Duelling', in *A Great Effusion of Blood? Interpreting Medieval Violence*, ed. Mark D. Meyerson, Daniel Thiery and Oren Falk (Toronto: University of Toronto Press, 2004), 101.

[9]   Thomas Gallant, 'Honor, Masculinity and Ritual: Knife Fighting in Nineteenth-Century Greece', *American Historical Review* 105 (2000): 363.

sources, the role of women in what might be termed the 'pre-official' handling of infanticide cases. Secondly, I shall look at the input of female observers and onlookers into cases where a woman was the victim of homicidal violence. And, lastly, I shall examine the input of women witnesses and other participants into what was the most normal form of fatal homicide in the period in question: male-on-male violence resulting in a fatality.

Recent research on infanticide (notably by Laura Gowing, who has also published on the related topic of illegitimate birth) has stressed its status as a criminal offence which was not only sex-specific but also operated very much within the female sphere, and the Cheshire sources confirm this impression.[10] Obviously, for an infanticide case to be recorded, it had to enter the essentially male world of the legal system. But before that happened, infanticide narratives reveal an essentially female world: a world of gossip among women, of friendship between women, of female agency once a case had been discovered and of female knowledge about pregnancy and birth.

Midwives, clearly, were an essential element. Sometimes called in by constables or justices of the peace, sometimes acting on their own initiative, they played a crucial role in questioning suspected infanticidal mothers and investigating the circumstances of the birth. In 1734, a woman named Dorothy Maddocks of Shocklach gave birth to a child which she was suspected of having killed, although she herself seems to have died shortly after the birth. Elizabeth Jackson, a midwife, interrogated Elizabeth Taylor, who had been a fellow-servant with the deceased Maddocks in the house of a yeoman named Thomas Peers, who was suspected to be the father of the child. Jackson asked to see the dead child, which Taylor with some difficulty pulled out of a drawer where it had been hidden in a coarse cloth, Jackson deposing that the child was 'distorted in such a manner as it could not be possibly brought into the world in such a shape'.

---

[10]   Laura Gowing, 'Secret Births and Infanticide in Seventeenth–Century England', *Past and Present* 156 (1997): 87–115, and 'Ordering the Body: Illegitimacy and Female Authority in Seventeenth-Century England', in *Negotiating Power in Early Modern Society: Order, Hierarchy and Subordination in Britain and Ireland*, ed. Michael J. Braddick and John Walter (Cambridge: Cambridge University Press, 2001), 43–62. Cheshire infanticide prosecutions for our period are discussed in J. R. Dickinson and J. A. Sharpe, 'Infanticide in Early Modern England: The Court of Great Sessions at Chester, 1650–1800', in *Infanticide: Historical Perspectives on Child Murder and Concealment, 1550–2000*, ed. Mark Jackson (Aldershot: Ashgate, 2002), 35–51, while Garthine Walker, 'Just Stories: Telling Tales of Infant Death in Early Modern England', in *Culture and Change: Attending to Early Modern Women*, ed. Margaret Mikesell and Adele Seeff (Newark: University of Delaware Press, 2003), 98–115, bases her study largely on Cheshire materials; see also Walker's discussion of infanticide in her monograph *Crime, Gender and the Social Order in Early Modern England* (Cambridge: Cambridge University Press, 2003), 148–58. There is a burgeoning literature on the history of infanticide in England, of which the most important work for our purposes is Mark Jackson, *New-Born Child Murder: Women, Illegitimacy and the Courts in Eighteenth-Century England* (Manchester: Manchester University Press, 1996).

Jackson asked why the child had not been 'laid out streight', and Taylor explained that she (Maddocks) had had no help, and when asked by the midwife why no 'neighbouring women' had been called in to help, replied that Maddocks 'would never consent to it'. Jackson asked Taylor who had cut the child's umbilical cord ('navel string'), and was told Maddocks had done it herself, which, the midwife opined, 'might probably destroy the said child'. Jackson asked what had become of the afterbirth, and Taylor explained that Maddocks had burnt it. Jackson then asked Taylor who had helped her lay out Maddocks's body, and when she was told that Thomas Peers, Taylor's and Maddocks's master, was 'the only person that assisted her in laying out the body', the midwife, who obviously had a clear notion of the gendering of such matters, asked Taylor 'if it was not indecent for a man to lay hands upon a woman in that condition'. Jackson obviously had a clear idea of how a childbirth should be organized, and was bringing that presupposition to bear when trying to establish the facts which lay behind the death of Maddocks's child.[11]

It is unclear if Elizabeth Jackson was sent to Thomas Peers's house by an official, or whether she went on her own initiative. What is obvious is that her status as a midwife gave her something of an expert status in her own mind, presumably in the village, and definitely in the eyes of Thomas Pulestone, the justice of the peace who took her deposition and those of other witnesses to this case. But this and other infanticide cases also demonstrate that other women felt that they had an interest in cases of newborn child killing, and that they had relevant expertise which they wished to deploy.

In a deposition of 3 March 1678, a spinster (her age is not given) named Mary Moses of Aldford parish admitted to giving birth to a child – which, she claimed, was born dead – while her parents were out of the house between 10 a.m. and noon on Saturday 3 March, as well as to hiding it in her bed and burying it 'in the backside of her father's house' while her parents were at church the next day. On her account, the child remained undiscovered until the morning of 2 April, when two women, Mary Ibottson and Mary Pullein, examined her.

We have a very full account of what happened from Mary Ibottson, a woman aged about 40. On 30 March, returning from Chester market, she heard that some people had claimed that she was unwilling to go and 'search ye body of Mary Moses', which suggests that rumours about the birth were already current. Mary called on two other women, Mary Pullein and Elizabeth Haswell, and asked them to go with her 'to see if the said Mary Moses wolde suffer them to see her breast, as she was reported to be with child'. On arrival, Mary Moses refused to let them do so, adding the very telling qualification that they might do so if they 'had authority from the churchwardens to do the same'. Ibottson went to question Mary a second and third time, and on this last occasion the young girl asked the older woman 'wherefore she would be so crewel towards her', to which Ibottson replied that 'her very counten[an]ce did betray her'. Eventually, after

---

further pressure, Mary Moses bared her breasts, and Ibottson and Mary Pullien, who was also present, established that she had given birth. Ibottson asked where the child and 'yt w[hi]ch midwives call the afterbirth' had been buried, and went with four other women to find them. When this was done, the parish constable was called in and arrested Mary Moses. Evidence also came from another older woman (Mary Pullein was aged 60, as was another witness, Elizabeth Haswell, while Mary Powell was aged 50). These women give a slightly different story, emphasizing the roles of a midwife called Mary Watson and of George Harrison, one of the township's constables, in orchestrating the questioning of Moses. But what is evident is that this mobilization was seen as desirable, and that a large number of women from the parish became involved. Elizabeth Haswell said that when she came to the Moses residence, she found other women 'to the number of about a dozen' already there, while Mary Powell reported going to the house 'alonge with the reste of her women neigbours'.[12]

The type of aggressive questioning directed by Mary Ibbotson at Mary Moses was not uncommon, nor was the involvement of a wide spectrum of local women. What these stories indicate is the way in which the discovery of infanticide could lay down moral markers. Let us consider another case, that of Ann Clough, accused of killing her newborn child in 1686.[13] Once news of the finding of the dead child spread, local women rapidly became involved. Rebecca Hamanway, a 55-year-old woman, married to a clothworker, told how a woman called Ann Nixson, a spinster aged 26, came to her and called her to see the child, and reported that on arrival 'she found other neighbours there with Anne Clough & saw a man child lye & handled it & shewed it to the rest of the women then p[re]sente & turned it & saw neither wound nor blench upon it'. A woman called Margaret Barker asked if anybody had taken the child from Clough, who replied that she had to help herself at the time of birth. Hamanway deposed that 'whatev[er] this exam[inant] asked the said Ann Clough she wept and gave no answer'. Ann Nixson told how she had heard Ann Clough groaning as she was going to church the previous Sunday, 'as formerly she used to having had the fitts for a long time before', and although she noted that Ann was 'somewhat bigger in her belly', she did not at that stage suspect that she was with child. But Alice Grimditch told her that Ann Clough's mother had, in turn, told her that Ann was with child, upon which Nixson's mistress told her 'to goe for neighbours', which Nixson 'forthwith did'. Alice Grimshaw, too, told how her mistress 'ordered her to send for wifes' – that is, wives, mature female neighbours. When the neighbours arrived at the house where Clough lived, the house of a Mrs Ashton, according to another witness, a 60-year-old widow, Ashton 'tould this exam[inant] and the rest of the women then p[re]sent what a misfortune has hapned in her house that the s[ai]d Ann Clough

---

[12]   TNA CHES 38/41, examinations relating to Mary Moses of Aldford. At trial, Moses was sentenced to death but subsequently reprieved (TNA, CHES 21/4, f. 176[a] v).

[13]   TNA CHES 38/41, examinations relating to Ann Clough of Great Budworth.

had born a child'. An illegitimate birth, let alone an infanticidal one, was clearly regarded as a disgrace to a respectable household.[14]

The female involvement in infanticide cases is understandable enough: these cases operated initially in the female sphere, with chastity, personal and collective female honour, knowledge about pregnancy and childbirth, and the good name of the household, perhaps even of the village, at stake. But female involvement was clearly present in other types of homicide, especially, of course, in those where a woman was a victim. I would like to take two case histories to illustrate this point.

The first comes almost at the end of 1798, and is recorded in depositions, a contemporary pamphlet and a newspaper report of the trial. It involved the killing of a woman named Sarah Malone, or Statham, by a man called John Thornhill.[15] Sarah Statham was a woman of about 40, previously married to an Irishman named Patrick Malone, who had deserted her, leaving her with two children. She had been involved with Thornhill, butler in the household of a local rector, the Reverend Archdeacon Egerton Leigh, and there were rumours that she was pregnant by him. In January 1798, her body was found in a millpond at Lymm, where she lived. The coroner's jury initially returned a verdict of killing by persons unknown, but suspicions became focused on Thornhill, and he was eventually arrested for the murder of Statham and convicted for her murder at the court of Great Sessions. A key element focusing suspicions against him was the information of a local widow called Phoebe Daniel, who had lived in the same house as Statham. In the pamphlet describing Thornhill's trial, Daniel is reported to have given the following evidence before the court:

> I saw the prisoner on the Tuesday following [i.e., following the discovery of Stratham's body], the 9th of January, at the door of the Spread-Eagle, in Lymm, and spoke to him: I was then going before the coroner. I said to the prisoner, it was a sad accident; he answered, it was. I then said to him 'I don't say to you John, as Nathan said to David, Thou art the man: but if you are, conscience will speak'. To which the prisoner made no answer, though there was time for him to do so, before I was called to the coroner, which I was almost immediately afterwards.[16]

And we have a very full account of what Phoebe Daniels said when she entered the Spread Eagle and gave her evidence to Thomas Hollins, the coroner. She

---

[14] Clough, however, was acquitted at her trial (TNA, CHES 21/4, ff. 286r, 287r; CHES 24/144/1).

[15] Very full depositions taken at the inquest on Statham by coroner John Hollins survive in TNA CHES 24/179/5. Thornhill's subsequent trial and conviction formed the subject matter of *The evidence on the trial of John Thornhill, for the murder of Sarah Statham, at Lymm, in Cheshire. For which he was executed, at Chester, on Monday the twenty-third of April, 1798, etc.* (Chester: W. Minshull, 1798), while his trial and execution were reported in the 27 April 1798 edition of the *Chester Courant*.

[16] *Evidence of the Trial of John Thornhill*, 4–5.

recounted how she had last seen the deceased at about 8 p.m. the previous Friday, when Statham went to put her 5-year-old daughter to bed. About two hours later, Statham's son, a 13-year-old who was already working as a weaver, came in, and Daniel asked him where his mother had gone, he replying that he did not know. Daniel expressed disquiet about Statham, as it was 'a very rough night', whereupon the young Statham said that his mother had gone to see her brother, also resident in Lymm, because his child was sick, although for some reason his mother had wanted the matter kept secret. Daniel told how she had eventually decided that Friday evening that Statham was keeping company with Thornhill, and that she 'has no reason to suppose any one kept her company besides John Thornhill since she knew her'. She said that she had discussed Statham's pregnancy with her, that Statham had told her that the child was Thornhill's, and that he was denying it among his fellow servants at the Leigh residence, adding that 'his denying that the child was his only made the sin the greater'. Daniel was obviously very concerned over Statham: John Pass, Archdeacon Leigh's gardener, deposed before the coroner how 'on Saturday last the said Phoebe Daniel came to him and told him that she was almost off her senses in consequence of the deceased having been missing all night from eight o'clock the preceding night',[17] adding that she 'then asked if John Thornhill had been out'. Both her evidence at the trial (she was the first witness called) and her previous evidence to the coroner make it evident that she had decided that Thornhill was responsible for her friend's death, and that she was anxious to implicate him.

The second case I would like to examine in some detail occurred in 1729, and involved the death of Sarah Dod, wife of Samuel Dod of Peckforton.[18] On the evening of 11 December of that year, Sarah Dod had entered the alehouse of William Penkett. Penkett told how Owen Wright and Samuel Smith were also there, and how they asked Dod to drink with them. She replied that 'she w[ou]ld not drink any of their cold drink but w[ou]ld drink any thing with them which was hott and good for that she had been at the mill & was very cold'. So the two men provided mulled ale laced with a 'knoggin' of warmed brandy to which sugar was added, and Dod sat by the fire drinking it with them. A little later, so Penkett recounted, Dod fell from her seat by the fire, and 'laid upon the s[ai]d Sam[ue]l Smith & her feet under the grate of the kitchen fire'. Penkett thought she was drunk, and 'he desir'd the s[ai]d Samuel Smith to help him carry her to bed which they did & laid her there'.

Very shortly afterward Sarah Dod was dead. A witness named Elizabeth Cheswise told how Ann Penkett, William's wife, came to her house that same evening and asked her to come over to the Penkett house, 'for Sarah Dod was dead'. Cheswise asked how Dod had come to her death so suddenly, 'having seen her about three hours before very well'. An unnamed girl of about 10, apprentice to William Penkett, 'made answer Samuel Smith had murdered her', whereupon

[17]   TNA CHES 24/179/5.

[18]   TNA CHES 38/41, examinations relating to the death of Sarah Dod.

her mistress exclaimed, 'you young bitch hold your tongue you will have us hang'd'. So Cheswise went to see Dod's body, and told how she found her 'lying dead partly on her left side with one of her legs off the bed and her face and neck black & her nose turned on one side. And when she strip'd her there was the sign of a dirty hand on her buttocks'. George Burghall, Dod's brother-in-law, was called to the Penkett house the next day, and found her 'lying on her side on a bed & her face swell'd black'. He continued: 'upon which he s[ai]d this woman had had some harm done to her but that he cou'd not get any account how she came by her death'.

What had almost certainly happened was that Samuel Smith had raped Sarah as she lay insensible, possibly already dead. Ann Penkett may have been unwilling to say too much before Elizabeth Cheswise, but the deposition she gave the examining justices was quite explicit. She had gone up to see how Dod was shortly after her husband and Smith had put her to bed, and found 'the s[ai]d Samuel Smith to lye upon her and saw his head & body move upon her'. She asked Smith what he was doing, but he 'gave no answer but got off the bed and as this examinant verily believes put up his breeches, upon which this examinant looked on the bed, and found Sarah Dod dead with her cloathes all put up to her waste and in a very dirty condition'.

Far fuller information, in fact the longest statement in this set of depositions, was given by a woman named Mary Madely of Beeston. She was staying at Penkett's house that Saturday night. On arrival, she saw Samuel Smith, whom she described as a shoemaker, emerging from 'a little parlour or chamber' with his 'wigg a cross on his hand', and he 'appeared as if he was frighted … and this examinant looking at him saw the knees of the s[ai]d Smith's breeches very dirty and also his finger nails, and he looked very simply'. Penkett's wife then gave her a candle and showed her into the room from which Smith had emerged, where she found 'a person lying upon the bed in a very indecent manner upon her face with her legs, thighs and breech all bare & naked, & some parts very dirty'. She returned to the main part of the house and asked who the person was, and 'one of the company by the fire told her it was Samuel Dod's wife'. Madeley then asked Ann Penkett 'why she let her lye in such a condition', and went together with Ann Penkett with a cloth and a pot of water to clean Dod up. Madely told how she 'made her as clean as she could and pull'd down her cloathes and let her lye on her face supposing she was asleep'. She further declared:

> she being one who striped or laid straight this Sarah Dod that night found her to be much abused in her private parts more than she can with modesty express, and that she verily believes it was the s[ai]d Samuel Smith who had so abused her no one having been with her after she came from her; and likewise her chin & breast were black and much discolour'd, and further that Penkett's wife told this examinant that when she saw the s[ai]d Samuel Smith lye on the s[ai]d Sarah Dod she told her husband of it & he bid damn her what did she concern herself.

William Penkett does not, in fact, on Madeley's evidence, emerge very well from the story. When she took the pot of water downstairs after cleaning Sarah Dod up, 'William Penkett being at the door asked whether she had turned her with the pizzle upwards or whether she thought he had been in the wrong hole and that nobody ever was kill'd with kissing'.

So we have one case in which a woman seems to have been instrumental in focusing suspicions on a male murderer, and another where a woman not only took control of the care for what proved to be a dead woman but also gave a detailed deposition to the examining magistrates with an account of the state of the body and a clear idea of who was responsible for the killing. Let us now turn to a less detailed case, in which a woman gave comfort to another in the last hours of her life and also helped establish who had killed her.

In this instance, the evidence begins with a statement by a woman who was asked to help with another woman who was very ill. Giving evidence on 24 February 1686, Isabel, the wife of a husbandman named Thomas Davey of Bostock, told how she had been called out of her house between 2 and 3 a.m. on 16 February by Samuel Buckley. Buckley was anxious that she should go to his house to see to Mary Eaton, whom, on entering the house, she found 'lyinge upon her back on the floore with her arms abroade in her cloathes & cald to her but she nev[er] spake nor stird'. Buckley claimed that Eaton had injured herself by falling in the fire, but Davey could not see any signs of burning on her clothes, and the evidence of various witnesses suggested a rather different story. During an argument with Eaton, Buckley, who was apparently a staunch adherent of the Duke of Monmouth, spoke in praise of the Protestant hero, upon which Eaton told him 'he [i.e., Monmouth] was a bastard & the said Samuel was the son of a whore'. The argument escalated, and Buckley threw a 'fire stick' at her, whereupon she fell.

Davey gave evidence about the nature of Eaton's wounds, which she said were more extensive than those seen by the coroner, and she seems to have taken a presiding role as a number of women came to see Eaton. Thus Jane Wrench, 33-year-old wife of a yeoman, recounted how she,

> Hearing that Mary was not well & alsoe hearing that there was some suspition that she might receive some harm by Samuell Buckley, went to see her on the said Wednesday eveninge & finding her very ill wished the said Isabell Davey being then p[re]sent to aske the said Mary whether the said Samuel Buckley had any way hurt her whereupon the said Isabell layd her head to the said Mary Eaton's & asked her whether Samuell had harmed her this exam[inant] heard the s[ai]d Mary make a noyse but w[ha]t she said to Isabell this exam[inant] could not understand but Isabell tould this exam[inant] the s[ai]d Mary said yea; & this exam[inant] saw the said Mary twice after before she died & saw her in a very sad condicion.

Davey was clearly trying to ensure that Buckley should be implicated, and another woman was happy to give supporting evidence. Margaret Barker, a husbandman's wife aged 30 or so, stated how, as she was going to Bostock mill a few days before the fatal incident, she fell into conversation with Mary Eaton, who complained that she was very much abused verbally by Buckley, and that 'shee would go to James Ouldfield for a warrant for the said Samuel Buckley for he had tould the said Mary that he would be her death & she was afraide of her life of him & weary of her life'.[19]

The female involvement in these cases where a woman was the victim of a homicide, although differing from that found in the cases of infanticide, again creates an impression of female agency and female involvement. Phoebe Daniel and Isabel Davey a century before her seem determined that the male killer of a woman acquaintance should be brought to justice, and with Davey we have a woman who took the injured party into her care in the last few days of her life. With Mary Madely we have a case of a woman who again was determined to bring a killer to justice, who played a part in cleaning up what she thought was an insensible woman, her sense of decency clearly being offended by the way in which Dod had been left, and who gave clear and (again as far as her sense of decency would allow) detailed evidence about the state of Dod's injuries to the examining magistrates.

As might be expected, the involvement of women is less pronounced in what was the most common form of non-infanticidal homicide in these Cheshire materials – fights between men, frequently originating in an alehouse after the consumption of alcohol, which led to an unexpected fatality and which frequently resulted in a conviction for manslaughter. Even so, a female presence, and at times an active one, can be discerned in a number of such cases.

If many of these incidents of male-on-male violence took place in alehouses, women were frequently present as proprietors, wives of proprietors or servants. Thus Hannah Hudson, an alehouse-keeper's wife, deposed that in 1755 she had tried to intervene in a fight between John Hollinworth and Thomas Bann:

> She begged of them to be quiet and said that Thomas was an old man and lame of an arm and desired 'em to drop their argument and be quiet and endeavoured to prevent them ... saith that she offered [i.e., attempted] to pull John Hollinworth off Thomas Bann but could not. And then shrieked and called out aloud for some good Christian to save Thomas Bann. Saith that her husband came down stairs and she went to the door and called out murder. And when she came to him again his water was running from him, And then and there instantly dyed.[20]

A similar attempt to stop two men from fighting was made in 1673 by an alehouse-keeper's wife named Margery Pierson. She told how a fortnight previously Richard Downes and Richard Davenport had come into her husband's house and had fallen out over the price one was to pay the other for loading turfs. The two men 'fell to foule words & both gott up & offered to fight', at which point

---

[19]   TNA, CHES 38/41, examinations relating to the death of Mary Eaton.
[20]   TNA, CHES 24/164/3.

she 'desired them not to fight in her house' and, taking hold of Davenport, 'wished him to be quiet, who answered I will be quiet if he will let me', whereupon Downes said, 'we will fight in the park', and walked out. Shortly afterwards Downes returned and insulted Davenport, saying, according to another witness, 'come out then courdly rogue & I will give thee satisfaction', whereupon Davenport broke loose from Margery Pierson's restraining hands and went out and fought his antagonist, inflicting fatal injuries on him.[21]

More generally, we find women giving evidence about instances of homicidal violence they had seen, or having their help enlisted for the benefit of men who had been injured in fights. A good example of the former came in 1795, when Thomas Smith was killed by Richard Wood outside the alehouse of Robert Parker in Nantwich. One woman, Martha Hilditch, told how she had been drinking with Smith, and how she had attempted to quieten Wood down. Another woman, a spinster named Jane Hilditch, gave her account of the story. She had seen Wood lurking near a small house near Parker's inn, and then saw him making an unprovoked attack on Smith. Hilditch declared that 'she never heard any ill language pass between the said Smith and Wood which she must otherwise have heard as she was leaning through a window of her master's house about eight or ten yards distant'. Jane Hilditch was obviously very keen to hear and see what was going on in the street outside her employer's residence.[22]

And, finally, there were cases of women being called upon to aid fatally injured men. Perhaps the most dramatic example came in yet another alehouse brawl, when George Massey inflicted fatal injuries on John Joseph in an alehouse in Shotwick in 1721. Agnes Hartley, probably a servant in the alehouse, witnessed Massey injuring Joseph with a skillet he threw at him, and she then held Joseph up for a quarter of an hour, not wishing him to fall to the floor, until he said he was recovered. At that point, the two men started fighting and fell on the floor together, and Hartley ran to get the parish constable. And, of course, women frequently helped men fatally injured in brawls. One such incident occurred at Bromborough in 1730, when two men called upon to carry out their statutory duties to repair the roads fell into a fight after disputing over the relative qualities of their respective teams of horses. Fatal injuries were inflicted on one of the men, Thomas Cook, when he was thrown down on a rock by his adversary, John Tellett. One of the witnesses to the incident, Thomas Warbutton, told how he was lifted off the rock by 'one or two women who were present'.[23] We return to Oren Falk's notion of 'auxiliaries' in acts of violence, the 'assorted sideliners' who witnessed violent incidents, and who in some cases helped to clear up the mess which followed them.

This essay has been very much a preliminary investigation of some largely unexploited documentation and a largely unexplored subject area. What I hope

---

[21]   TNA, CHES 38/41, examinations relating to the death of Richard Downes.

[22]   TNA, CHES 24/178/4.

[23]   TNA, CHES 38/41, examinations relating to the death of Thomas Cooke.

to have done is to demonstrate that if we are to understand homicide as a cultural entity, we have not only to think about the perpetrators and victims of homicide but also to take into account the actions and statements of the 'assorted sideliners' whose involvement, even if we build in all the caveats about the difficulties of interpreting this type of deposition evidence, can tell us so much about perceptions of, and reactions to, violence in the past. This general conclusion is, I hope, especially relevant when we take seventeenth- and eighteenth-century women into consideration. Female involvement in infanticide investigations is perhaps now a familiar issue, although surely the obvious need felt by 'respectable' women within a community to investigate and distance themselves from the infanticidal mother of illegitimate children demands more detailed investigation. What is perhaps less expected is the sound of women's voices as they construct narratives around non-infanticidal killings. We tend to regard such killings as essentially masculine affairs, and see female involvement largely in terms of women victims of homicidal violence, and especially of domestic homicide.[24] But the women we have come across in these Cheshire materials demonstrate a much broader range of female involvement, albeit usually unwilling, in early modern English violence.

They also demonstrate the extent of female agency in the operation of the criminal law in seventeenth- and eighteenth-century England. I have already argued for the importance of women as accusers and witnesses in witchcraft cases.[25] The evidence I have explored here, albeit perhaps less conclusively, argues for what may be an unexpected level of female involvement in homicide cases: variously trying to defuse violent situations, aiding the victims of violence or simply witnessing violent acts. Women were allotted very little formal agency in the operation of the criminal law in early modern England. But their less formal interventions, and the witness statements they made to coroners, justices of the peace, and (insofar as these can be documented) at trials themselves, all point to the importance of female participation in homicide cases and, indeed, to their importance as historical agents in the broader culture of early modern England.

---

[24]   It is worth remembering, of course, that domestic violence as an historical phenomenon is subject to varying interpretations: see Elizabeth A. Foyster, *Marital Violence: An English Family History, 1660–1875* (Cambridge: Cambridge University Press, 2005).

[25]   James Sharpe, 'Women, Witchcraft and the Legal Process', in *Women, Crime and the Courts in Early Modern England*, ed. Jenny Kermode and Garthine Walker (London: UCL Press, 1994), 106–24.

Works Cited

Primary Sources

Manuscript Sources
Cheshire and Chester Archives and Local Studies, Chester; CR 580: Crown Books.
The National Archives, Kew, CHES 21/4–7: Courts of Great Sessions of Chester and Flint: Crown Books; CHES 24/171/1 – 24/179/5: Courts of Great Sessions of Chester and Flint: Files; CHES 38/41: Palatinate of Chester: Miscellanea.

Printed Primary Source
The evidence on the trial of John Thornhill, for the murder of Sarah Statham, at Lymm, in Cheshire. For which he was executed, at Chester, on Monday the twenty-third of April, 1798, etc. Chester: W. Minshull, 1798.

Secondary Sources

Dickinson, J. R., and J. A. Sharpe. 'Infanticide in Early Modern England: The Court of Great Sessions at Chester, 1650–1800'. In *Infanticide: Historical Perspectives on Child Murder and Concealment, 1550–2000*. Edited by Mark Jackson. Aldershot: Ashgate, 2002. 35–51.
Falk, Oren. 'Bystanders and Hearsayers: Reassessing Participant Roles in Duelling'. In *A Great Effusion of Blood? Interpreting Medieval Violence*. Edited by Mark D. Meyerson, Daniel Thiery and Oren Falk. Toronto: University of Toronto Press, 2004. 98–130.
Foyster, Elizabeth. *Marital Violence: An English Family History, 1660–1857*. Cambridge: Cambridge University Press, 2005.
Gallant, Thomas. 'Honor, Masculinity and Ritual: Knife Fighting in Nineteenth-Century Greece'. *American Historical Review* 105 (2000): 359–82.
Gowing, Laura. 'Ordering the Body: Illegitimacy and Female Authority in Seventeenth-Century England'. In *Negotiating Power in Early Modern Society: Order, Hierarchy and Subordination in Britain and Ireland*. Edited by Michael J. Braddick and John Walter. Cambridge: Cambridge University Press, 2001. 43–62.
———. 'Secret Births and Infanticide in Seventeenth-Century England'. *Past and Present* 156 (1997): 87–115.
Hindle, Steve. *The State and Social Change in Early Modern England, c. 1550–1640*. Basingstoke: Macmillan, 1999.
Jackson, Mark. *New-Born Child Murder: Women, Illegitimacy and the Courts in Eighteenth-Century England*. Manchester: Manchester University Press, 1996.
Langbein, John H. *Prosecuting Law in the Renaissance: England, Germany, France*. Cambridge, MA: Harvard University Press, 1974.

Miller, William Ian. *Humiliation: And Other Essays on Honor, Social Discomfort, and Violence*. Ithaca, NY: Cornell University Press, 1993.

Riches, David. 'The Phenomenon of Violence'. In *The Anthropology of Violence*. Edited by David Riches. Oxford: Blackwell, 1986. 1–27.

Sharpe, James. 'Women, Witchcraft and the Legal Process'. In *Women, Crime and the Courts in Early Modern England*. Edited by Jenny Kermode and Garthine Walker. London: UCL Press, 1994. 106–24.

Walker, Garthine. *Crime, Gender and Social Order in Early Modern England*. Cambridge: Cambridge University Press, 2003.

————. 'Just Stories: Telling Tales of Infant Death in Early Modern England'. In *Culture and Change: Attending to Early Modern Women*. Edited by Margaret Mikesell and Adele Seeff. Newark: University of Delaware Press, 2003. 98–115.

Chapter 8
'Angels with Dirty Faces': Violent Women in Early Modern Scotland

Anne-Marie Kilday

The study of violence and violent activity is one that has engaged scholars for generations. It has only been relatively recently, however, and especially in relation to the early modern period, that any analysis of this type has involved violent female behaviour. Traditionally, historians have tended to marginalize women's involvement in violent criminal activity in that era, arguing that it was uncharacteristic and uncommon. As Pieter Spierenburg has argued, violence was a male culture in which women did not participate.[1] Instead, more attention has been paid to women's role as victims, and to male offenders, who were believed to dominate criminal indictments as far as aggressive behaviour was concerned.[2] The reasons for this anomaly are not clear. Scholars have long held the view that women never strayed from the boundaries of acceptable behaviour, that females relished their role as the 'gentler sex', and that as a result they steadfastly remained within familiar and fixed ideological limits.[3] Furthermore, the only perceived exceptions

---

[1] Pieter Spierenburg, 'How Violent Were Women? Court Cases in Amsterdam, 1650–1810', *Crime, History and Societies* 1 (1997): 27.

[2] See, for instance, John M. Beattie, 'The Criminality of Women in Eighteenth Century England', *Journal of Social History* 8 (1975): 80; Clive Emsley, *Crime and Society in England, 1750–1900*, 2nd ed. (London: Longman, 1996), 152; Sharon Howard, *Law and Disorder in Early Modern Wales: Crime and Authority in the Denbighshire Courts, c. 1660–1730* (Cardiff: University of Wales Press, 2008); James A. Sharpe, *Crime in Early Modern England 1550–1750*, 2nd ed. (London: Longman, 1999); and Garthine Walker and Jennifer Kermode, introduction to *Women, Crime and the Courts in Early Modern England*, ed. Jennifer Kermode and Garthine Walker (London: UCL Press, 1994), 4. For more on women's role as victims, see Anna Clark, *Women's Silence, Men's Violence: Sexual Assault in England 1770–1845* (London: Pandora, 1987); Elizabeth A. Foyster, *Marital Violence: An English Family History, 1660–1857* (Cambridge: Cambridge University Press, 2005); and Frank McLynn, *Crime and Punishment in Eighteenth-Century England* (London: Routledge, 1989), ch. 6.

[3] These notions were reinforced by the constructs of femininity supported by contemporary writing in chapbooks, novels and conduct books. For further information, see Hannah Barker and Elaine Chalus, eds, *Gender in Eighteenth-Century England: Roles, Representations and Responsibilities* (London: Longman, 1997); Robert B. Shoemaker, *Gender in English Society, 1650–1850: The Emergence of Separate Spheres?* (London:

to break away from this general rule were women of 'unstable' character and mental ineptitude. Their signified abnormality rendered any objective analysis problematic.

Much of the existing historiography relating to criminal women has concentrated on gender-specific offences such as witchcraft, scolding, prostitution or infanticide, which emphasize the mysterious or deviant nature of female criminality rather than illustrating any of the more mainstream aggressive tendencies so regularly associated with male offenders.[4] Thus discussing violent female activity as a phenomenon that might be a central part of life in the earlier modern period has proved surprisingly difficult for historians.[5]

The main purpose of this chapter will be to investigate the historiographical hypothesis put forward by scholars such as John Beattie and James Sharpe, not only that women were less commonly indicted for violent behaviour compared with men but also that they were less brutal when committing criminal offences.[6] Rather than being directly involved in the perpetration of violent offences, women are said to have been on the periphery of criminal action, operating as decoys or lookouts and thus merely supporting the deviancy of their male associates.[7] This premise has been widely supported by criminologists and criminal

---

Longman, 1998); Joy Wiltenburg, *Disorderly Women and Female Power in the Street Literature of Early Modern England and Germany* (Charlottesville: University Press of Virginia, 1992); and Sandra Clark, *Women and Crime in the Street Literature of Early Modern England* (Basingstoke: Palgrave Macmillan, 2003).

[4]   See Sharpe, *Crime in Early Modern England*, 157–59; James A. Sharpe and Richard Golden, eds, *English Witchcraft, 1560–1736* (London: Pickering and Chatto, 2003); Martin Ingram, '"Scolding Women Cucked or Washed": A Crisis in Gender Relations in Early Modern England?', in *Women, Crime and the Courts in Early Modern England*, ed. Jennifer Kermode and Garthine Walker (London: UCL Press, 1994), 48–80; Mark Jackson, *New-Born Child Murder: Women, Illegitimacy and the Courts in Eighteenth-Century England* (Manchester: Manchester University Press, 1996); and Anne-Marie Kilday, *A History of Infanticide in Britain c. 1600 to the Present* (Basingstoke: Palgrave, 2013).

[5]   Exceptions to this general trend include Jennine Hurl-Eamon, *Gender and Petty Violence in London, 1680–1820* (Columbus: Ohio State University Press, 2005); Randall Martin, *Women, Murder and Equity in Early Modern England* (London: Routledge, 2008); Robert B. Shoemaker, *Prosecution and Punishment: Petty Crime and the Law in London and Rural Middlesex, c. 1660–1725* (Cambridge: Cambridge University Press, 1991); and Garthine Walker, *Crime, Gender and Social Order in Early Modern England* (Cambridge: Cambridge University Press, 2003). In the Scottish context more particularly, see Anne-Marie Kilday, *Women and Violent Crime in Enlightenment Scotland* (Woodbridge: Royal Historical Society/Boydell Press, 2007), ch. 2, and Robert Falconer, *Crime and Community in Reformation Scotland: Negotiating Power in a Burgh Society* (London: Pickering and Chatto, 2013).

[6]   See Beattie, 'Criminality', 82.

[7]   See Beattie, 'Criminality', 90, and Sharpe, *Crime in Early Modern England*, 155.

historians alike for many years. Indeed, research has suggested that throughout Europe and throughout time, women rarely participated in violent criminal activity.[8]

Arguably, however, this contention has contributed much to the marginalization of the phenomenon of violent female criminality within the mainstream scholarship of crime history.[9] The main purpose of this article will be to challenge this hypothesis with reference to the experience of women from lowland Scotland during the late eighteenth and early nineteenth centuries. In this essay, lowland Scotland is taken to mean the region south of the Forth-Clyde Valley. This region was chosen for a variety of reasons, not least because it was the hub of economic and social modernization; it was also the area where most of the Scottish population resided during the premodern period.

The evidence contained in this analysis is based on a detailed study of 1,061 indictments for violent crime which were brought before the Scottish Justiciary Court between 1750 and 1815. After its formation in 1672, the Justiciary Court dealt with the majority of the most serious offences committed north of the border, and the judiciary had a reputation for meticulous record-keeping and legal prowess.[10] The comprehensive nature of the Justiciary Court material has allowed an in-depth investigation of the nature of violent crime in the lowlands of Scotland,

---

[8]   See, for instance the references at note 2 above, as well as Raymond Gillespie, 'Women and Crime in Seventeenth-Century Ireland', in *Women in Early Modern Ireland*, ed. Margaret MacCurtain and Mary O'Dowd (Edinburgh: Edinburgh University Press, 1991), 43–52; Julius R. Ruff, *Crime, Justice and Public Order in Old Regime France: The Sénéchaussées of Libourne and Bazas, 1696–1789* (London: Croom Helm, 1984); and Brian Henry, *Dublin Hanged: Crime, Law Enforcement and Punishment in Late Eighteenth-Century Dublin* (Blackrock: Irish Academic Press, 1994). An exception to this general thesis would be episodes of popular disturbance, where women were regular participants in the riots and tumults that took place. See John Bohstedt, 'Gender, Household and Community Politics: Women in English Riots 1790–1810', *Past and Present* 120 (1988): 88–122, and Malcolm I. Thomis and Jennifer Grimmett, *Women in Protest 1800–1850* (London: Croom Helm, 1982). However, as these offences usually involved the destruction of property, rather than personal confrontation, their inclusion in any analysis of 'violent' crimes is problematic.

[9]   See, for example, Barbara Hanawalt, 'The Female Felon in Fourteenth-Century England', *Viator* 5 (1974): 251–73; James S. Cockburn, ed., *Crime in England, 1550–1800* (London: Methuen, 1977); Sharpe, *Crime in Early Modern England*, *passim*; James A. Sharpe, *Crime in Seventeenth-Century England – A County Study* (Cambridge: Cambridge University Press, 1983); John M. Beattie, *Crime and the Courts in England 1600–1800* (Oxford: Clarendon Press, 1986); McLynn, *Crime and Punishment, passim*; Emsley, *Crime and Society, passim*; Carol Smart, *Women, Crime and Criminology: A Feminist Critique* (London: Routledge and Kegan Paul, 1977); and Otto Pollak, *The Criminality of Women* (Philadelphia: University of Pennsylvania Press, 1950).

[10]   For further discussion, see Anne-Marie Kilday, *Women and Violent Crime in Enlightenment Scotland*, ch. 2.

the extent of women's involvement in these types of offences and the response of the authorities towards such forms of illegal behaviour.[11]

Predominantly, the types of violent offences for which lowland women were indicted before the Justiciary Court fall under the general term of 'crimes against the person', which consist of homicides, assault (both verbal and physical), infanticide and popular disturbances. Due to the proportionately high levels of female participation in the crimes of infanticide and popular disturbances, these offences cannot be investigated within the scope of this chapter. Here, therefore, attention is directed to the two most serious crimes against the person: homicide and assault.

During the premodern period, Scots law defined homicide as a crime 'by which life is taken away, and the person of a human creature is destroyed'.[12] Unlike its English counterpart, Scots law was relatively uncomplicated when it came to establishing the boundaries of homicidal behaviour. Issues of premeditation, which dominated legal debate south of the border, were not such a concern in Scotland. North of the border, the courts were more preoccupied with trying to prove that a given homicide had taken place, rather than whether or not it was a 'forethocht felony'. In addition, the principle in English law of *feme covert*, whereby a married woman was not deemed responsible for criminal activity if her husband was present when she was carrying out the offence, did not apply in Scots law. Married women were just as culpable as single women in Scotland, and the circumstances surrounding their illegality, in terms of the rationale behind their actions, were rarely an issue.[13] Already, then, we see a different approach to criminal women than has been suggested by the historiography to date. Rather than relegating criminal women to mere supporting roles in criminal enterprises, the Scottish authorities believed that, in criminal matters, women were capable of behaving as independent actors. Female offenders in Scotland were not protected from the law; rather, they were treated in much the same way as their male counterparts.

The relatively uncomplicated nature of Scots law enabled a clear and precise categorization of homicide to be made. Four kinds of homicide were recognized

---

[11]   The Justiciary Court, for the most part, was the institution where the most 'serious' criminal cases were indicted, in particular, those where a capital conviction could result. Violent and habitual offenders were also more likely to be brought to the Justiciary Court than casual petty criminals. Consequently, it must be remembered that any study of accused individuals brought before the Justiciary Court is likely to be biased towards the most 'serious' offenders.

[12]   David Hume, *Commentaries on the Law of Scotland, respecting the Description and Punishment of Crimes*, 2 vols (Edinburgh, 1797), vol. 1, ch. 6, 179.

[13]   For further discussion of *feme covert* and its applicability in England, see Shoemaker, *Gender in English Society*, 297, and Peter King, 'Gender, Crime and Justice in Late Eighteenth- and Early Nineteenth-Century England', in *Gender and Crime in Modern Europe*, ed. Margaret L. Arnot and Cornelie Usborne (London: UCL Press, 1999), 64. See also the chapter by Krista Kesselring in the present volume.

by the courts across Scotland – aggravated murder, murder, culpable homicide and murder 'free from all blame'.[14] This last section included casual and justifiable homicide.[15]

Of the homicidal charges brought before the Justiciary Court between 1750 and 1815 relating to lowland Scotland, 216 related to murder, 53 related to culpable homicide, and there was 1 case of justifiable homicide.[16] If all these cases are taken together to show the overall incidence of homicide indictments in the premodern period, the gender disparity in this respect is significant. Some 71% of the cases (or 213 out of 270 indictments) were brought against men and 29% (or 57 cases out of 270 indictments) were brought against women.[17] Although the figures are not directly comparable, due to variations in legal context and in the types of criminal records researched, it is interesting to note that the findings of this study with respect to the incidence of homicide indictments appear similar to those uncovered elsewhere, in terms of the male predominance in this kind of violent activity.[18] Beattie, for instance, in his sampling of the Surrey judicial records between 1663 and 1802, noted that of 284 charges for murder and manslaughter, 87% were against men and 13% were against women.[19] Likewise, Sharpe, in his study of the Essex assizes between 1620 and 1680, found that of 310 homicide suspects, 84% were male and only 16% were female.[20] The general trend that seems to emerge

---

[14]   For further discussion, see Hume, *Commentaries*, vol. 1, ch. 6, 191–291.

[15]   Casual homicide occurred when an individual was killed by accident. Justifiable homicide occurred when an individual was killed by an 'officer' executing his duty. For further discussion, see W. David H. Sellar, 'Forethocht Felony, Malice Aforethought and the Classification of Homicide', in *Legal History in the Making: Proceedings of the Ninth British Legal History Conference: Glasgow, 1989*, ed. William M. Gordon and Thomas D. Fergus (London: Hambleton, 1991), 55–56.

[16]   When the charge against the accused was murder or culpable homicide, I have counted the offence as that for which he or she was eventually convicted. If the individual was acquitted, I have used the witness testimony, the Advocate Depute's declaration and/ or the judge's interlocutor on the relevancy of the libel to arrive at the type of homicide implied in the indictment; this was the case in only a negligible number of the indictments.

[17]   It should be remembered that this study cannot reflect actual crime levels, only the crimes indicted before the Justiciary Court. Many crimes must have gone unreported, contributing to the so-called Dark Figure of criminal statistics. For further discussion, see Anne-Marie Kilday, 'Women and Crime in South-west Scotland, 1750–1815: A Study of the Justiciary Court Records' (PhD thesis, University of Strathclyde, 1998), esp. 3–4, 22 (relating to homicides) and 37–39 (relating to assaults).

[18]   This qualification concerning comparability holds true for any of the comparisons made in this article. Evidence from studies elsewhere is included merely as a matter of interest.

[19]   Beattie, 'Criminality', 85.

[20]   My calculations on the evidence presented; see Sharpe, *Crime in Seventeenth Century England*, 124. Most studies do not offer specific data concerning the gender breakdown in cases of alleged homicides and indeed other offences. See, for example, Henry, *Dublin Hanged*, 77–99, and Ruff, *Crime, Justice and Public Order*, 68–105, who

from these historians is that, with respect to homicide, 'A strikingly lower level of criminality of women'[21] is in evidence.

In fact, 57 lowland Scottish women were brought to the Justiciary Court between 1750 and 1815, charged with committing an act of homicide. Forty-eight of those women were charged with murder and nine with culpable homicide. The overwhelming majority of the accused, some 81%, were single women, and more than half of these were 'relicts', or widows. This is because the most frequent victim of female homicidal activity in lowland Scotland was the husband of the accused. The other notable characteristic of the women indicted for murder and culpable homicide at the Justiciary Court was that they overwhelmingly perpetrated their offences in 'urban' areas.[22] Some 68% of those accused had allegedly killed in the towns, whereas 32% had allegedly killed in the country. This figure serves to confirm the work of the Scottish criminal historian Ian Donnachie, who claims that in the first half of the nineteenth century, 'law breaking was widespread throughout the Scottish countryside, but it was still relatively limited by urban standards'.[23] Whether this statement also applies to assault will be examined in due course. For now, it is enough to say that the most common *locus operandi* for homicide amongst the indicted lowland Scottish women was urban rather than rural in nature.

Running parallel to the argument that women committed far fewer offences compared to men is the contention by some that when women did participate in crime, their offences were usually committed without violence. The modern criminologist Carol Smart suggests that in general 'Violent offences ... do not appear to be easily reconciled with the traditional conceptualization of feminine behaviour. Murder and other violent acts against the person appear to be the

---

prefer instead to provide statistics on the lack of women's involvement in crimes against the person in general.

[21]   Beattie, 'Criminality', 80.

[22]   The references used to determine which of the locations were urban and which were rural were as follows: John G. Bartholomew, ed., *The Survey Gazetteer of the British Isles Topographical, Statistical and Commercial, Compiled from the 1911 Census and the Latest Official Returns* (Edinburgh: John Bartholomew and Co., 1914); *Place Names and Population in Scotland: An Alphabetical List of Populated Places Derived from the Census of Scotland* (Edinburgh: HMSO, 1967); and Samuel Lewis, *A Topographical Dictionary of Scotland Comprising the Several Counties, Islands, Cities, Burgh and Market Towns, Parishes and Principal Villages with Historical and Statistical Descriptions; Embellished with Engravings of the Seals and Arms of the Different Burghs and Universities*, 2 vols (London: S. Lewis, 1846).

[23]   Ian Donnachie, '"The Darker Side": A Speculative Survey of Scottish Crime during the First Half of the Nineteenth Century', *Scottish Economic and Social History* 15 (1995): 5. See also Ian Donnachie, 'Profiling Criminal Offences: The Evidence of the Lord Advocate's Papers during the First Half of the Nineteenth Century in Scotland', *Scottish Archives* 1 (1995): 85–92.

complete antithesis of the gentle, retiring, caring role of the female sex'.[24] It would appear to follow from this that if a woman was to commit an act of homicide, she would favour doing so in a manner that did not involve overt violence but rather act in a way that was relatively 'appropriate' for a member of the so-called gentler sex.[25]

Poisoning fits well with this description. Indeed, of all the methods used by women in murder cases brought before the Justiciary Court, poisoning was by far the most favoured approach, accounting for 20 of the 48 cases, the next most popular being strangulation (6 cases). However, women did not necessarily turn to poisoning due to revulsion at being involved in a violent crime, nor did they do so to compensate for a lack of physical strength. It is much more likely that women predominantly chose poisoning as it was much easier to conceal, both in administration and effect. It was for example, a lot less conspicuous and simpler for a woman to go to an apothecary to acquire rat poison than to go and purchase a firearm. It was also relatively easy for a woman, in the role of nursemaid or food preparer, to administer the poison. Also, as Pollak implies, as the symptoms of poisoning were not unlike those for other contemporary diseases, the actual act of murder was often hidden, unless there was any suggestion of foul play, such as an unexpectedly rapid death.[26] Of course, it could be argued that men could also resort to such tactics to commit homicide. However, they were less likely to be in a position or role which enabled them to administer the poison in the first instance without raising suspicion, and indeed of the 168 murder cases from lowland Scotland brought against men, only 6 involved poisoning.[27]

Certainly, poisoning showed a clear degree of premeditation, and in the English courts in the early modern period it was 'detested because it tapped a profound male fear of female deviousness; it was the ultimate horror even to conceive of the possibility that the polite yet secretive female might harbour dark homicidal urges under the mask of gentility'.[28] In Scotland in the eighteenth century, poisoning, perhaps in the context of the relatively recent witch-hunt, was considered threatening and deviant. Those brought before the Justiciary Court at this time for an alleged homicide involving poisoning were always charged with murder and never the lesser offence of culpable homicide. Having said this, however, not one of the 26 defendants involved in these cases was convicted. This was because the cause of death had to be clearly proven in poisoning cases.[29] Although this

---

[24] Smart, *Women, Crime and Criminology*, 16.

[25] For further discussion, see Carol Z. Wiener, 'Sex Roles in Late Elizabethan Hertfordshire', *Journal of Social History* 8 (1975): 49.

[26] For further discussion, see Pollak, *Criminality*, 17–18.

[27] For further discussion of the use of poison as a tool for committing homicide, see Katherine D. Watson, *Poisoned Lives: English Poisoners and Their Victims* (London: Hambledon and London, 2004).

[28] McLynn, *Crime and Punishment*, 119.

[29] For further discussion, see Hume, *Commentaries*, vol. 1, ch. 6, 288–90.

prerequisite did not deter prosecutors from doing their utmost to gain a conviction, cases were difficult to prove conclusively.

A good illustration of this (there are indeed many which could be cited) was the case of Jean Semple, who was accused of poisoning her husband, David Baird. The case was heard in Ayr during the summer of 1773.[30] Witnesses testified to a long history of abuse against the husband by his spouse, even quoting her exclamation that she would eventually 'ding the life out of him'. It was then testified by an apothecary that Jean Semple had bought some rat poison from him, despite the fact that the family kept several cats to stop rodent infestations. The deceased's eldest son, William Baird, swore on oath that his father, after eating porridge and milk, complained of 'a dry boke ... a great drouth [drought] and a pain in his Belly'. Despite this, his mother did not send for a doctor for three days, and David Baird subsequently died on the third of December 1772. A subsequent autopsy showed that the cause of death was arsenic poisoning.

Despite all of the evidence for the prosecution, the case turned on the testimony of Beana Cumming, a witness who had overheard a conversation between a Doctor Graham and the deceased, in which the former said to the latter, 'I gave you the poison to be given to the rats, not to be taken by yourself. Go home to your wife and drink a quantity of milk'. Jean Semple was found not guilty, was released from the bar and set at liberty. Poisoning cases in Scotland, as elsewhere, were notoriously difficult to prove in the early modern period.

Even though poison was the most popular *modus operandi* in female murder cases, accounting for 20 of the 48 cases, as mentioned previously, of the remaining 28 cases, 26 involved the use of overt violence.[31] These women, far from committing crimes in a feminine or gentle manner, were often brutal and bloodthirsty. In these instances, the need to be violent transcended gender and its associated stereotypes. Strangulations, drownings, batteries, slashings with razors, stabbings with knives, 'dashing brains out' with pokers and cudgels and stonings all appear in the remaining 26 cases. Certainly, the aggressive nature of these women cannot be doubted. Two examples further illustrate this.

The first involves charges brought before a Glasgow court in 1767 against Agnes Dougall. The indictment accused that in May 1767, Agnes had killed her 8-year-old daughter, Joanna, by slitting her throat with a table knife whilst they were out walking. When the defendant was asked how she could do such a thing to her own child, Agnes replied, 'the authorities gard [made] her do it, for that the Church Elders had threatened to put her into the Correction House for fornication and upon that account she had taken revenge upon her Child which had been begotten out of wedlock'.[32] Another case was brought against Isobel McLean in 1787. She was accused of the murder of her husband, Henry Small. Isobel had battered her husband, kicked him and trod on him. She then attacked him in the

---

[30]   National Records of Scotland (NRS) JC (Justiciary Court Records), 13/18.

[31]   In two cases, the method of murder was unspecified.

[32]   NRS JC 26/180.

legs with a razor. Whilst he was on the floor languishing from his wounds, Isobel then jumped on top of him and bit and tore at his facial flesh with her teeth. In consequence of the many wounds he had received, and the blood loss he had suffered, Henry Small died soon afterwards.[33]

The crime of culpable homicide is defined as 'a killing caused by fault which falls short of the evil intention required to constitute murder'.[34] Even in the nine charges of this nature brought against women in lowland Scotland during the period in question, six involved brutal attacks on the victim, the *modus operandi* in the remaining three cases being unspecified. Take, for example, the case of culpable homicide brought against Jean Inglis, a Dumfriesshire woman, in 1755.[35] This case was a private prosecution brought by the victim's husband, who described the accused as a midwife and former close companion of the deceased Margaret Sutherland. Jean Inglis was called for after Margaret Sutherland had gone into labour. Instead of caring for the woman in labour as would be expected of a midwife, Inglis 'bolted the door and rushed furiously upon her patient with a broken bottle, using her most barbarously and inhumanely and cutting out her bowel'. After her ordeal, Margaret Sutherland suffered 'a most extraordinary flooding' and died four days later.

The other culpable homicide cases contain similar evidence. It is clear that the line between degrees of 'evil intention' was a very fine one. Nevertheless, these cases were still categorized as culpable homicides because death was not instantaneous.

Another feature of female homicide in lowland Scotland between 1750 and 1815 is that in 77% of cases women acted alone. Men also predominantly murdered alone, but the incidence of their doing so was proportionately less than that of their female counterparts – 62% of the cases brought against them at the Justiciary Court. The exceptions to homicidal felons acting alone occurred when murders were committed in the furtherance of another offence, most typically violent thefts of one sort or another. These crimes were seen as being the 'grossest' of all violent activity by the authorities concerned and were most common when the victim offered resistance to being robbed or having property stolen.[36] However, such incidents were not that common. As McLynn argues, 'people who were driven by want, hunger, or greed to rob were not thereby disposed to murder, even when it might be expedient and prudent for them to do so'.[37] It would seem therefore that, rather than being seen as a means to an end, murder during the committal of another crime was only resorted to in the most desperate of situations.

---

[33] NRS JC 26/243.

[34] Mairi Robertson, gen. ed., *The Concise Scots Dictionary* (Aberdeen: Aberdeen University Press, 1985), 127.

[35] NRS JC 26/156.

[36] See, for instance, Beattie, *Crime and the Courts*, 78.

[37] McLynn, *Crime and Punishment*, 43.

There were obvious exceptions to this, and one such example was the case of the Adam sisters, Margaret and Agnes, which was brought in 1774. The court heard that on the 29th of October 1773, the sisters went into a Paisley inn to have a drink. When the other customers had left the premises, the sisters attacked the shop owner, a woman called Janet McIntyre. After locking the shop from the inside, the sisters attacked their victim, hitting her repeatedly over the head with a poker and then strangling her with their bare hands. They then stole just over 10 shillings from her person before making their escape.[38]

There is one further important identifiable aspect that links almost all of the primary source evidence relating to the incidence of indicted female homicidal activity in lowland Scotland. In the overwhelming majority of cases, the victim and the offender were either related or acquainted. This seems to be a fairly common feature of this type of violent crime. Sharpe, Beattie, McLynn and Ruff all agree that the majority of women brought to court upon a charge of homicide in the early modern period 'were accused of killing someone within their own domestic circle or at least their own neighbourhood'.[39] Indeed, between 1750 and 1815, some 58% of *all* family homicides were charged against lowland Scottish women. Furthermore, if the number of cases in which the victim simply 'knew' his or her aggressor is added to this, the figures are even more startling: 88% of all homicides charged against females were allegedly committed against relations or acquaintances, compared with 27% of the cases charged against males.

Some explanations for this gender disparity relate to the apparently limited social activity of women.[40] Women were clearly less likely than men to become involved in disputes with strangers of a kind that might result in homicidal violence. As women were said rarely to visit taverns and alehouses, they generally were not offered and therefore did not accept challenges to fights and brawls, and as a result, they were less likely to be placed in a situation where a murder or culpable homicide charge could result. However, little evidence exists from the Justiciary Court material to confirm these arguments. Whatever the case, it is clear that Donnachie's comment that 'There was an almost equal mix of intra-family and extra-family murder',[41] which is based on his study of the Lord Advocate's papers of early nineteenth-century Scotland, cannot be readily applied to the material studied here.

The motives for homicides both within the domestic sphere and beyond are hard to determine from the indictments of the Justiciary Court due to the relative lack of importance which the Scottish courts placed on the issue of premeditation. Where

---

[38]   NAS JC 26/198.

[39]   Beattie, 'Criminality', 83. See also Ruff, *Crime, Justice and Public Order*, 80; McLynn, *Crime and Punishment*, 46 and 117; and James A. Sharpe, 'Domestic Homicide in Early Modern England', *Historical Journal* 24 (1981): 29–48.

[40]   For further discussion, see Beattie, 'Criminality', 84, and McLynn, *Crime and Punishment*, 122–23.

[41]   Donnachie, '"The Darker Side"', 14.

motives can be discerned from the evidence, they are very much case specific, and this makes it virtually impossible to draw any meaningful conclusions about the background to this type of violent crime – indeed, there were rarely witnesses to homicidal acts. Nevertheless, it is possible to draw some tentative conclusions. It is clear that in the lowlands between 1750 and 1815, the most common victim in domestic homicides was the husband. As Sharpe suggests, 'domestic strife was a familiar enough phenomenon. ... It is only to be expected that such strife would sometimes erupt into acts of overt violence'.[42] Although Sharpe is writing with reference to seventeenth-century England, his comments are readily applicable to late eighteenth- and early nineteenth-century Scotland, and even to the present day. Smart describes most domestic homicides as being 'victim precipitated', that is, cases where 'the eventual victim was the original aggressor'.[43] It must often have been the case that women on the receiving end of years of physical and mental abuse (with divorce or abandoning the household not an option in economic terms or otherwise) built up tensions, jealousies and hatred over that time which would eventually result in a sudden outburst of spontaneous violence. This could take the form of either a 'hot-blooded' act of homicide or a simple act of self-defence. The evidence of the instruments used in the committal of these offences by the indicted women of lowland Scotland lends weight to this argument. With the exception of poison and two cases involving stones, the assaults were carried out using household objects near at hand when tempers frayed, such as razors, kitchen knives, pokers and cudgels.

Indeed, it is perhaps surprising that *more* wives did not kill their husbands in the light of the dictatorial and abusive relationships that are suspected to have existed at this time. However, for many women living as economic dependents in already impoverished conditions, the removal of the breadwinner from the household, no matter how beneficial and attractive a prospect in the short-term, would only have worsened the long-term situation for her and the mouths she had to feed.

It is harder to determine the motives for the killing of other family members and also of neighbours and acquaintances, although monetary disputes were often the initial source of tension in these instances. Of course, in some cases no motive existed at all, as the accused individual concerned was clearly insane, but only in the most severe cases was this brought to the attention of the court.[44]

In terms of the indictments for homicide brought before the Justiciary Court in relation to lowland Scotland between 1750 and 1815, the hypothesis cited at the outset of this chapter that in general women were insignificant participants in violent criminality appears to have been proven to apply, at least in part. Although some interesting patterns develop from a close analysis of female homicidal

---

[42] Sharpe, 'Domestic Homicide', 31.

[43] Smart, *Women, Crime and Criminology*, 17.

[44] Only three males and one female were declared insane by the court in relation to all the alleged offences committed in lowland Scotland and indicted at the Justiciary Court between 1750 and 1815.

activity, the incidence of such activity is relatively rare in comparison with the male involvement in murder and culpable homicide. It is perhaps plausible to argue that as women's social spheres were relatively restricted, they were less likely to carry weapons, less likely to become involved in fatal brawls with strangers or to accept challenges to duels, and in turn therefore more likely to be restricted in the types of violent offences they committed, at least in comparison to men.

However, the fact that more than half of the indicted lowland Scottish women had used extreme violence in their homicidal activities suggests that, although their crimes were relatively few in number, they could behave just as aggressively in the committal of this type of criminal activity as their male counterparts. Consequently, the second part of the hypothesis being tested – namely, that women committed crimes less violently and less aggressively than men – cannot be readily applied to the lowland Scottish women indicted for homicide at the Justiciary Court in the early modern period.

According to Beattie, 'Assault charges could arise from such a wide variety of events and behavior. ... they do not form a category of offence that can be usefully analyzed from the court records'.[45] Sharpe concurs with Beattie, in this respect at least, when he suggests that the wide-ranging definition of assault makes that crime a poor 'barometer of violence'.[46] The problem which both these scholars faced in their research is that in England assault was very much a non-specific umbrella-term for every offence from a life-threatening incident down to a petty squabble. As a result of this, coherent analysis of the English experience of assault appears to have been difficult to achieve.

In Scotland, even though the definition of assault in the eighteenth and nineteenth centuries was 'an intentional physical attack upon the person, either seriously threatened or actually accomplished',[47] when a given case actually came to court, the categories of the offence were much more specific. Attempted murder, 'common' aggravated assault,[48] aggravated assault of authority, rape and sexual assault[49] and a series of minor offences, such as gross insult and abuse, violent threatenings and writing incendiary letters, were all charged in the indictments and warrants of the Justiciary Court. The clear distinction between crimes of this nature makes a closer scrutiny of the offence more practical in the case of lowland Scotland between 1750 and 1815, than it would be for contemporary England, or indeed contemporary Ireland or France for that matter, where similar problems to

---

[45]   Beattie, *Crime and the Courts*, 75–76.

[46]   Sharpe, *Crime in Seventeenth Century England*, 119. For further expansion of this opinion, see 117–19.

[47]   Archibald M. Anderson, *The Criminal Law of Scotland*, 2nd ed., part 2 (Edinburgh: Bell and Bradfute, 1904), 158.

[48]   I have used the word 'common' to distinguish this type of assault from assault against authority.

[49]   As no women were charged even with being accessory to this offence between 1750 and 1815, it does not warrant close attention in this study.

those encountered by Beattie and Sharpe exist.[50] In any case, as assault in general terms was the most common single crime against the person that was brought before the Justiciary Court in lowland Scotland, a 'closer scrutiny' of this type of offence is surely vital for any understanding of indicted violent criminality during the period under review.

Although comparisons with other studies can be imperfect for the reasons suggested above, it is still interesting to note that Sharpe calculates women's participation in assault in seventeenth-century Essex at 8.1% of the total number of cases,[51] and Beattie at nearly 20% for eighteenth-century Surrey.[52] However, in lowland Scotland between 1750 and 1815 women were involved in 37%, or 291 out of 791 indictments.[53] In addition, if a similar analysis is done of individual types of assault, in some instances it is clear that women participated just as often if not more frequently than men in certain types of violent offences against the person. This point will be considered in more detail below.

Two hundred and ninety-one lowland Scottish women were brought before the Justiciary Court between 1750 and 1815 charged with committing an act of assault.[54] More women were indicted for this type of criminal behaviour than for any other at the Justiciary Court during the 65-year period being analyzed. Assault charges constituted some 30% of all the offences brought to the Justiciary Court against lowland Scottish women between 1750 and 1815. In a significant 73% of cases, the alleged crime was committed in a rural area. This evidence would appear to be in conflict with the contention of Donnachie that Scottish crimes, and especially violent offences, were committed predominantly in urban

---

[50]   For instance, as well as Beattie, *Crime and the Courts*, 75–76, and Sharpe, *Crime in Seventeenth-Century England*, 117–19, Gillespie, 'Women and Crime', 43–51, dealing with seventeenth-century Ireland, and Ruff, *Crime, Justice and Public Order*, 70–105, dealing with the south-west of France in the eighteenth century, do not distinguish between categories of assault, although Ruff makes the distinction between physical and verbal 'violence'.

[51]   My calculation on the evidence presented; see Sharpe, *Crime in Seventeenth-Century England*, 117.

[52]   This figure is given in relation to the general category Beattie denotes as 'Assault and Wounding', rather than 'Assault on Constables, etc.'. This is the only distinction he makes relating to the crime of assault; see Beattie, 'Criminality', 85.

[53]   This figure rises to 40% if comparisons between men and women are made in only the crimes for which women were indicted, i.e., discounting rape and other sexual offences.

[54]   Fourteen of these women were declared 'fugitate' by the court. This means their names had been called out three times in court and at the door of the courthouse, but they had failed to appear to answer to the charges against them. Consequently, the individuals were declared outlaws and had all of their movable goods and gear confiscated to the use of the Crown, rendering them bankrupt. In some instances, the full-length indictments were reduced to minute form when the court realized that a defendant was absent, and as a result, certain details relating to a case were not recorded. However, this was not true of the 14 instances referred to here.

locations.[55] This fact also stands in stark contrast to the evidence from the homicide indictments, where the favoured *locus operandi* was the town rather than the country. Also, as was not the case with recorded homicides, lowland Scottish men and women rarely acted alone when perpetrating assaults. Although the difference in male cases between those acting alone and those acting with others is only slightly in favour of the latter, in the case of women the difference is significant: 90% of women were charged along with co-accused (including relatives), and only 10% acted alone. Rather than being involved in face-to-face confrontation as individuals, women were more likely to join others (both male and female), not necessarily to compensate for a lack of physical prowess, but more likely because of a common interest or motive. Perhaps this was often in the face of a perceived threat to their personal livelihood or that of their family. One woman wielding a stick and throwing stones might not be taken as seriously as a group of 20 doing so. It is to the various methods employed by the lowland Scottish women indicted for assault that this study will now turn.

The first types of assault to be addressed are attempted murder and 'common' aggravated assault. Considered together, these offences counted for more than a third of all the assault charges brought against lowland Scottish women at the Justiciary Court between 1750 and 1815. However, in comparison with male involvement in this type of crime against the person, Beattie's hypothesis, mentioned above, that women were less often involved in crimes of a violent nature appears to hold true.[56] Lowland Scottish men were more than twice as likely to commit an act of attempted murder or 'common' aggravated assault as their female counterparts.[57] Consequently, although women were slightly more involved in these types of offences than they were in homicides, a similar lack of participation in violent criminal activity relative to men is still in evidence.

There are, however, clear distinctions between women's participation in homicidal activity and their involvement in 'common' aggravated assault and attempted murder. Unlike homicide, where poisoning was a predominant *modus operandi*, the methods used by women to commit attempted murder and 'common' aggravated assault were much more overt and brutal in nature. Beatings with sticks, stonings, and, to a lesser extent, attacks with knives and other instruments both sharp and blunt are common in the indictment evidence. Women would also use their hands in these kinds of assaults, but not nearly to the same extent as their male counterparts, where this method overwhelmingly predominated due to their frequent participation in brawling and fist fights. A few examples will serve

---

[55]   Donnachie, "'The Darker Side"', 5.

[56]   Beattie, 'Criminality', 82.

[57]   Two hundred and forty lowland Scottish men were indicted for these offences, compared to 109 women. In percentage terms, this meant that 69% of the indicted attempted murders and 'common' aggravated assaults were committed by lowland Scottish men and 31% by lowland Scottish women.

to demonstrate the aggressive and violent nature of the indicted lowland Scottish women's acts of attempted murder and 'common' aggravated assault.

The first of these involved a Wigtown woman, Agnes Keir, in 1766. The court heard that Agnes harboured ill-feelings towards her husband, Alexander, expressing on several occasions 'the strongest desire of his death'. On the night of Saturday the 28th of September 1765, Agnes became increasingly annoyed by her husband's complaints about the meal she had prepared. In consequence of their disagreement, she seized a chopping knife and hit her husband on the shin, making a large wound and fracturing his leg in several places.[58] Another case was brought before the High Court of Justiciary in Edinburgh in 1750 involving charges against Mary McFarlane and her two daughters. They stood accused of the assault of their former servant Elizabeth Algie. Algie had lost several articles of the defendants' clothing after taking some washing to be laundered. As a result, the defendants beat their servant in the face with their fists, tore her clothes from her and then shut her out of their house in the dead of night, with the intention that she should freeze to death or be attacked.[59]

With regard to women committing an act of attempted murder or 'common' aggravated assault in the furtherance of another offence, the evidence suggests that the indicted women would far more readily commit an assault in these circumstances than a homicide. However, as in the majority of cases the ultimate objective was theft in one form or another, these crimes will not be dealt with here in any detail. Overall, the lowland Scottish evidence relating to the women indicted for attempted murder and 'common' aggravated assault at the Justiciary Court between 1750 and 1815 shows that women were not afraid to behave aggressively when the situation warranted that kind of behaviour. Evidence to substantiate this suggestion comes in that category of crimes against the person known as the assault of authority.

In 82% of the cases charged against women between 1750 and 1815 relating to lowland Scotland, the assault of authority was coupled with the crime of deforcement. Deforcement is defined by Hume as 'the hindrance or resistance to officers of the law, in the execution of their duty'.[60] Together, these two crimes were considered extremely serious offences by the Scottish law courts. As Hume explains, a crime of this nature

> cannot be considered by the law as a venial transgression. The reprehension due to it, is not only on account of the high damage which may attend the hindrance, etc. in the particular instance; but also, and more especially, because it is a contempt of the authority of the King, as represented by his Courts of Justice, and in the course of legal process; and is thus a matter of evil and very dangerous

---

[58]   NRS JC 26/177.

[59]   NRS JC 3/27.

[60]   Hume, *Commentaries*, vol. 1, ch. 8, 386.

example, which tends to the unhinging of government, and to intercept the benefits of the state of civil union.[61]

Given the apparent serious nature of this type of offence, it might be expected that female participation in such crimes would be somewhat limited, in line with the other 'heinous' offences studied. Beattie's investigation into female criminality in eighteenth-century England would appear to confirm this theory, as less than a fifth of the total number of individuals indicted for 'assaults on constables' were women.[62] However, in lowland Scotland during the period in question, 181 cases of aggravated assault of authority were brought against women, compared to 180 brought against men. Unfortunately, for the reasons previously stated, no other study gives comparable data for these types of offences, but in the Scottish case, at least, this type of 'female militancy' was not uncommon. Highland women, for instance, were consistently at the forefront of the resistance against oppression in the context of the Highland Clearances.[63] The weapons used to carry out these attacks on authority in the Highland areas were much the same as those employed by the women in south-west Scotland decades earlier. In 170 of the 181 cases cited, sticks and stones were the favoured implements.

A few examples may help to illustrate the type of behaviour exhibited by lowland Scottish women in their assaults on authority. The first is a case that was brought to the High Court of Justiciary in Edinburgh in 1758, and was charged against seven women. The assize found it proven that all of the women attacked John McChlery, a Sheriff Officer in Newton Stewart who had come to collect fines levied against individuals who had been retailing alcohol without a licence. The women laid violent hands on McChlery and attacked him with clubs and sticks, causing a great effusion of blood. One of the women sat on the victim's face, causing his nose to break, and others rubbed manure in his hair, whilst forcing the warrants he had brought into his mouth. They then tore his clothes from him, and dragged him towards the sea. It is the victim's belief that the women would have drowned him, had he not been rescued by some passersby.[64]

The second example is a case brought before the South Circuit Court in 1781 against five individuals, three of them women. The court heard that on the 3rd of November 1780, revenue officers seized a box of tea at Port William (Wigtownshire). The defendants then tried to rescue the box of tea by violently assaulting the chief customs official. They dragged the man to the ground, and as the male defendants held him down, the female defendants attacked him with razors and then 'beat him and abused him most cruelly wherein his lower lip was

---

[61]   Hume, *Commentaries*, vol. 1, ch. 8, 386.

[62]   My calculation of the evidence presented; see Beattie, 'Criminality', 85.

[63]   Malcolm MacLean and Christopher Carrell, eds, *As an Fhearann = From the Land* (Edinburgh: Mainstream, 1986), 23.

[64]   NRS JC 26/161.

torn off to the great effusion of his blood and danger of his life'.[65] In their actions against authority, the women of lowland Scotland clearly showed that they were ready, willing and able to fulfil the role of protector whenever necessary and to use whatever force was required to do so.

In cases of attempted murder or 'common' aggravated assault, as with homicides, victims were seldom strangers. Sharpe quotes Malinowski's observation that 'aggression, like charity, begins at home'[66] and then cites William Gouge, who said that 'the nearer and dearere any persons be, the more violent will be that hatred which is fastened on them'.[67] While this was undoubtedly the case in lowland Scotland, the reported incidence of attempted murder and 'common' aggravated assault committed by females within the domestic circle is relatively slight, certainly in comparison with homicide. Only 26% of the lowland Scottish women indicted for an attempted murder or a 'common' aggravated assault at the Justiciary Court between 1750 and 1815 were alleged to have committed an offence of this nature in the home.[68]

Motives for attempted murder and 'common' aggravated assault in the domestic sphere could stem from the mere refusal to do a prescribed task, accusations of impropriety in terms of either relationships or criminal activity, self-defence or even the accidental breakage of crockery: 'trivial disagreements tended to lead rapidly to blows.'[69] Typically, however, all these motives were very much related to the environment in which the eventual act of aggression was to occur. Outside the home, motives were more diverse in origin.

An overwhelming percentage – 74% – of all offences of this nature allegedly perpetrated by lowland Scottish women were committed against neighbours and acquaintances, compared with 36% of those charged against lowland Scottish men. According to Lawrence Stone, 'Quarrels, beatings and lawsuits were the predominant pastimes of the village' in England during the early modern period, where 'intense ... personal hostility of one individual towards another' meant that 'expressions of hatred' reached high 'levels of frequency, intensity and duration'.[70] This atmosphere of antagonism seems to have been prevalent also in the lowland of Scotland in the eighteenth century, as Marion Stewart describes for Dumfries at that time: 'There was a great deal of brawling and violence, drunkenness and assault' and what she terms a 'general rumbustiousness'.[71]

---

[65]   NRS JC 26/223.

[66]   Bronislaw Malinowski, quoted in Sharpe, *Crime in Seventeenth-Century England*, 120.

[67]   William Gouge, quoted in Sharpe, *Crime in Seventeenth-Century England*, 120.

[68]   The few instances of this type of indictment – only 28 cases – are most likely a result of under-reporting.

[69]   Lawrence Stone, *The Family, Sex and Marriage, 1500–1800* (London: Weidenfeld and Nicolson, 1977), 93.

[70]   Stone, *Family*, 94–95 and 99.

[71]   Marion M. Stewart, '"In Durance Vile": Crime and Punishment in Seventeenth- and Eighteenth-Century Records of Dumfries', *Scottish Archives* 1 (1995): 71.

Disputes involving women and their neighbours and acquaintances that resulted in violent assault were motivated by a variety of factors, such as money or disputes over land ownership, property damage, trespassing, ridicule and slander, drunkenness and a prolonged history of bitterness between the parties involved. Often, assaults took place as a result of a need for defensive action in the face of a real or perceived threat to someone's material well-being. There are indeed numerous examples throughout history and also in the present day of women going to great and at times inordinate lengths to protect their family and its livelihood. It would be surprising if the maternal instincts of women in lowland Scotland in the late eighteenth and early nineteenth centuries were any different. Whether or not such 'threats' existed, or whether these women suffered from paranoia or hypersensitivity, is more difficult to determine. What one family sees as a menace, another might disregard completely.

Some similarities can be drawn between the motives of the lowland Scottish women indicted for ordinary assault and those charged with assault of authority. Rarely acting alone, and as in the cases of attempted murder and 'common' aggravated assault, the women involved in these offences were reacting to anticipated perceived threats to their own or their families' livelihood. Predominantly, in lowland Scotland, the victims of these attacks were law officers, messengers, constables, sheriff-officers and the like, attempting to serve warrants of arrest on the spouse, close relative or acquaintance of their aggressor. The threat of the removal of the breadwinner from the household or a loved one from the community was a startling enough prospect for these women to be stimulated into overt action.

Women were also involved in crimes in which the ultimate intention was the seizure of goods (whether smuggled or otherwise) without payment of duty. Although the resulting assault and deforcement of revenue and excise officers was proportionately more often associated with male offenders, just over a quarter of the lowland Scottish women charged with assault of authority were accused of these types of offences.

Aside from the zeal of the authorities to prosecute offenders involved in assaults of this nature and the protective instincts which have been previously mentioned, what other theories can be offered to explain the considerable level of female participation in these acts of manifest violence? In the case of aggravated assaults against law officers in which women predominated, it could be argued that in many instances the men whom these officers were trying to arrest (as it was indeed, on the whole, a male upon whom they were trying to serve a warrant) were hardly likely to make their job an easy one and must often have been in hiding, leaving the women to face the authorities. Less deviously, the lack of male participation in this particular offence could be attributed to their being out at work, away on business or overseas on military service at the time the authorities arrived to arrest them. The officers' insistence on thoroughly and often recklessly searching the premises, regardless of the woman's explanations for the absence of her spouse, may well have incited many women to enlist the help of others to deforce and assault the sheriffs and constables who were invading, disrupting and vandalizing their households and property.

In cases of offences against revenue and excise officers, where men and women often joined forces in their attacks, but where females regularly made up the vanguard, it could be supposed that the offenders believed the authorities would behave more leniently towards the women on account of their sex. But this is not a very convincing argument. It is more likely that, in simple economic terms, the household could not afford to have the male wage-earner arrested. Women, in their role of mothers and homemakers, could be easily replaced by a relative, if taken into custody; men, in their role as providers, could not.

In general terms, lowland Scottish men far outnumbered their female counterparts in indictments for assault at the Justiciary Court between 1750 and 1815. This would seem to confirm Beattie's assertion, cited at the outset of this chapter, that women committed crime, and violent crime in particular, less often than men. However, further analysis of the evidence shows that in the category of assault of authority, at least, there were actually *more* lowland Scottish women indicted than lowland Scottish men. In addition, of the individuals indicted for all types of assault, women behaved just as violently as men, using whatever degree of violence was deemed necessary to meet their ends. Scottish women were active, independent participants in violent criminality. The way in which the lowland Scottish women indicted for assault differed from their male counterparts, however, was that, although often spontaneous, female criminal activity of this nature was frequently motivated and therefore regularly premeditated, albeit in varying degrees from case to case. Lowland Scottish men, on the other hand, were predominantly involved in sporadic acts of *random* violence.

Overall, then, it seems that the incidence of lowland Scottish women being brought before the Justiciary Court charged with the crimes against the person of homicides and assaults does suggest that women committed these types of offences less frequently than their male counterparts. However, only in murder and culpable homicide cases did they commit their offences less aggressively than the men similarly accused. Certainly, what this work has shown is that attempts by historians to dismiss female criminal activity, and violent female criminal activity in particular, due to its lesser incidence, and then to infer as a result that women must have behaved less aggressively in the committal of such offences than their male counterparts, cannot be justified.

Works Cited

Primary Sources

Manuscript Sources
National Records of Scotland. Justiciary Court Records, JC 3/27; JC 13/18; JC 26/156; JC 26/161; JC 26/177; JC 26/180; JC 26/198; JC 26/223; JC 26/243.

Printed Primary Source

Hume, David. *Commentaries on the Law of Scotland, respecting the Description and Punishment of* Crimes. 2 vols. Edinburgh, 1797. [National Library of Scotland H.27.a.10].

Secondary Sources

Anderson, Archibald M. *The Criminal Law of Scotland*, part 2, 2nd ed. Edinburgh: Bell and Bradfute, 1904.

Barker, Hannah, and Elaine Chalus, eds. *Gender in Eighteenth-Century England: Roles, Representations and Responsibilities*. Harlow: Longman, 1997.

Bartholomew, John G., ed. *The Survey Gazetteer of the British Isles Topographical, Statistical and Commercial, Compiled from the 1911 Census and the Latest Official Returns*. Edinburgh: John Bartholomew and Co., 1914.

Beattie, John M. *Crime and the Courts in England, 1600–1800*. Oxford: Clarendon Press, 1986.

———. 'The Criminality of Women in Eighteenth-Century England'. *Journal of Social History* 8 (1975): 80–116.

Bohstedt, John. 'Gender, Household and Community Politics: Women in English Riots 1790–1810'. *Past and Present* 120 (1988): 88–122.

Clark, Anna. *Women's Silence, Men's Violence: Sexual Assault in England 1770–1845*. London: Pandora, 1987.

Clark, Sandra. *Women and Crime in the Street Literature of Early Modern England*. Basingstoke: Palgrave Macmillan, 2003.

Cockburn, James S., ed. *Crime in England, 1550–1800*. London: Methuen, 1977.

Donnachie, Ian. '"The Darker Side": A Speculative Survey of Scottish Crime during the First Half of the Nineteenth Century'. *Scottish Economic and Social History* 15 (1995): 5–24.

———. 'Profiling Criminal Offences: The Evidence of the Lord Advocate's Papers during the First Half of the Nineteenth Century in Scotland'. *Scottish Archives* 1 (1995): 85–92.

Emsley, Clive. *Crime and Society in England, 1750–1900*. 2nd ed. London: Longman, 1996.

Falconer, Robert. *Crime and Community in Reformation Scotland: Negotiating Power in a Burgh Society*. London: Pickering and Chatto, 2013.

Foyster, Elizabeth A. *Marital Violence: An English Family History, 1660–1857*. Cambridge: Cambridge University Press, 2005.

Gillespie, Raymond. 'Women and Crime in Seventeenth-Century Ireland'. In *Women in Early Modern Ireland*. Edited by Margaret MacCurtain and Mary O'Dowd. Edinburgh: Edinburgh University Press, 1991. 43–52.

Hanawalt, Barbara. 'The Female Felon in Fourteenth-Century England'. *Viator* 5 (1974): 251–73.

Henry, Brian. *Dublin Hanged: Crime, Law Enforcement and Punishment in Late Eighteenth-Century Dublin*. Blackrock: Irish Academic Press, 1994.

Howard, Sharon. *Law and Disorder in Early Modern Wales: Crime and Authority in the Denbighshire Courts, c. 1660–1730*. Cardiff: University of Wales Press, 2008.

Hurl-Eamon, Jennine. *Gender and Petty Violence in London, 1680–1820*. Columbus: Ohio State University Press, 2005.

Ingram, Martin. '"Scolding Women Cucked or Washed": A Crisis in Gender Relations in Early Modern England?' In *Women, Crime and the Courts in Early Modern England*. Edited by Jennifer Kermode and Garthine Walker. London: UCL Press, 1994. 48–80.

Jackson, Mark. *New-Born Child Murder: Women, Illegitimacy and the Courts in Eighteenth-Century England*. Manchester: Manchester University Press, 1996.

Kilday, Anne-Marie. *A History of Infanticide in Britain c. 1600 to the Present*. Basingstoke: Palgrave, 2013.

———. 'Women and Crime in South-west Scotland, 1750–1815: A Study of the Justiciary Court Records'. PhD thesis, University of Strathclyde, 1998.

———. *Women and Violent Crime in Enlightenment Scotland*. Woodbridge: Royal Historical Society/Boydell Press, 2007.

King, Peter. 'Gender, Crime and Justice in Late Eighteenth- and Early Nineteenth-Century England'. In *Gender and Crime in Modern Europe*. Edited by Margaret L. Arnot and Cornelie Usborne. London: UCL Press, 1999. 44–74.

Lewis, Samuel. *A Topographical Dictionary of Scotland Comprising the Several Counties, Islands, Cities, Burgh and Market Towns, Parishes and Principal Villages with Historical and Statistical Descriptions; Embellished with Engravings of the Seals and Arms of the Different Burghs and Universities*. 2 vols. London: S. Lewis, 1846.

MacLean, Malcolm, and Christopher Carrell, eds. *As an Fhearann = From the Land*. Edinburgh: Mainstream, 1986.

McLynn, Frank. *Crime and Punishment in Eighteenth-Century England*. London: Routledge, 1989.

Martin, Randall. *Women, Murder and Equity in Early Modern England*. London: Routledge, 2008.

Place Names and Population, Scotland: An Alphabetical List of Populated Places Derived from the Census of Scotland. Edinburgh: HMSO, 1967.

Pollak, Otto. *The Criminality of Women*. Philadelphia: University of Pennsylvania Press, 1950.

Robertson, Mairi, gen. ed. *The Concise Scots Dictionary*. Aberdeen: Aberdeen University Press, 1985.

Ruff, Julius R. *Crime, Justice and Public Order in Old Regime France: The Sénéchaussées of Libourne and Bazas, 1696–1789*. London: Croom Helm, 1984.

Sellar, W. David H. 'Forethocht Felony, Malice Aforethought and the Classification of Homicide'. In *Legal History in the Making: Proceedings of the Ninth British Legal History Conference: Glasgow, 1989*. Edited by William M. Gordon and Thomas D. Fergus. London: Hambledon, 1991. 43–59.

Sharpe, James A. *Crime in Early Modern England 1550–1750*. 2nd ed. London: Longman, 1999.

———. *Crime in Seventeenth Century England – A County Study*. Cambridge: Cambridge University Press, 1983.

———. 'Domestic Homicide in Early Modern England'. *Historical Journal* 24 (1981): 29–48.

Sharpe, James A., and Richard Golden, eds. *English Witchcraft, 1560–1736*. London: Pickering and Chatto, 2003.

Shoemaker, Robert B. *Gender in English Society, 1650–1850: The Emergence of Separate Spheres?* London: Longman, 1998.

———. *Prosecution and Punishment: Petty Crime and the Law in London and Rural Middlesex, c. 1660–1725*. Cambridge: Cambridge University Press, 1991.

Smart, Carol. *Women, Crime and Criminology: A Feminist Critique* London: Routledge and Kegan Paul, 1977.

Spierenburg, Pieter. 'How Violent Were Women? Court Cases in Amsterdam, 1650–1810'. *Crime, History and Societies* 1 (1997): 9–28.

Stewart, Marion M. '"In Durance Vile": Crime and Punishment in Seventeenth and Eighteenth Century Records of Dumfries'. *Scottish Archives* 1 (1995): 63–74.

Stone, Lawrence. *The Family, Sex and Marriage, 1500–1800*. London: Weidenfeld and Nicolson, 1977.

Thomis, Malcolm I., and Jennifer Grimmett. *Women in Protest 1800–1850*. London: Croom Helm, 1982.

Walker, Garthine. *Crime, Gender and Social Order in Early Modern England*. Cambridge: Cambridge University Press, 2003.

Walker, Garthine, and Jennifer Kermode. 'Introduction' to *Women, Crime and the Courts in Early Modern England*. Edited by Jennifer Kermode and Garthine Walker. London: UCL Press, 1994. 1–25.

Watson, Katherine D. *Poisoned Lives: English Poisoners and Their Victims*. London: Hambledon and London, 2004.

Wiener, Carol Z. 'Sex Roles in Late Elizabethan Hertfordshire'. *Journal of Social History* 8 (1975): 38–60.

Wiltenburg, Joy. *Disorderly Women and Female Power in the Street Literature of Early Modern England and Germany*. Charlottesville: University Press of Virginia, 1992.

Chapter 9
'The lowest and most abandoned trull of a soldier': The Crime of Bastardy in Early Eighteenth-Century London[1]

Jennine Hurl-Eamon

Illegitimate pregnancies placed eighteenth-century women in a legal grey area. As Theodore Barlow told justices in 1745, 'the getting of Bastards' was 'of a mixt Nature', being, to varying degrees, both a crime committed by the pregnant woman and a crime against her.[2] Even more overtly than other crimes, bastardy focused upon the poor, its policing motivated above all by the fear that illegitimate babies would have to be maintained by the parish. Abandoned wives or single women who found themselves pregnant without a good way to provide for their offspring faced – at best – a humiliating interview before a Justice of the Peace, where they had to recount details of the intercourse which led to the pregnancy, and identify the father.

At worst, two JPs sitting at petty sessions could sentence a woman to life imprisonment, if she had previously born a bastard kept on parish charity.[3] Her behaviour was not only an 'example and encouragement of Lewdness'; it also

[1]   The quotation comes from Henry Fielding, *Amelia*, 4 vols (London: A. Millar, 1752), 1: 50. Research for the chapter was funded by a Faculty Research Grant from the Social Sciences and Humanities Research Council of Canada. The author also wishes to thank Nicholas Rogers for commenting on an earlier draft and generously lending his microfilm copy of the Westminster Bastardy Examinations. John Black also kindly provided suggestions on the earlier draft, along with his unpublished work on the subject, both of which were extremely helpful. Their criticisms have benefited the final product enormously, but I take full responsibility for any errors that remain.

[2]   Theodore Barlow, *The Justice of the Peace, a Treatise Containing the Power and Duty of That Magistrate, etc.* (London, 1745), 582.

[3]   First offenders could also be imprisoned up to one year, 'to be punished daily, for therefore she is sent thither, (as I conceive)' (Michael Dalton, *The Country Justice* [London, 1705], 41). For an example of an order against a second offender, see the order against Sarah Fildes in William Hunt, *The Justicing Notebook of William Hunt, 1744–1749*, ed. Elizabeth Critall (Devizes: Wiltshire Record Society, 1982), 85, entry 182.

'defraud[ed] the impotent and aged *true Poor* of the Parish' by placing an ill-gotten babe in the relief queue.[4]

The latter fact motivated much of the legal activity against bastard-bearers in eighteenth-century England. Like the crime of infanticide, bastard-bearing subjected its female suspects to community surveillance.[5] Pregnant women in this category could trust no one; ratepayers were likely to report any single woman, widow or deserted wife with a big belly.[6] Once JPs became aware of her presence within the parish, they compelled her to appear before them and identify the father. Those who refused to do so could face punishment, such as Pheebe Hams, who was incarcerated in 1751 after saying 'That if the Justices insisted That she should declare the Father of her last Child She would go away and leave her 3 Children to the Parish'.[7] Elizabeth Brace, on the other hand, who appeared before the same Hackney justice two years later to say that she did not know the father of her baby due to her abundance of sexual partners, was not punished.[8]

As a resident of Hackney, just north of the City, Brace may offer insight into the distinct character of the administration of bastardy offences in the eighteenth-century metropolis. Historians may disagree over the details of the way in which the poor relief laws were administered in England, but they all concede that the provincial overseers of the poor functioned quite differently from those in the capital.[9] London's population size and density made it impossible to police the

---

[4]   J. Bond, *A Compleat Guide for Justices of Peace, etc.* (London, 1707), part 2, 41–42; emphasis added. Feminine lewdness alone could – in theory – merit serious punishment. The law stated that even a woman whose baby was not a burden on public funds could nonetheless be publicly whipped (Bond, *Compleat Guide*, 39; William Nelson, *The Office and Authority of a Justice of Peace, etc.* [London, 1711], 85; Giles Jacob, *The Compleat Parish-officer, etc.* [London, 1729], 121).

[5]   Laura Gowing, *Women, Touch and Power in Seventeenth-Century England* (New Haven, CT: Yale University Press, 2003), 138–48.

[6]   Barlow, *Justice of the Peace*, 59, includes the example of an information by a yeoman's wife of a woman pregnant with a bastard. Constables were also obligated to present the names of 'Mothers of Bastards, … or such as are likely to be chargeable to the Parish wherein they reside' (P. S., *A Help to Magistrates, and Ministers of Justice, etc.* [London, 1721], 135). The few extant JPs' notebooks suggest that overseers were alerted about questionable pregnancies and it was they who brought the complaint to a JP, but occasionally the woman came forward voluntarily. For an example of the latter, see Hunt, *Justicing Notebook*, 46, entry 292, and Henry Norris, *Justice in Eighteenth-Century Hackney: The Justicing Notebook of Henry Norris and the Hackney Sessions Book*, ed. Ruth Paley (London, 1991), 145, entry 899.

[7]   Norris, *Justice*, ed. Paley, 179, entry 1063. Paley notes that Hams's illegitimate daughter was 'not actually chargeable to the parish'.

[8]   Norris, *Justice*, ed. Paley, 199, entry 1137, n. 1.

[9]   See Dorothy Marshall, *The English Poor in the Eighteenth Century: A Study in Social and Administrative History* (New York: A. M. Kelley, 1969), 164–67; J. S. Taylor, 'The Impact of Pauper Settlement, 1691–1834', *Past and Present* 73 (1976): 60–61; K. D. M. Snell, 'Pauper Settlement and the Right to Poor Relief in England and Wales',

poor as closely, which most likely worked to the advantage of both the women and men involved in illegitimacy proceedings. Hackney officials would be unable to countenance outright defiance such as that shown by Pheebe Hams, but were not driven to punish Brace, since she appeared to answer their questions as well as she was able. The fact that Brace could not identify a man to indemnify the parish for the cost of her baby was of less concern to these and other officials in greater London.[10]

At the same time, the multitude of parishes within its bounds meant that there was not a uniform character to metropolitan poor relief. As John Black found in his study of three widely distributed London parishes, 'both benign care and brutality could exist in close proximity'.[11] Even St Luke's Chelsea Parish, which enjoyed the former reputation, was more likely to require unwed mothers with legal settlements in its own parish to marry when they named fathers who had a settlement outside the parish.[12] Otherwise, of course, the baby would become the financial responsibility of Chelsea, while a marriage made both mother and child someone else's problem. The same fiscal concerns prompted officials of Hackney to remove Robert and Elizabeth Crew's pregnant daughter to another London parish where she had her last legal settlement, and order their arrest when word came that they had again given her refuge.[13]

It is impossible to ignore, however, that London's illegitimate babies presented less imposing costs to its parishes than those of the rest of the country, simply because their survival rate was so low. Tim Hitchcock credits metropolitan workhouses, lying-in hospitals and foundling hospitals with providing 'readymade institutional dumping grounds for the products of failed attempts at contracting a marriage'.[14] He cites the extraordinarily high proportion of children who died while in institutional care; the 61.02% death rate for the London Foundling Hospital was comparatively modest.[15] Contemporaries were aware of this as well. In addition

---

Continuity and Change 6.3 (1991): 390; and Norma Landau, 'Who Was Subjected to the Laws of Settlement? Procedure under the Settlement Laws in Eighteenth-Century England', *Agricultural History Review* 43.2 (1995): 144.

[10] Her outright refusal of an examination by JPs placed Hams in a special legal category, but Brace was still subject to a range of punishments for simply delivering a bastard child. By the statute 7 Jac. c. 4, such a woman could face up to a year in a house of correction. JPs rarely seem to have applied such penalties in practice.

[11] John Black, 'Illegitimacy and the Urban Poor in London, 1740–1830' (PhD thesis, Royal Holloway and Bedford New College, University of London, 1999), ch. 2, 62.

[12] John Black, 'Illegitimacy and the Breakdown of Plebeian Courtship in St Luke's Chelsea Parish 1733–1810' (BA dissertation, University of North London, 1994), ch. 4.

[13] Norris, *Justice*, 109, entry 641, 23 April 1733.

[14] Tim Hitchcock, '"Unlawfully begotten on her body": Illegitimacy and the Parish Poor in St Luke's Chelsea', in *Chronicling Poverty: The Voices and Strategies of the English Poor, 1640–1840*, ed. Tim Hitchcock, Peter King and Pamela Sharpe (Basingstoke: Macmillan, 1997), 80.

[15] Hitchcock, '"Unlawfully begotten"', 77.

to Daniel Defoe, Dorothy George cites Jonas Hanway as saying in 1766 that the London practice of fathers paying the parish a lump sum to release them from all responsibility for their illegitimate offspring often constituted a bit of a windfall for the parish, due to the strong possibility of the infant's life 'being but so many days'.[16]

This does not mean that ratepayers were not as resentful of bastards 'dropped' on their parish, however. Even in greater London, the taint of bastardy imparted its own shame, as women like Mary Regatty could attest. When Regatty came before Justice Narcissus Lutrell in Fulham to renew her alehouse licence, he refused, saying, 'she is a whore & has had sevll bastards & putt the Parish to an hundred pounds charge' after 'indecent actions' with 'Captain Merryweather & one Parker'.[17] The disgrace of bastardy remained with a woman long after her child had left the parish rolls, in London as well as the provinces.

This essay will explore the crime of bastardy in London by focusing on one particular group of offenders: the women who charged military men with being the fathers of their illegitimate infants. The existing research on illegitimacy in eighteenth-century London has been marshalled in pursuit of a variety of goals. Not only has it addressed longer-term demographic trends in courtship and sexuality, but it has also looked at specific examples of the circumstances behind illegitimacy, examining everything from the locations of sexual encounters to the role of parish relief structures in affecting sexual behaviour.[18] Although previous work has acknowledged the visible presence of military fathers in bastardy cases,

---

[16]   Jonas Hanway, *An Earnest Appeal for Mercy to the Children of the Poor* (1766), quoted in M. Dorothy George, *London Life in the Eighteenth Century*, 2nd ed. (Chicago: Academy Chicago Publishers, 1984), 215. S. C., *Legal Provisions for the Poor: Or, a Treatise of the Common and Statute Laws Concerning the Poor, Either as to Relief, Settlement, or Punishment, etc.*, 3rd ed. (London, 1715), 83, notes the greater likelihood of overseers from districts 'especially about *London*' to 'take a Sum of Money in Gross' from putative fathers, rather than requiring them to enter a bond for continual maintenance payments.

[17]   We know of the event because Clift later charged Lutrell with defamation (London Metropolitan Archives, DL/C/259 f 112, Clift c. Lutrell, 21 June 1720). Sara Heller Mendelson, '"To shift for a cloak": Disorderly Women in the Church Courts', in *Women and History: Voices of Early Modern England*, ed. Valerie Frith (Concord, Ontario: Irwin Publishing, 1997), 6–10, acknowledges the shame of bastardy allegations.

[18]   See Richard Adair, *Courtship, Illegitimacy and Marriage in Early Modern England* (Manchester: Manchester University Press, 1996); Nicholas Rogers, 'Carnal Knowledge: Illegitimacy in Eighteenth-Century Westminster', *Journal of Social History* 23.2 (1989): 355–76; Hitchcock, '"Unlawfully begotten"', 70–86; John Black, 'Illegitimacy, Sexual Relations and Location in Metropolitan London, 1735–85', in *The Streets of London from the Great Fire to the Great Stink*, ed. Tim Hitchcock and Heather Shore (London: Rivers Oram Press, 2003), 101–18; Alysa Levene, Samantha Williams and Thomas Nutt, eds, *Illegitimacy in Britain, 1700–1920* (Basingstoke: Palgrave Macmillan, 2005); and Samantha Williams, 'The Experience of Pregnancy and Childbirth for Unmarried Mothers in London, 1760–1866', *Women's History Review* 20.1 (2011): 67–86.

no study has probed the dynamics behind it, or singled out this particular group with any depth.

Soldier-fathers are an interesting category for several reasons. Their reputation among contemporaries, visible in the popular novels, plays and ballads of the age, held them to be especially likely to father bastards. This was exacerbated by a 1685 law that prevented most soldiers from marrying. Although the rules and culture that surrounded them seemed to equate army life with licentious bachelorhood, not every soldier appears to have embraced this. Roger Lee Brown found a small group of soldiers who married clandestinely at the Fleet in this period.[19] Others – among them the bastard-begetters discussed in the following pages – seem more likely to have engaged in less formal unions of relatively significant duration. Although Rebecca Probert has effectively routed claims that common-law marriage was prevalent and accepted in England before Hardwicke's Marriage Act, this small group of military unions shows an attempt to replicate emotional marriage without legal recognition.[20] This also revises, somewhat, the rakish image of military masculinity popular in the eighteenth century and today.

By conducting an intensive analysis of 117 women laying their children to military fathers between 1712 and 1752 in bastardy examination records from Westminster and Chelsea, this essay will consider the crime from two angles.[21] Given that these women were simultaneously victims and perpetrators of crime, this essay will explore each identity separately. Such an approach leads to conclusions that contribute to the larger picture of women and crime in eighteenth-century England.

The first section will treat them as victims of crime by investigating the widely held belief that unwed mothers would maliciously accuse innocent men of begetting bastards upon them. Such a notion could strike fear in the hearts of men, for whom allegations of illicit fatherhood posed some hardship. Beyond the ignominy of begetting a bastard, a man so charged was likely to be fined a significant amount, or imprisoned or whipped if he was unable to pay.[22] Military

---

[19]   Roger Lee Brown, 'The Rise and Fall of the Fleet Marriages', in *Marriage and Society: Studies in the Social History of Marriage*, ed. R. B. Outhwaite (London: Europa Publications, 1981), 126, shows that some soldiers married clandestinely at the Fleet in this period, but never accounted for more than 8.2% in a single year (1700), in contrast to sailors, who made up more than 25% of Fleet marriages in 1710, and craftsmen, who were consistently well over 30% of the grooms at the Fleet.

[20]   Rebecca Probert, 'Common-Law Marriage: Myths and Misunderstandings', *Child and Family Law Quarterly* 20.1 (2008): 1–22.

[21]   The latter has been published in *Chelsea Settlement and Bastardy Examinations, 1733–1766*, ed. Tim Hitchcock and John Black (Leicester: London Record Society, 1999).

[22]   The bastard-begetter had three options: he could enter into an agreement with the parish to make a one-time payment that would indemnify him of all future responsibility (as was more often the case in London by this period); he could enter into a bond to ensure that he would compensate the parish with a weekly fee until the child reached (at least) the age

men were considered prime targets for such false allegations. By delving into some of the circumstances outlined in the Westminster and Chelsea examinations, this section will negate the perception of bastard-bearers as malicious prosecutors.

The second section shifts the emphasis to bastard-bearers as perpetrators of crime. It considers a significant group among military bastard-bearers whose self-perception differed considerably from the state's view. It examines evidence of affection and loyalty between certain unwed parents, and shows marked distinctions between the sexual behaviour of some men in the ranks and their officers. It will argue that, although the state regarded bastardy fairly indiscriminately as an economic and moral crime, certain unwed mothers understood things quite differently.

I

A prominent image of bastard-bearers held them to be especially likely to make false claims in order to extort money or a promise of marriage from an innocent man. The women accusing military men were viewed with particular scepticism. The *Report of the Royal Commission on the Poor Laws* stated it to be 'common practice' by the nineteenth century 'in garrisons in particular, ... to swear the child to a soldier, from whom nothing can be recovered and who can only be sent to the tread-wheel for a short time'.[23] Christian Davies, the cross-dressing British soldier immortalized by Daniel Defoe, was charged with fathering a bastard by a woman who calculated Davies to be 'the best able to provide for her in her month, and to take care of her bastard'. She confessed herself 'tempted to disprove her effectually' by announcing her true sex, but decided against it, taking on the costs of the child until its death in infancy.[24]

One fictional army captain identified false bastardy charges as one of the only things 'that a woman could do to a man', apart from poxing or gelding him, or picking his pocket.[25] Another fictional officer, Farquhar's rakish Captain Plume, pretends that the mother of his bastard lied, 'g[iving] out that [he] was the father in hopes that' his wealthy connections would offer greater gain than the 'true' father, who (he claimed) was his sergeant.[26] In this case, of course, the audience is expected to know that it is actually Plume who is telling the falsehood, but his

---

of 8 (or be imprisoned if he lacked sufficient sureties); or he could, if single, simply marry the woman. Legal experts acknowledged that – even for men – the crime of bastardy was 'a Disgrace and an Injury to his Reputation' (Nelson, *Office and Authority*, 87).

[23]   *The Poor Law Report of 1834*, ed. S. G. and E. O. A. Checkland (Harmondsworth: Penguin Books, 1974), 263.

[24]   Daniel Defoe, *The Life and Adventures of Mrs Christian Davies, Commonly Called Mother Ross* (1740, reprinted London, 1929), 38–39.

[25]   Joseph Browne, *State Tracts: Containing Many Necessary Observations, etc.* (London, 1715), 219.

[26]   George Farquhar, *The Recruiting Officer: A Comedy* (London, 1706), Act II, scene ii.

lie is dependent upon the popular belief that girls would foist their bastards upon officers in order to make money from their predicament.

If this sort of activity had been frequent, it seems likely that the bastardy examinations would offer periodic hints. The only evidence in the 30 years of parish examinations studied here is limited to two depositions. The first comes from a servant in the lodgings of Captain Clayton, and the second (to be addressed in more detail later) is from Eliza Stone, who had a sham marriage with a soldier. Captain Clayton's servant gave birth to an illegitimate daughter in the autumn of 1720. She identified Clayton's footman as the father. This is the only clear case where an officer's servant named someone other than the officer as having begotten a bastard upon her.[27]

Of course, it is possible that the footman was indeed her lover, and it is also plausible that other officers acted like Farquhar's Captain Plume, and persuaded the unfortunate girls to marry one of their subordinates, relinquishing charges against them.[28] Something of the sort occurred in St Martin's Parish in 1709. Witnesses came forward with evidence that Catherine Weatherell's 18-month-old daughter was illegitimate. It appeared that the baby's father, an army captain, had paid nurses to take care of Weatherell during her lying-in and the subsequent birth, and had persuaded her to pass herself off as the wife of a spurious sergeant. Weatherell professed herself to have taken 'the name of Mrs. Hill & ... the character of a serjeants wife ... to hide her shame'.[29]

Weatherell's story is remarkable for its rarity, however. The significant proportion of commissioned officers among the military men charged with begetting bastards suggests that such recourse was far from a universal, or perhaps even a frequent choice. There are thus sufficient grounds for confidence that the Westminster and Chelsea women identifying soldier fathers were telling the truth.

There was also little incentive for women to claim a soldier or other lower-class man as the father in an officer's stead. John Black's extensive research into bastardy records in various metropolitan London parishes in the eighteenth century led him to deem it 'unlikely' that any woman would falsely swear a poorer man to be the father. Black additionally observed that most accused fathers paid up, and did not take advantage of the appeal process available to them in cases of wrongful affiliations, a fact which strengthens the probability that few false allegations

---

[27] City of Westminster Archives Centre (CWAC), bastardy examinations for the United Parishes of St Margaret and St John the Evangelist, vol. 4, E2577, fol. 120, deposition of Mary Tedbury, 28 October 1720.

[28] Recruiting officer Captain Plume impregnated a young woman, and told his sergeant that he 'must father the child'. The sergeant lamented that 'her friends will oblige [him] to marry' her, and that he was already currently married to six other women. A later scene depicts the sergeant foreboding the likelihood of yet another marriage when his captain found a new country girl upon whom to prey. See Farquhar, *The Recruiting Officer*, Act I, scene i, and Act III, scene i.

[29] CWAC, bastardy examinations for St Martin's Parish, F5001, fols 94–95, deposition of Catherine Weatherell, 11 May 1709.

made it to the courts.[30] Black also established the accuracy of the examinations by correlating the information contained therein with baptismal records. Simply put, there is little archival evidence to uphold contemporary notions that unwed mothers lied to parish officials.[31]

Sympathy for the myth of malicious prosecution extended to the bench, having the paradoxical effect of making women even more likely to tell the truth.[32] Even the woman who brought allegations against 'Jack the Fool' – the dubious hero of a 1682 comedy – was told to 'seek another father for [her] Child', and immediately ordered by the judge to be punished.[33] That punishment was at least a public whipping, but might have been life imprisonment.[34] While it seems likely that few JPs were as punitive as the fictional magistrate protecting Jack the Fool, they were still very wary of allowing innocent men to face the repercussions of false affiliations.

Thomas Nutt's investigation of the Chelmsford petty sessions' records in the early nineteenth century shows that JPs were assiduous in testing women's stories, and in giving putative fathers a chance to offer proof of their innocence. Nutt concludes that few, if any, bastards could have been maliciously attributed to the wrong man with any success.[35] Although eighteenth-century London officials may have been slightly less diligent than those of Chelmsford 100 years later, wrongful allegations would still have been difficult to advance. Magistrate Henry Norris kept one of the few surviving justicing notebooks in the north London district of Hackney in the 1730s. Norris's notes reveal the significant care he took before

---

[30]　Black, 'Illegitimacy and the Urban Poor', 135–39.

[31]　Black, 'Illegitimacy and the Urban Poor', 46–47.

[32]　Joseph Shaw, *Parish Law, etc.* (London, 1734), 165, acknowledges that 'daily Experience shews, that many People are wrongfully accused in These Cases', necessitating that JPs speak to the putative father before making their decision.

[33]　*The Birth, Life and Death of John Frank* (London, 1682), unpaginated.

[34]　See Somerville Dingley, *The Parish Officer's Companion* (London, 1786), 184; Henry Care, *English Liberties, etc.* (London, 1703), 140; and Jacob, *Compleat Parish-officer*, 122. JPs' notebooks indicate that the penalty was indeed handed out. See Edmund Tew, *The Justicing Notebook (1750–64) of Edmund Tew, Rector of Boldon*, ed. Gwenda Morgan and Peter Rushton (Bristol: Boydell Press, 2000), 145.

[35]　Thomas Nutt, 'The Paradox and Problems of Illegitimate Paternity in Old Poor Law Essex', in *Illegitimacy in Britain, 1700–1920*, ed. Alysa Levene, Samantha Williams and Thomas Nutt (Basingstoke: Palgrave Macmillan, 2005), 105–11. Nutt has reinforced his point in a subsequent article with greater geographic breadth, entitled 'Illegitimacy, Paternal Financial Responsibility, and the 1834 Poor Law Commission Report: The Myth of the Old Poor Law and the Making of the New', *Economic History Review* 63.2 (2010): 346. It emphasizes the success of 'the mechanisms of the old poor law for enforcing paternal financial responsibility', contrary 'to the assertions made by the Commissioners who stressed the futility of the system'.

drawing up orders against putative fathers, but strict measures to ensure payment of those whose culpability was established.[36]

Faced with a cold, sceptical JP, who intended to perform due diligence in questioning her story, few illicit mothers would have considered it worth the risk to lie. Even when they were believed, women who named fathers with little means to indemnify the parish might have to pay for their illegitimate offspring themselves. In the likely event that they could not cover the costs, they might be incarcerated or whipped. Although it is doubtful these punishments were enforced with as much efficiency in eighteenth-century London, it is still difficult to find motivation for most women falsely to accuse a poor man of fathering the child of a wealthy man.[37]

A 1762 examination from another London parish provides a glimpse of a mother who clearly chose not to lie, despite considerable pressure to do so from her baby's father:

> this Examinant ... saith that since she found herself with Child she acquainted the [father] therewith who then offered her six Guineas if she would swear the Child or Children to any other person or marry any young man she liked & pulled out three Guineas [and eventually a total of six]...but this Examinant refused to swear it to any other person but sayd she would take the six Guineas and he never should be troubled on account of the child but he refused to pay the money unless she this Examinant would swear it to some other person and hath threatened to present this Examinant and put her in the pillory or transport her if she should offer to trouble him on account of getting her wth. Child.[38]

Though she gave no explanation for her refusal falsely to accuse another man, one can only assume that fear of and respect for laws against malicious testimony played a role. This furthers the probability that the identifications of soldier fathers in the Westminster and Chelsea examinations were genuine.

The record of Eliza Stone offers the only other hint of a couple's conspiracy. Eliza Stone married soldier Jacob Stone at the Fleet on 30 September, when she was very pregnant. She gave birth a month later, and made a deposition the

---

[36] Hunt, *Justicing Notebook*, entries 545 and 547 (5 and 19 June 1732), for example, show desire for 'further consideration' of Elizabeth Townsend's claim that William Ward fathered her illegitimate son, with no indication that an order ever came against Ward. Conversely, entry 566 (7 August 1732) reveals that Samuel Bayley, who was too poor to indemnify the parish for his bastard daughter and whose marital status prevented him from marrying the mother instead, was committed to 'new Prison'. He 'languished' there and was released only when he caught a life-threatening disease, forcing Petty Sessions' justices to finally relinquish all hope of 'getting the charges the Parish hath been at' (95–96, 98–99).

[37] Hitchcock, '"Unlawfully begotten"', 79–81, expresses doubts about the likelihood of London bastard-bearers facing punishment.

[38] Examination of Elizabeth Woodfin, 14 May 1762, St Leonard's Shoreditch Settlement and Bastardy Examination Books, quoted in Black, 'Illegitimacy, Sexual Relations and Location', 109.

following February naming barber and peruke-maker John May as the father. Four days later, she was examined again (perhaps because May refuted her claim to his fatherhood and told bastardy officers of her Fleet wedding). At her second examination, Eliza admitted to her marriage to Jacob, but claimed that 'John May gave her away and gave the minister for marrying her five shillings and for the certificate one shilling'.[39]

Ultimately, this record again shows the likelihood that most bastard-bearers named the man they genuinely believed to have fathered their child, once they found themselves before parish officers. It appears to present a situation where May attempted to marry Eliza off in order to avoid his responsibility to support her and his child, and found the most willing candidate: a soldier. Eliza probably wound up in front of the JPs because Jacob had accepted some sort of payment from May to marry her, and then deserted her after the baby's birth. Her testimony about May's payment for the wedding was particularly damning.

Jacob Stone thus raises the spectre of another stereotype about military men. Eighteenth-century stories and songs abounded with accounts of soldiers abandoning wives and children to follow the drum. The ballad of the 'Rambling Soldier' depicts him courting 'all damsels ... and marry[ing] none', having left broken hearts and ruined women throughout the British Isles.[40] Countless others reinforce the notion of soldier lovers as the antithesis to commitment and responsibility.[41]

This begs the question of whether it is possible that many of the soldiers named as bastard-begetters in Westminster and Chelsea were knaves who had conspired with the true father and his lover to take credit for the child. The unwed mother would then gain a husband, the soldier would receive payment and the true father would avoid the full costs of bastardy. Though this image fits with literary stereotypes of irresponsible soldiers and lying bastard-bearers, it is unconvincing.

It is difficult to imagine no other woman acting as Eliza Stone did after her soldier husband's desertion, and telling JPs the name of the true father, since she

---

[39]   CWAC, bastardy examinations for the United Parishes of St Margaret and St John the Evangelist, vol. 4, E2577, fol. 232, deposition of Eliza Stone, 26 Feb. 1732/33. Documentation of the Fleet wedding was provided in the form of a certificate appended to fol. 231, stating that Jacob Stone had married Eliza Stone, witnessed by Ann Hodgkins. Note also that Eliza described Jacob as a 'common soldier', though the wedding certificate listed him as a 'Batechlor & Perukemaker', probably to get around the fact that soldiers could not marry without permission.

[40]   'The Rambling Soldier' (London: J. Pitts, 1819–44), Bodleian Library, Harding B 11(835).

[41]   See also Eliza Fowler Haywood, *The History of Miss Betsy Thoughtless*, 2nd ed., 3 vols (London: T. Gardner, 1751), 3: 147, and Samuel Richardson, *Familiar Letters: Letters Written To and For Particular Friends ... Directing not only the Requisite STYLE and FORMS to be Observed in Writing Familiar Letters; But how to Think and Act Justly and Prudently, in the Common Concerns of Human Life, etc.*, 4th ed. (London: J. Osborn, J. and J. Rivington; Bath: J. Leake, 1750), 84–85.

could obtain more funds through him than she could on parish rates as a deserted wife.[42] Indeed, it is implausible that most pregnant women would agree to marry a soldier in the first place for this very reason. The army's regulations against marriage would offer a further obstacle to tempting soldiers to enter such illicit agreements.[43] The bribe would have to be inordinately high to persuade a soldier falsely to admit to fathering a bastard.

This does not, however, negate the possibility that, rather than trying to contract a marriage, some London women conspired with their lovers to affiliate the child with an unsuspecting soldier. This option would have appeal because it allowed the mother access to higher parish funds to provide for her baby; it simultaneously released the true father from the obligation to refund those costs to the parish (or be imprisoned if he could not), and pinned responsibility on a nameless man in uniform who would not be able to answer the charge. Such a scenario is impossible to validate or negate entirely. However, the fact that the majority of examinations accusing soldiers give details of name, address and regimental affiliation suggests that this strategy was not widely pursued.[44]

Implicit in all this remains the notion that soldiers were less responsible for their bastards than civilian men. In many ways, low-ranking military men did seem better able to escape the financial penalties of bastardy laws than most. The 'Common Soldier's Case' that came before King's Bench in 1752 formally asserted that 'the common soldiers of the army, maintained and kept for the support of our liberties and property', were exempt from the obligation to maintain their wives and children incumbent on other civilian men.[45] Could uniformed men use this immunity to vagrancy laws as justification to avoid bastardy payments? There is a paucity of information on the mechanisms by which the parishes took their

---

[42]   *The Poor Law Report of 1834*, ed. S. G. and E. O. A. Checkland, 265–67.

[43]   Although my book, *Marriage and the British Army in the Long Eighteenth Century: 'The Girl I Left Behind Me'* (Oxford: Oxford University Press, 2014), argues that soldiers found ways of circumventing the army's anti-marriage policy, it emphasizes the fact that love and the desire to marry and head a family drove these violations, and that only a small (albeit a significant) minority of soldiers were married. Richard Holmes, *Redcoat: The British Soldier in the Age of Horse and Musket* (London: HarperCollins, 2001), 293, describes a soldier who received 100 lashes and confinement merely for *asking* to marry his love. He estimates that a paltry 7% of men in the British Army were married.

[44]   Sixty-four percent of the 117 military fathers named by Westminster Bastardy deponents had lovers who knew their regiment and/or current location. Mary Morrison, for example, first had intercourse with infantryman William Radford 'at a house at Brussels in Flanders ... and several times after in other places', but ended up in Chelsea where he was an out pensioner of the Royal Hospital. Her continual proximity to Radford is more than a coincidence and is unlikely to have occurred without his cooperation and assistance. See *Chelsea Settlement and Bastardy Examinations*, 50–51, deposition of Mary Morrison, 11 October 1745.

[45]   One Wilson King's Bench 33: *English Reports*, vol. 95, 646. I am grateful to Kim Kippen for providing me with this case.

pound of flesh from military bastard-begetters in the early eighteenth century, but evidence from the following century provides some indications.

The Middlesex Sessions' papers include the record of Joshua Milnes, an infantryman who 'was apprehended by order of the churchwardens of the parish of St James, Westminster' for fathering an illegitimate child in 1824, and ended up in debtor's prison 'in consequence of his not having any more money than the pay of a private soldier' to compensate the parish for the costs.[46] A decade later, the parliamentary enquiry into the Poor Law – while lamenting parishes' inability to recover funds from soldiers – acknowledged that the guilty ones were at least located and incarcerated at hard labour. Lacking the funds to compensate the parish, unable to take the usual alternative of marrying the mother, soldiers were 'sent to the tread-wheel' in the local prison.[47]

Whether their early eighteenth-century counterparts were so consistently found and brought to account is more obscured. David Christiansen's unpublished PhD thesis on military men in Newcastle argues 'that soldiers were very rarely brought to task for their role in fathering children outside wedlock'.[48] In theory, however, they were no more exempt from punishment than other men. The Articles of War promised to release errant men to civilian authorities whenever they required it, with the additional assurance that 'Reparation' be made, 'so far as part of the Offenders Pay can Enable him'.[49] Studies of Germany indicate that its army consistently handed over men attempting to escape responsibility for begetting a bastard, and there seems little reason to suspect the British Army of acting any differently.[50]

Few of the orders to pay the parish have survived, and still fewer refer to military men. Despite the paucity of records, those remaining illuminate the parish's efforts to follow up each accusation.[51] More than two years after he had

---

[46] London Metropolitan Archives, MJ/SP1824/04/054. Milnes had entered into a recognizance to pay the funds, which was then estreated due to his poverty. A note on the reverse side of the document indicated the courts' sympathy, ordering that Milnes now 'be discharged from the Estreat'.

[47] *The Poor Law Report of 1834*, ed. S. G. and E. O. A. Checkland, 263.

[48] David Christiansen, 'From the Glorious Revolution to the French Revolutionary Wars: Civil-Military Relations in North-East England during the Eighteenth Century' (PhD thesis, University of Newcastle-upon-Tyne, 2005), 112.

[49] *Rules and Articles for the Better Government of Our Horse and Foot-guards and All Our Other Land-forces, etc.* (London, 1718), articles 16 and 32, 8–9, 23.

[50] Peter H. Wilson, 'German Women and War, 1500–1800', *War in History* 3.2 (1996): 133.

[51] I can find little direct evidence of the mechanisms by which these civilian courts ensured the cooperation of military officials in cases involving soldiers' begetting bastards on parish women. *A Collection of Decisions of the Court of King's Bench upon the Poor's Laws, etc.* (London, 1770[?]), mentions the case of *Rex v. Teriam*, M. 13 G. MSS, where it is clear that an army captain gave officials a certificate showing that a bastard-bearer's husband was in the army in Ireland. The fact, however, that the legal treatises and justicing

impregnated Mary Bennett, soldier Robert Moore was successfully compelled to accept the costs of his daughter's care. Though himself quartered and unable to keep her, he 'put [her] to Nurse' at a home in Knightsbridge.[52] Officials certainly do not appear to have thrown up their hands in surrender when a military father was named; they pursued army fathers of all ranks. A note in the St Martin's Parish examinations book for 1718 succinctly states, 'Colo Burr reputed father ... to be taken up' eight months after the birth of his illegitimate daughter.[53] John Black found an account of Chelsea overseers expending significant time and energy to locate a soldier in 1793. When they finally found him at the Tower of London serving guard duty, he proved himself unable to pay, and they dropped the matter.[54]

The innocuous fate of the London Tower guard was probably more typical than that of Moore. What is significant in both cases, however, is that parish officials did not simply dismiss soldier-father identifications as lost causes and refuse to follow them up. In pursuing each paternity charge with relative zeal, the magistracy ensured that men accused of paternity had a chance to answer the charges against

---

handbooks say little may be itself significant. Shaw, *Parish Law*, 164–65, includes an example of a naval commander being named in an examination of a woman newly delivered of a bastard. His naval status is remarked upon nowhere else in the text, nor is it suggested that the Admiralty Board should have any role in compelling his appearance or payment. The strongest evidence I can find that soldiers were set apart as a more difficult group to police in bastardy cases is a reference to a precedent-setting case whereby petty sessions' JPs were adjudged to have exceeded their bounds in asking an employer to pay half of the costs of maintaining a bastard because 'he did suffer a souldier to get the child upon the body of his maid servant' (*English Reports*, vol. 82, Styles Rep. 207, 649–50). The decision was overturned at King's Bench, because the Elizabethan bastardy act exempts parties other than the parents from punishment. This leaves a frustratingly brief trace of the idea that it may have been especially difficult to extract money from soldier fathers. One cannot but imagine, however, that if this were an extremely pervasive problem, one would find more evidence. These silences speak volumes. Were there problems in dealing with the military over bastardy payments, surely they would be acknowledged with more clarity, and remedies called for more vociferously. National Army Museum 1968-06-43-65, fol. 36, is a letter to the officer commanding the Depot of the Seventh Hussars, dated 1 April 1815, requesting that he 'procure the Examination of William Smith, a private in your regiment'. In this case, the object is to determine Smith's parish of settlement because he is married and his wife has sought relief from the parish, but the letter stands as evidence that parish officials communicated with regiments.

[52]   CWAC, bastardy examinations for St Margaret's Parish, vol. 1, E2574, fol. 34, statement relating to Bastard Jane Moor [*sic*], undated (c. October 1712). Mary Cooley, née Bennett, was committed to a house of correction, and this precipitated the order for Moore to provide for the little girl. It is unclear whether the mother's prison sentence emerged from bastardy charges or an unrelated offence.

[53]   CWAC, settlement examinations for St Martin's Parish, F5012, fol. 220, statement related to Elizabeth Howard, undated (c. 1718).

[54]   Black, 'Illegitimacy and the Breakdown of Plebeian Courtship', ch. 5.

them. This made it dangerous falsely to allege soldiers as fathers in bastardy cases, and reaffirms the probability that women would have been reluctant to do so.

To add to this, the record of soldier Robert Moore also offers hints that army life did not valorize cutting personal ties and shirking familial duties. Christian Davies, the woman who successfully impersonated a soldier for many years, gained the respect of her comrades in arms by taking responsibility for a bastard laid to her. 'It is well known' throughout the regiment, her biography boasted, 'that she had a child lain to her, and took care of it'.[55] Patricia Lin's work on state provision for military families in this period also uncovered soldiers who 'dedicated themselves to fulfilling their parental responsibility'.[56] My own research has further indicated that some London soldiers went to great lengths to protect and provide for the mothers of their children, suggesting that responsible fatherhood was esteemed in both military and civilian cultures.[57] Most recently, Joanne Bailey noted that the 'masculine warrior ideal' of the eighteenth century encompassed notions of 'affectionate fatherhood'.[58] The next section of this chapter will build on these insights.

Let me return to the main point of this section, however. This image of soldiers claiming responsibility for illegitimate offspring casts further doubt upon the idea that women falsely affiliated their bastards with military men to ensure that no one would answer the charges and that the parish could not collect. Nicholas Rogers's study of later Westminster examinations substantiates this. He uncovered a marked decline in military fathers in the course of the eighteenth century, rather than the steady rise one would expect to support the allegations expressed in the parliamentary enquiry of 1834.[59] By concentrating on women who accuse soldiers, this investigation raises more doubts about the likelihood of many bastard-bearers giving false depositions.

II

The taint of bastardy hung closely around cultural representations of romance with military men. A popular play said that military recruiting parties left as many

---

[55]   Defoe, *Life and Adventures*, 80.

[56]   Patricia Y. C. E. Lin, 'Caring for the Nation's Families: British Soldiers' and Sailors' Families and the State, 1793–1815', in *Soldiers, Citizens and Civilians: Experiences and Perceptions of the Revolutionary and Napoleonic Wars, 1790–1820*, ed. Alan Forrest, Karen Hagemann and Jane Rendall (Basingstoke: Palgrave Macmillan, 2009), 111.

[57]   Jennine Hurl-Eamon, 'Insights into Plebeian Marriage: Soldiers, Sailors, and Their Wives in the *Old Bailey Proceedings*', *London Journal* 30.1 (2005): 26.

[58]   Joanne Bailey, *Parenting in England 1760–1830: Emotion, Identity, and Generation* (Oxford: Oxford University Press, 2012), 114. I am grateful to Joanne Bailey for providing me with this material prior to its publication.

[59]   Rogers, 'Carnal Knowledge', 359.

bastards behind 'as they carried out' in new recruits.[60] A fictional army captain proudly claimed to have fathered 'as many great Bellies in my time, as ever you saw Mole-Hills in an Acre of Fat Pasture'.[61] Londoners also sang of the soldier who seduced a virgin in a wood with the promise of marriage. The broken-hearted girl found herself pregnant and alone, the soldier having glibly told her that his captain required him to depart, but that he would sleep with her again if he came that way next spring.[62] 'Your mammy will not be angry', another soldier consoled his tearful lover after refusing to marry her, 'if you have a little drummer boy, / He'll come of a noble race'.[63]

Were the literary stereotypes true to life, one would expect to find a majority of liaisons in bastardy examinations to be like that of guardsman William Hutchenson and Elizabeth Adams, who were said to have copulated only once, 'in the stables at the Horse Guards', or infantryman Thomas Brown and Mary Stacey, whose sole encounter occurred 'at Hannah Gearys a noted Bawdy house in Thieving Lane'.[64] Adams and Stacey sound like the debauched girls depicted with military men in popular song and literature.

In the Westminster and Chelsea records, however, they are significant for their uniqueness. No other accounts mention men in the ranks at bawdy houses or in stables, and almost none depict other locations – such as alleys or parks – that would imply a temporary tryst.[65] John Black's study of similar records for a longer period additionally notes that the illegitimate children of soldiers tended to be conceived in peacetime, under circumstances more conducive to relationships than casual encounters. This, he argues, belies the common image that military bastards were the product of demobilized men engaging in 'a casual sexual spree'.[66]

Indeed, for the Westminster and Chelsea examinations, soldier John Bull stands out as the only man in the ranks to have been charged with impregnating

---

[60]   Farquhar, *The Recruiting Officer*, Act I, scene i.

[61]   Browne, *State Tracts*, 219.

[62]   'The Nightingale's Song: or The Soldier's Rare musick, and Maid's Recreation, etc.' (London: W. Onley, 1689–1709), Bodleian Library, Douce Ballads 2 (166b).

[63]   'The Soldier's Cloak' (Nottingham: Burbage and Stretton, 1797–1807), Bodleian Library, Harding B 12(162).

[64]   CWAC, bastardy examinations for the United Parishes of St Margaret and St John the Evangelist, vol. 5, E2578, fol. 44, deposition of Elizabeth Adams, 31 August 1738, and fol. 212, deposition of Mary Stacey, 19 September 1747.

[65]   Most prostitutes, of course, would not appear in the bastardy examinations, because JPs would have immediately incarcerated bastard-bearers for whom it was clear that no father could be identified to pay for his offspring. The fact that there were no more accounts of rushed copulations with soldiers like those of Adams and Stacey is nonetheless telling, for Rogers's study found clear evidence of female promiscuity in similar accounts of sex with civilian men ('Carnal Knowledge', 362–63). Black also found traces of prostitution in the bastardy examinations and showed that outdoor locations were clear signs of such commercial sex ('Illegitimacy, Sexual Relations and Location', 103–4).

[66]   Black, 'Illegitimacy and the Urban Poor', 161–68.

more than one woman.[67] In a clear majority of cases, the women who identified low-ranking military men as fathers of their illegitimate offspring had multiple encounters with the same man over a lengthy period, suggesting an emotional as well as physical relationship.[68]

Table 9.1   Bastard-begetters: Breakdown by occupation

Bastard-Begetter	All*	Cohabitants*
Commissioned Officers	6	0
Soldiers and N.C.O.s	10	34
Gentry†	13	15
Lower-Class Men‡	71	51
n (total of known occupation)	750	47

Source: Bastardy Examinations for St Margaret and St John the Evangelist, Westminster, 1712–52, and Chelsea, Middlesex, 1733–50.

*as percentage of total number of bastard-begetters of known occupation. Note that there were 114 examinations where the father's occupation was not listed; only 4 of these described cohabitating relationships.

†Includes titled men ('Sir', 'Esquire', etc.) and professionals (e.g., physicians, attorneys).

‡Includes servants, artisans, labouring men and the like.

A quick glance at Table 9.1 shows that military men were far from the only illicit lovers in early eighteenth-century Westminster and Chelsea. Soldiers and their officers account for less than 20% of all men named as putative fathers in the bastardy examinations. Of course, they may be disproportionately represented; the percentage of military personnel may have been a much smaller segment of the city's male population than the 16% visible in the bastardy examinations. The lack of appropriate data for this period makes this virtually impossible to determine. Black's findings at least show that *all* occupational categories of the local male population could be found in the bastardy records, so soldiers certainly did not constitute an 'exceptional substratum' of bastard-begetters.[69]

---

67   See CWAC, bastardy examinations for St Margaret's Parish, vol. 2, E2575, fol. 103, deposition of Jane Grace, 14 March 1720/1, and fol. 115, deposition of Margaret Juffkins, 19 July 1721. It is possible that there were two different men named 'John Bull', but the proximity of the accusations makes this less likely.

68   Seventy-four percent – almost three-quarters – of the 117 military fathers named by Westminster Bastardy deponents were described as having had multiple sexual encounters, rather than just one or two, with the same woman. Rogers found the same lack of 'hit and run' sexual behaviour such as one might expect of promiscuous individuals. One must acknowledge, however, the possibility that some of the accounts exaggerate the number of times a couple had sex. JPs' handbooks include the term 'several times' in their examples of the text of a typical bastardy examination record. Use of such a phrase understandably strengthened the allegations against the putative father.

69   Black, 'Illegitimacy and the Urban Poor', 149.

Equally, their numbers may be higher because they were an especially negligent group. A bastardy examination might not be generated if the man stepped forward and quickly married his pregnant lover or paid the necessary sums to satisfy poor law officials. However, extant JPs' notebooks suggest that most accused fathers offered remedy to the parish only *after* the mother's bastardy examination elicited a warrant against them.[70] Thus, rather than being definitive evidence of irresponsible soldiers, this indicates only their especially unfortunate situation in being prohibited to marry and extremely poorly paid.[71]

Contemporary literature virtually ignored the possibility of any real or lasting affection within military marriages. Novelist Henry Fielding portrayed an encounter between a drummer from an Irish infantry regiment and a woman he met on the road between Bristol and Froome. Not even particularly taken with her looks (describing her as 'about thirty Years old ... [and] not very handsome, but well enough for a soldier'), he 'made Love to her in our military way' simply because she was a woman and he the only soldier in his small party without one. As he avers, 'We struck a Bargain within a Mile, and lived together as Man and Wife' for the rest of the journey.[72] Popular perception held that soldiers' unions were loveless, viewed as purely pragmatic by both parties.

If reality matched the literary picture of soldiers taking wives only for the duration of a campaign and carousing and womanizing at every opportunity, then the military men in Westminster or Chelsea – far from the battlefield – should have been eager for only the most casual of encounters. Instead, Table 9.1 shows that privates', corporals' and sergeants' illicit unions had more traces of fidelity and affection than those of their civilian counterparts (labourers, journeymen and apprentices). A disproportionately high number of low-ranking soldiers lived as cohabitants with the women who were pregnant by them. Though soldiers and non-commissioned officers made up only 10% of the bastard-begetters in the Westminster and Chelsea parishes, they comprised a full 34% of the couples who claimed to be living as husband and wife at the time of the illegitimate pregnancy.[73]

This number could be even larger, but it includes only those bastard-begetters described explicitly as 'cohabitants' with the mothers in question. Soldiers and women described simply as 'lodging' together without the accompanying phrases 'cohabiting as Man and Wife' may refer to relationships conducted between fellow tenants in the numerous multi-residential dwellings of eighteenth-century London.

---

[70]	See Tew, *The Justicing Notebook*; Norris, *Justice*; and Hunt, *Justicing Notebook*.

[71]	See Hurl-Eamon, 'Insights', 27, 30–32, and Jennine Hurl-Eamon, 'The Fiction of Female Dependence and the Makeshift Economy of Soldiers, Sailors, and Their Wives in Eighteenth-Century London', *Labor History* 49.4 (2008): 481–501, for evidence of the poverty of men in the ranks.

[72]	Henry Fielding, *Joseph Andrews* (London: A. Millar, 1742), vol. 2, ch. 12, 268.

[73]	Black, 'Illegitimacy and the Urban Poor', 189, noted the 'numerous soldiers' who entered into long-term consensual unions in the London parishes of his study, and his tables 6.10 and 6.11 illustrate the disproportionately high numbers from this occupational group represented among the consensual unions of St Mary Le Strand and Shoreditch parishes.

Thus, Table 9.1 does not even include in its numbers the depositions of women like Elizabeth Whitthall, who told officials that she had conducted her relationship with infantryman James Pyle for an extended period 'in the house ... where he and she ... then Lodged'.[74] Nor does it include relationships such as that of Mary Brewster, alias Young, and soldier Daniel Young, who also 'lodged' together and shared the soldier's surname, obviously considering themselves to be married but not explicitly described as 'cohabiting' in Mary's deposition.[75] If anything, therefore, it seems likely that the number of military cohabitants is under-represented in the group.

Perhaps even more telling, these mothers named their illegitimate babies after the soldiers who had impregnated them. They gave sons their father's forename. The data is sparse – many examinations took place during the pregnancy – and, of those that recorded a birth, most did not state the name of the child, or else the child was a daughter. In other cases, a son's name was given, but the putative father had only a surname, or no occupation by which to categorize him. Though the group of named boys known to have been born to enlisted men is small, it is in direct proportion to military men's representation in the bastardy records as a whole.[76]

Naming has been little studied in bastardy cases. The marked exception is John Black's unpublished bachelor's thesis on the Chelsea bastardy examinations. In it, he acknowledged that 'the naming of a child was a link with the absent father and a reflection that many of these births were part of a process of courtship which was expected to end in marriage'.[77] Black did not go on to analyze this data for any variations among fathers' different occupational groups, however. An essay by Tim Hitchcock noted, only in passing, that one London woman named her illegitimate son after the father, but this was the only case.[78] He used it to show that she must have had feelings for her lover, but he did not develop the point.

Quantitative research into naming has focused overwhelmingly on legitimate children. Recent British research is helpful, in that it has established the higher propensity of parents – rather than godparents – to choose names after the seventeenth century.[79] Studies of naming patterns have rarely been taken as

---

[74] CWAC, bastardy examinations for St Margaret's Parish, vol. 2, E2575, fol. 2, deposition of Elizabeth Witthall, 5 January 1718/9.

[75] CWAC, bastardy examinations for the United Parishes of St Margaret and St John the Evangelist, vol. 4, E2577, fol. 204, deposition of Mary Brewster alias Young, 15 February 1730/31.

[76] There were 19 (15%) records of named sons with military men implicated in a total of 130 records where a son's name and an alleged lover's name and occupation were known. This is roughly the same proportion as the number of military men in the records as a whole (120 of 864).

[77] Black, 'Illegitimacy and the Breakdown of Plebeian Courtship', ch. 4.

[78] Hitchcock, '"Unlawfully begotten"', 73.

[79] Jeremy Boulton, 'The Naming of Children in Early Modern London', in *Naming, Society and Regional Identity*, ed. David Postles (Oxford: Leopard's Head Press, 2002), 147–67.

indicators of emotional ties, probably because, when studies focus on legitimate babies, they reasonably presume parents' affection for them. Instead, studies link choice of names to expressions of political affiliation, kinship, class identity or religious conviction.

The fascinating contributions of this research show the potential for quantitative analyses of naming. The hitherto under-explored field of naming patterns for illegitimate infants presents an especially valuable opportunity, because it is one of the only occasions where maternal decision-making is more clearly in evidence. The choice of a name for her bastard son was one of the few ways that a woman could make a statement to the world. The Westminster and Chelsea bastardy examinations suggest rather strongly that some women proclaimed their love for the child's father – and perhaps their sense that his son had legitimacy in their eyes, if not in those of the parish.

The argument could be raised that, in this particular context, naming is an indication less of genuine affection for the father than of a simple desire to establish his link to the infant: a pseudo-legitimacy. In the same way that early modern rape victims often wanted to marry their attacker, unwed mothers may have felt that naming their son after his father would give him more of the appearance of a legal father. Neither of these scenarios, it could be argued, had anything to do with love. This theory breaks down, however, when we look at the proportion of namesakes accorded to officers as opposed to enlisted men.

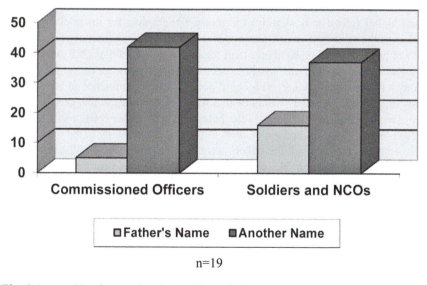

n=19

Fig. 9.1   Naming tendencies: Military fathers

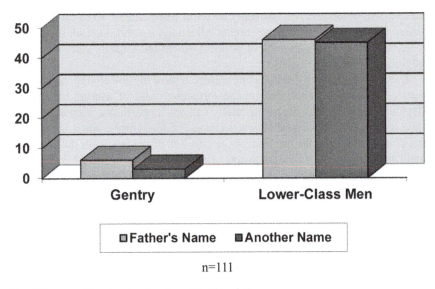

n=111

Fig. 9.2   Naming tendencies: Civilian fathers

Figure 9.1 shows that women impregnated by military men tended to choose *not* to name their baby after him. For civilian men, by contrast, there were fairly equal numbers of those who inspired their partners to name sons after them as of those who did not (see Figure 9.2). In an even more illuminating way, though, Figure 9.2 shows that the likelihood of women giving sons their father's name was higher (albeit only slightly) for gentry fathers than for lower-class fathers, whereas the military men of higher social standing actually garnered a significantly lower proportion of such tributes than their soldier subordinates.[80] From a purely mercenary standpoint, one would expect mothers to be more eager to link their sons with an officer father, who could perhaps use his influence to advance the boy in later life, than they would be to affiliate him with a humble private.

These figures instead point to the potential for a deeper relationship between lower-ranking soldiers and the mothers of their bastards. Many of the women who named sons after their soldier fathers were living as their wives at the time of the birth. Just as interesting, however, are the records of sons bearing the name of a father not cohabiting with his mother. Mary Hills told the Petty Sessions' JPs that she was a virgin when she first slept with guardsman Richard Graden in a private house on Tufton Street. One year later, in the same house, she gave birth to a son, whom she had baptized as 'Richard' and attributed to a long-term sexual

---

[80]   While the difference between having namesakes and not was an additional 3% for gentry fathers and 1% for lower-class civilians, commissioned officers were 37% less likely to have offspring named after them, and low-ranking soldiers were only 21% less likely.

relationship with Graden.[81] Though they never lived together, it seems likely that she felt an emotional bond with Graden, and possibly even saw herself in a wifely role. Unlike most of the women impregnated by officers, a distinct group of soldiers' women gave sons their father's forename. In doing so, they marked a familial relationship in one of the only ways available to them.

Illegitimate children of both sexes were occasionally given fathers' surnames as well. Chelsea officials learned of Sarah Norton's dubious parentage only after her mother (also named Sarah) died and she found herself in need of parish relief at the age of 16. A family friend testified that 'William Norton, a soldier in the Scotch Guards, was the reputed father of the said girl', but was uncertain whether 'the said William Norton was ever married to the said Sarah Norton [Sr.] (though she went by his name)'.[82] A quantitative analysis of surnames of both male and female infants is more difficult to perform, since the records tend to mention only the forename with which an infant was baptized. Black's analysis of later Chelsea records yields hints that unwed mothers did adopt lovers' surnames on occasion, most likely as an attempt to cast a veil of legitimacy over the relationship and the status of its progeny.[83]

Another look at the bastardy examinations explains why officers' illicit offspring were not given their names. The Westminster and Chelsea records suggest that officers who engaged in extramarital sex were more licentious than their civilian counterparts, and less likely than their men to develop an emotional attachment to the objects of their conquest. Like their men, officers were subject to occupational constraints over their romantic entanglements. Officers could consort with but not marry working-class women. Military authorities considered marriage below one's station 'demean[ing] to the officer's status', and his career would be severely harmed by such indiscretion.[84]

Table 9.1 shows that no officers cohabited with their lovers, in contrast to civilian men of similar status, who did occasionally live out of wedlock with women. One of the latter, a 'gentleman' named Richard Hull, lived with Margaret Innis for seven years in residences from Edinburgh to Chelsea.[85] Attorney Alexander Wigginton likewise 'Cohabited as man and wife' for 'about four or five years' with Mary Edwards.[86]

---

[81] CWAC, bastardy examinations for St Margaret's Parish, vol. 2, E2575, fol. 152, deposition of Mary Hills, 23 February 1721.

[82] *Chelsea Settlement and Bastardy Examinations*, 1–2, deposition of Margaret Abbot, 3 October 1733.

[83] Black, 'Illegitimacy and the Breakdown', ch. 4.

[84] Holmes, *Redcoat*, 296.

[85] CWAC, bastardy examinations for the United Parishes of St Margaret and St John the Evangelist, vol. 4, E2577, fol. 70, deposition of Margaret Innis, 20 June 1727.

[86] CWAC, bastardy examinations for St Margaret's Parish, vol. 2, E2575, fol. 145, deposition of Mary Edwards, 3 January 1721.

Descriptions of officers' illicit sex also had more predatory undertones, resonant with their aggressive womanizing behaviour on campaign.[87] Almost a quarter of the claims against officers depict them seducing the servant girls in their lodgings.[88] Captain Thomas Welding had sex only once with servant Letitia Davis, who declared herself a virgin before the encounter that resulted in her pregnancy.[89] Elizabeth Turner became the prey of Captain Copeney within a week of being hired at his lodging house. He had sex with her 'several times' during the month in which she remained at the post.[90] Servant Catherine Weatherell claimed that Captain Hugh White, 'by Inticements solicitations & great promises', broke down her defences and got her pregnant.[91] He paid for the child's support (telling the nurse to count the months to ensure the baby was his), but refused to marry her.

One cannot conclude that these encounters were all non-consensual, but the documents occasionally show clear signs of victimization. 'The life of a maidservant in early-modern England was one fraught with perils', R. C. Richardson argues, presenting numerous examples of young women who suffered the tragic consequences of sexual advances by their master, his male relatives or lodgers.[92] The London bastardy examinations involving military men add more anecdotes to this tragic saga. Ann Macfarling told parish officers that the man she knew as 'Captain Fisher' had carnal knowledge of her only once, the day before his departure from the home where she worked as a maid. She had few resources to determine his whereabouts, and knew only that he 'went into Lancashire ... where he is said to have a wife and family'.[93]

A man named Captain Duce bears the dubious distinction of being the most licentious of Westminster's military bastard-begetters, having three bastards charged against him. He met and had sex with Ann Archer at a coffee house, and then took her back to his lodgings at Killigrew Court in Scotland Yard.[94] He also brought Margaret Evans and Jane Jones to Killigrew Court, and it seems likely that other women trysted with the captain but were fortunate enough to avoid

---

[87]   This is outlined at length in the third chapter of my book, *Marriage and the British Army in the Long Eighteenth Century*.

[88]   Fifteen servants brought claims against military men. Of these, 10 charged commissioned officers, and an additional three named sergeants.

[89]   CWAC, bastardy examinations for the United Parishes of St Margaret and St John the Evangelist, vol. 4, E2577, fol. 224, deposition of Letitia Davis, 2 September 1732.

[90]   CWAC, bastardy examinations for St Margaret's Parish, vol. 1, E2574, fols 269 and 271, deposition of Elizabeth Turner, 28 March 1718.

[91]   CWAC, bastardy examinations for St Martin's Parish, F5001, fol. 95, deposition of Catherine Weatherell, 11 May 1709.

[92]   R. C. Richardson, 'A Maidservant's Lot', *History Today* 60.2 (2010): 25.

[93]   CWAC, bastardy examinations for St Margaret's Parish, vol. 2, E2575, fols 129 and 136, deposition of Ann Macfarling, 8 November 1721.

[94]   CWAC, bastardy examinations for St Margaret's Parish, vol. 2, E2575, fol. 67, deposition of Ann Archer, 10 June 1712.

pregnancy.[95] Black's extensive study of three metropolitan parishes between 1740 and 1809 yielded only six promiscuous men, with only two described in any detail. One of the two was Lieutenant Jeremiah Viguers, who impregnated two of the servant girls in the house where he lodged.[96]

Duce's exploits pale in comparison to those of London's most notorious military rake, however. Colonel Charteris was convicted of rape in 1730 and was known as the 'Rape-Master General of Great Britain'. His liberties with servant girls were widely condemned by all levels of society, and crowds attacked him when they caught a glimpse of him in the street and defiled his grave after his death in 1732. Westminster bastardy examiners saw the Colonel in 1724, when a pregnant Isabella Cranston claimed that he had taken her virginity 'in the house of Mrs. Jolly in Suffock [*sic*] Street (to which place she was decoyed under pretence of being hired into service)'.[97] No accounts of contact with men in the ranks mention such trickery.

It is difficult to hear bastard-bearers' voices in the parish examinations, governed as they were by the strict legal rules about form and wording, but there are occasional glimpses of soldiers' cohabitants constructing their relationship as one of love and fidelity – as a marriage. A distinct subgroup of women who were brought before Westminster and Chelsea JPs lived in committed relationships with men in the lower ranks of the British Army. Marriage had been largely prohibited for these men by a 1685 regulation. Officers' illicit sex clearly fell within the strictures of army life, but that of their men proved more resistant. Despite their inability to marry, certain soldiers formed strong relationships with women who considered themselves wives.[98] The children they brought into the union were illegitimate only in the eyes of the state.

III

This investigation of bastardy among military couples offers some fascinating insights about English women and crime more broadly. First, when the law viewed

---

[95] CWAC, bastardy examinations for St Margaret's Parish, vol. 2, E2575, fol. 124, deposition of Margaret Evans, 4 October 1721 and Jane Jones, 27 August 1719.

[96] Black, 'Illegitimacy and the Urban Poor', 178.

[97] CWAC, bastardy examinations for St Margaret's Parish, vol. 3, E2576, fol. 103, deposition of Isabella Cranston, 16 June 1724. This case did not generate a rape trial and has no relation to the three rape prosecutions against Charteris in 1722, 1728 and 1729.

[98] Black has come to a similar conclusion for long-term consensual unions of all occupational groups, based on other evidence. The London parish examinations he studied also provided information on the age of bastard-bearers, which allowed him to observe that women in cohabitant relationships were slightly older than the other single mothers, and slightly older than the age at first marriage of the female working-class population of the era, an indication that they 'perceived their status as equivalent to legal marriage, and/or as a decided alternative' (Black, 'Illegitimacy and the Urban Poor', 274).

bastard-bearers as victims (and almost every case accorded them a measure of victimhood), it actually offered them more power and authority than it did victims of another sexual crime: rape. Unlike the latter, bastard-bearers giving testimony of male sexual activity were given the benefit of the doubt far more often.[99] Their testimony was immediately acted upon, and it was up to their accused sexual partner to prove that the act had not taken place; he rarely could.

At the same time, both bastard-bearers and rape victims were perceived and depicted as likely to lie, to charge innocent men maliciously. The image of the malicious female prosecutor pervades both rape and bastardy cases, and has been discredited by several scholars for the former category.[100] This essay is the first to focus on the notion of false testimony in military bastardy cases. Contrary to popular perception, most women did not pin charges on nameless soldiers in order to spare officers or civilian men the social and economic costs of fathering a bastard. They knew the man's name, regiment and quarters, and they had little to gain and much to risk from a false allegation against a penniless soldier. More importantly, the courts' suspicion about the likelihood of malicious prosecution worked to ensure that it did not happen. Accused fathers had a chance to offer proof of their innocence, and questionable allegations were dismissed.

Unlike the notion of malicious prosecution in rape, however, this perception of false testimony in bastardy did not liberate many men. Of course, the death penalty hanging over rape accusations, in contrast to the much lighter penalties facing bastard-begetters, helps to explain this. Nonetheless, it is important to acknowledge bastardy as an unusual area of sex-related crime in early modern England, where the word of a promiscuous woman was commonly taken over that of her (alleged) male partner.

As criminals, too, military bastard-bearers had a measure of power and agency. Evidence of affection and loyalty, and of marked distinctions between the sexual behaviour of some men in the ranks and their officers, brings into question traditional notions of soldiers' romances. Despite regulations a few decades earlier that prevented most low-ranking men at arms from marrying, a distinct minority entered committed relationships with women in early eighteenth-century London.

The *Poor Law Report of 1834* acknowledged the possibility of a counterculture among bastard-bearers. It lamented the 'inconvenience' caused when the Irish of England's urban centres were married by Catholic priests, an arrangement

---

[99]   Dalton, *The Country Justice*, 40, and Richard Burn, *The Justice of the Peace, and Parish Officer, etc.* (London, 1756), vol. 1, 127, acknowledge that the mother's evidence is weighted very heavily over that of other witnesses, particularly the father.

[100]   Antony E. Simpson, 'The "Blackmail Myth" and the Prosecution of Rape and Its Attempt in 18th Century London: The Creation of a Legal Tradition', *Journal of Criminal Law and Criminology* 77.1 (1986): 101–50, and Laurie Edelstein, 'An Accusation Easily to Be Made? Rape and Malicious Prosecution in Eighteenth-Century England', *American Journal of Legal History* 42.4 (1998): 351–90.

that 'satisf[ied] the conscience of the wife' but had no legal basis.[101] This essay offers evidence that a similar practice existed among the military couples in early eighteenth-century Westminster and Chelsea. The progeny of these relationships were clearly illegitimate in the eyes of the state but may have been seen quite differently by the mothers themselves.

In this sense, bastardy can be viewed in a similar light to the social crimes outlined by E. P. Thompson, Douglas Hay, Peter Linebaugh and others.[102] All of these histories depict a criminalization of plebeian customs in the eighteenth century and conclude that many continued the behaviour as a form of protest against the new laws. The Westminster and Chelsea bastardy examinations reveal a group of soldiers' lovers who acted on a similar principle. Though authorities made it an offence for soldiers to marry without permission after 1685, women continued to act as they had before, in defiance of the regulation, forming committed relationships and having children.

Works Cited

Primary Sources

Manuscript Sources

Broadside Ballads Collection, Bodleian Library.

City of Westminster Archives Centre (CWAC). Bastardy examinations for St Margaret's Parish, vols 1–3, E2574–E2756; bastardy examinations for the United Parishes of St Margaret and St John the Evangelist, vols 4–5, E2577–E2758; bastardy examinations for St Martin's Parish, F5001; settlement examinations for St Martin's Parish, F5012.

London Metropolitan Archives. Bishop of London's Consistory Court Deposition, DL/C/259 f 112, Clift c. Lutrell; Middlesex Sessions Papers, MJ/SP1824/04/054.

National Army Museum, Chelsea. Letter Collection, 1968-06-43-65.

Printed Primary Sources

Barlow, Theodore. *The Justice of the Peace, a Treatise Containing the Power and Duty of That Magistrate, etc.* London, 1745.

The Birth, Life and Death of John Frank. London, 1682.

Bond, J. *A Compleat Guide for Justices of Peace, etc.* London, 1707.

Browne, Joseph. *State Tracts: Containing Many Necessary Observations, etc.* London, 1715.

---

[101]   *The Poor Law Report of 1834*, ed. S. G. and E. O. A. Checkland, 273.

[102]   E. P. Thompson, *Whigs and Hunters: The Origin of the Black Act* (London: Allen Lane, 1975); Douglas Hay et al., eds, *Albion's Fatal Tree: Crime and Society in Eighteenth-Century England* (London: Allen Lane, 1975); and Peter Linebaugh, *The London Hanged: Crime and Civil Society in the Eighteenth Century* (Cambridge: Cambridge University Press, 1992).

Burn, Richard. *The Justice of the Peace, and Parish Officer, etc.* London, 1756.

Care, Henry. *English Liberties, etc.* London, 1703.

Chelsea Settlement and Bastardy Examinations, 1733–1766. Edited by Tim Hitchcock and John Black. Leicester: London Record Society, 1999.

A collection of decisions of the Court of King's Bench upon the Poor's Laws, etc. London, 1770(?).

Dalton, Michael. *The Country Justice, etc.* London, 1705.

Defoe, Daniel. *The Life and Adventures of Mrs. Christian Davies, Commonly Called Mother Ross.* 1740; repr. London: Peter Davies, 1929.

Dingley, Somerville. *The Parish Officer's Companion, etc.* London, 1786.

English Reports, Vols 82, 95 (1900).

Farquhar, George. *The Recruiting Officer: A Comedy.* London: Bernard Lintott, 1706.

Fielding, Henry. *Amelia.* 4 vols. London: A. Millar, 1752.

———. *Joseph Andrews* [*The history of the adventures of Joseph Andrews, and of his friend Mr. Abraham Adams. Written in imitation of the manner of Cervantes, etc.*]. 2 vols. London: A. Millar, 1742.

Haywood, Eliza Fowler. *The History of Miss Betsy Thoughtless.* 2nd ed. 4 vols. London: T. Gardner, 1751.

Hunt, William. *The Justicing Notebook of William Hunt, 1744–1749.* Edited by Elizabeth Critall. Devizes: Wiltshire Record Society, 1982.

Jacob, Giles. *The Compleat Parish-officer, etc.* London, 1729.

Nelson, William. *The Office and Authority of a Justice of Peace, etc.* London, 1711.

Norris, Henry. *Justice in Eighteenth-Century Hackney: The Justicing Notebook of Henry Norris and the Hackney Sessions Book.* Edited by Ruth Paley. London: London Records Society, 1991.

P. S. *A Help to Magistrates, and Ministers of Justice, etc.* London, 1721.

The Poor Law Report of 1834. Edited by S. G. and E. O. A. Checkland. Harmondsworth: Penguin Books, 1974.

Richardson, Samuel. *Familiar Letters: Letters Written To and For Particular Friends. ... Directing not only the Requisite STYLE and FORMS to be Observed in Writing Familiar Letters; But how to Think and Act Justly and Prudently, in the Common Concerns of Human Life, etc.* 4th ed. London: J. Osborn, J. and J. Rivington; Bath: J. Leake, 1750.

Rules and Articles for the Better Government of Our Horse and Foot-Guards and All Our Other Land-Forces, etc. London: John Baskett, 1718.

S. C. *Legal Provisions for the Poor: Or, a Treatise of the Common and Statute Laws Concerning the Poor, Either as to Relief, Settlement, or Punishment, etc.* 3rd ed. London, 1715.

Shaw, Joseph. *Parish Law, etc.* London, 1734.

Tew, Edmund. *The Justicing Notebook (1750–64) of Edmund Tew, Rector of Boldon.* Edited by Gwenda Morgan and Peter Rushton. Bristol: Boydell Press, 2000.

Secondary Sources

Adair, Richard. *Courtship, Illegitimacy and Marriage in Early Modern England.* Manchester: Manchester University Press, 1996.

Bailey, Joanne. *Parenting in England 1760–1830: Emotion, Identity, and Generation.* Oxford: Oxford University Press, 2012.

Black, John. 'Illegitimacy and the Breakdown of Plebeian Courtship in St Luke's Chelsea Parish 1733–1810'. BA dissertation, University of North London, 1994.

———. 'Illegitimacy, Sexual Relations and Location in Metropolitan London, 1735–85'. In *The Streets of London from the Great Fire to the Great Stink.* Edited by Tim Hitchcock and Heather Shore. London: Rivers Oram Press, 2003. 101–18.

———. 'Illegitimacy and the Urban Poor in London, 1740–1830'. PhD thesis, Royal Holloway and Bedford New College, University of London, 1999.

Boulton, Jeremy. 'The Naming of Children in Early Modern London'. In *Naming, Society and Regional Identity.* Edited by David Postles. Oxford: Leopard's Head Press, 2002. 147–67.

Brown, Roger Lee. 'The Rise and Fall of the Fleet Marriages'. In *Marriage and Society: Studies in the Social History of Marriage.* Edited by R. B. Outhwaite. London: Europa Publications, 1981. 117–36.

Christiansen, David. 'From the Glorious Revolution to the French Revolutionary Wars: Civil-Military Relations in North-East England during the Eighteenth Century'. PhD thesis, University of Newcastle-upon-Tyne, 2005.

Edelstein, Laurie. 'An Accusation Easily to Be Made? Rape and Malicious Prosecution in Eighteenth-Century England'. *American Journal of Legal History* 42.4 (1998): 351–90.

George, M. Dorothy. *London Life in the Eighteenth Century.* 2nd ed. Chicago: Academy Chicago Publishers, 1984.

Gowing, Laura. *Women, Touch and Power in Seventeenth-Century England.* New Haven, CT: Yale University Press, 2003.

Hay, Douglas, et al., eds. *Albion's Fatal Tree: Crime and Society in Eighteenth-Century England.* London: Allen Lane, 1975.

Hitchcock, Tim. '"Unlawfully begotten on her body": Illegitimacy and the Parish Poor in St Luke's Chelsea'. In *Chronicling Poverty: The Voices and Strategies of the English Poor, 1640–1840.* Edited by Tim Hitchcock, Peter King and Pamela Sharpe. Basingstoke: Macmillan, 1997. 70–86.

Holmes, Richard. *Redcoat: The British Soldier in the Age of Horse and Musket.* London: HarperCollins, 2001.

Hurl-Eamon, Jennine. 'The Fiction of Female Dependence and the Makeshift Economy of Soldiers, Sailors, and Their Wives in Eighteenth-century London'. *Labor History* 49.4 (2008): 481–501.

———. 'Insights into Plebeian Marriage: Soldiers, Sailors, and Their Wives in the *Old Bailey Proceedings*'. *London Journal* 30.1 (2005): 22–38.

_____. *Marriage and the British Army in the Long Eighteenth Century: 'The Girl I Left Behind Me'*. Oxford: Oxford University Press, 2014.

Landau, Norma. 'Who Was Subjected to the Laws of Settlement? Procedure under the Settlement Laws in Eighteenth-Century England'. *Agricultural History Review* 43.2 (1995): 139–59.

Levene, Alysa, Thomas Nutt and Samantha Williams, eds. *Illegitimacy in Britain, 1700–1920*. Basingstoke: Palgrave Macmillan, 2005.

Lin, Patricia Y. C. E. 'Caring for the Nation's Families: British Soldiers' and Sailors' Families and the State, 1793–1815'. In *Soldiers, Citizens and Civilians: Experiences and Perceptions of the Revolutionary and Napoleonic Wars, 1790–1820*. Edited by Alan Forrest, Karen Hagemann and Jane Rendall. Basingstoke: Palgrave Macmillan, 2009. 99–117.

Linebaugh, Peter. *The London Hanged: Crime and Civil Society in the Eighteenth Century*. Cambridge: Cambridge University Press, 1992.

Marshall, Dorothy. *The English Poor in the Eighteenth Century: A Study in Social and Administrative History*. New York: A. M. Kelley, 1969.

Mendelson, Sara Heller. '"To shift for a cloak": Disorderly Women in the Church Courts'. In *Women and History: Voices of Early Modern England*. Edited by Valerie Frith. Concord, Ontario: Irwin Publishing, 1997. 3–18.

Nutt, Thomas. 'Illegitimacy, Paternal Financial Responsibility, and the 1834 Poor Law Commission Report: The Myth of the Old Poor Law and the Making of the New'. *Economic History Review* 63.2 (2010): 335–61.

———. 'The Paradox and Problems of Illegitimate Paternity in Old Poor Law Essex'. In *Illegitimacy in Britain, 1700–1920*. Edited by Alysa Levene, Samantha Williams and Thomas Nutt. Basingstoke: Palgrave Macmillan, 2005. 102–21.

Probert, Rebecca, 'Common-Law Marriage: Myths and Misunderstandings'. *Child and Family Law Quarterly* 20.1 (2008): 1–22.

Richardson, R. C. 'A Maidservant's Lot'. *History Today* 60.2 (February 2010): 25–31.

Rogers, Nicholas. 'Carnal Knowledge: Illegitimacy in Eighteenth-Century Westminster'. *Journal of Social History* 23.2 (1989): 355–76.

Simpson, Antony E. 'The "Blackmail Myth" and the Prosecution of Rape and Its Attempt in 18th Century London: The Creation of a Legal Tradition'. *Journal of Criminal Law and Criminology* 77.1 (1986): 101–50.

Snell, K. D. M. 'Pauper Settlement and the Right to Poor Relief in England and Wales'. *Continuity and Change* 6.3 (1991): 375–415.

Taylor, J. S. 'The Impact of Pauper Settlement, 1691–1834'. *Past and Present* 73 (1976): 42–74.

Thompson, E. P. *Whigs and Hunters: The Origin of the Black Act*. London: Allen Lane, 1975.

Williams, Samantha. 'The Experience of Pregnancy and Childbirth for Unmarried Mothers in London, 1760–1866'. *Women's History Review* 20.1 (2011): 67–86.

Wilson, Peter H. 'German Women and War, 1500–1800'. *War in History* 3.2 (1996): 127–60.

Chapter 10
Coverture and Criminal Forfeiture in English Law[1]

Krista Kesselring

'Why is the property of the woman who commits Murder, and the property of the woman who commits Matrimony, dealt with alike by your law?' Frances Power Cobbe had a hypothetical visitor from another world pose this question in her famous 1868 article, 'Criminals, Idiots, Women and Minors'.[2] In the nineteenth-century debates that surrounded married women's property law, reformers frequently drew comparisons between the legal effects of crime and those of marriage. At common law, a convicted felon forfeited all possessions real and personal. All too similarly, these reformers pointed out, a woman who married lost ownership or at least control of all her possessions because of the common law fiction that a husband's legal identity 'covered' that of his wife. One reformer offered the sardonic observation that

> the confiscation of a man's property is associated in our minds with felony or high treason; the confiscation of a woman's property with marriage. Of course I mean that is the idea of the more thoughtful among us, for the ugly fact that a woman's marriage is punished as a felony is concealed from the young under a bridal veil and orange blossoms.[3]

Upon occasion, reformers also noted the unhappy effects when these two legal practices coincided. One story told of a woman cruelly abused by her husband. When she finally succeeded in having him criminally convicted, she lost not just the abusive husband but also the legacy left her by her father. According to the

---

[1]   The author wishes to thank the participants in the conference 'Women and Crime in the British Isles and North America since 1500' (Lyons, France, 2008) for their useful feedback on the first version of this essay, and Tim Stretton for commenting on an early draft. He and Paul Cavill also provided useful references. The author wishes, too, to thank the Social Sciences and Humanities Research Council of Canada for funding the research from which this chapter derives. Please note that the spelling in all quotations from primary sources has been modernized.

[2]   Frances Power Cobbe, 'Criminals, Idiots, Women and Minors', *Fraser's Magazine*, December 1868, 5.

[3]   *Married Women's Property Committee Report of the Proceedings of the Annual Meeting, 1876* (Manchester, 1876), 21.

dictates of coverture, upon her marriage it had become her husband's property, and thus upon his conviction, it became the property of the crown.[4]

Polemical comparisons of the effects of coverture and criminal convictions were new to nineteenth-century debates, but the convergence of these two legal devices for the wives of felons had a long history. This essay examines the conjunction of coverture and criminal forfeiture, with a special focus on the early modern period. Given that most convicted felons were men, and that a good many of them were married, one must ask what effects criminal forfeiture had on the wives whose legal identity was 'covered' by that of their criminal partners. This chapter, then, deals only indirectly with female transgressors, instead focusing on the relationship between legal fiction and social fact, when married women who were at least discursively imagined as innocent suffered for the transgressions of their husbands. Justifications of coverture often referred to the wife's protection and maintenance; paeans to the law also highlighted a wife's diminished legal responsibility for her own minor misdeeds as a valuable consideration.[5] But while some married women may have escaped punishment for their own transgressions, others became liable to punishment for their husbands' crimes, stripped of much, if not all, of the familial property. One might then ask how, in turn, these effects on wives shaped the understanding and practice of criminal forfeiture. As suggested here, the consequences of forfeiture for the wives of the condemned came to serve as the basis for both the key criticisms and the chief defences of forfeiture. For some observers, these effects offered sure evidence that forfeiture constituted an unjust punishment that penalized the innocent rather than the guilty; for others, it was precisely the effects on the innocent that allowed a practice founded in feudalism to be reformulated as a valuable deterrent. The essay first offers an overview of both coverture and criminal forfeiture. It then turns to concrete examples and rhetorical constructions of their conjunction, demonstrating ways in which the gendered structure of property law – and the legal fiction of coverture at its heart – shaped English criminal law and its sanctions.

The forfeiture of property by married women and by felons had long histories, embedded in the very origins of the common law. The rationale for coverture shifted over time, from the wife being under the *dominium* of her husband to husband and wife being one person at law.[6] In its latter guise, which insisted upon the 'unity of

---

[4]   Cited in Lee Holcombe, *Wives and Property: Reform of the Married Women's Property Law in Nineteenth-Century England* (Toronto: University of Toronto Press, 1983), 66; see also 149.

[5]   See, for example, William Blackstone, *Commentaries on the Laws of England*, 4 vols (Oxford, 1765–69), vol. 1, 432–33. See, too, Marisha Caswell's essay in this volume.

[6]   See, for example, Maeve Doggett, *Marriage, Wife-Beating, and the Law in Victorian England* (Columbia: University of South Carolina Press, 1993); Frances Dolan, *Marriage and Violence: The Early Modern Legacy* (Philadelphia: University of Pennsylvania Press, 2008); and Tim Stretton, 'Coverture and Unity of Person in Blackstone's Commentaries', in *Blackstone and His Commentaries: Biography, Law, History*, ed. Wilfrid Robertson Prest (Oxford: Hart, 2009), 111–28.

person' of husband and wife, coverture proved one of the longer lasting of English legal fictions, an 'imaginative projection' that very much impinged upon socio-historical realities. Whatever the rationale, the immediate effects remained much the same. Upon marriage, a woman lost to her husband ownership of all her goods and chattels – that is, personal property – and lost control of any real property. Anything in the intermediate category of 'chattels real', such as leases on land, became her husband's during marriage but reverted to her ownership should both she and the property in question outlast him. Some exceptions existed, thanks in large part to equity courts. The twelfth-century development of the joint fee tail, or jointure, allowed property to be specifically settled upon a woman at marriage.[7] By the late sixteenth century, and increasingly over the years that followed, equity developed more mechanisms to protect the separate property interests of women who could afford its use.[8] For most women, however, the common law principles of coverture set the parameters of property ownership until the late nineteenth century. The first statutory moderation came with the Married Women's Property Act of 1870, and others followed in succeeding decades.[9]

Like coverture, criminal forfeiture had early roots. With parallels if not origins under the Anglo-Saxons, the practice of seizing an offender's possessions survived in altered guise throughout the Norman and Angevin reforms. The word 'felony' initially denoted disloyalty between lord and vassal, or a violation of the feudal bond, for which a vassal forfeited his lands to his lord.[10] Over time, 'felony' took on a new meaning, designating particularly heinous wrongs more generally. By the late 1100s, the standard formula held that felons lost all goods and chattels to the king and their real property to their lord, after the king had taken those lands

---

[7] Joseph Biancalana, *The Fee Tail and the Common Recovery in Medieval England, 1176–1502*, Cambridge Studies in English Legal History (Cambridge: Cambridge University Press, 2001), esp. 9, 13, 39, 141–45, 180.

[8] See Maria Cioni, *Women and Law in Elizabethan England, with Particular Reference to the Court of Chancery* (New York: Garland, 1985), *passim*, and for developments thereafter, see Susan Staves, *Married Women's Separate Property in England, 1660–1833* (Cambridge, MA: Harvard University Press, 1990). On the costs of marriage settlements, see Holcombe, *Wives and Property*, 46; on the costs in Chancery, estimated at a minimum of £50 per suit even in the late sixteenth century, see W. J. Jones, *The Elizabethan Court of Chancery* (Oxford: Clarendon Press, 1967), 309. Amy Erickson has argued that many couples of moderate means devised marriage settlements through common bonds; such bonds, however, would have been subject to felony forfeiture like other debts. See Amy Louise Erickson, 'Common Law versus Common Practice: The Use of Marriage Settlements in Early Modern England', *Economic History Review*, 2nd ser., 43 (1990): 21–39.

[9] Holcombe, *Wives and Property*, 175ff.

[10] Patrick Wormald, *The Making of English Law: King Alfred to the Twelfth Century*, vol. 1: *Legislation and Its Limits* (Oxford: Blackwell, 2000), 19, 144–49.

for a year and a day.[11] The king might in turn use these forfeitures as a source of patronage, granting the rights to collect them to favoured individuals. Whether the seizures went to the landlord, the king, or the king's grantee, however, the immediate effects on the felon remained much the same: the loss of all land, goods and chattels. As with coverture, over time, those with the resources to do so found a variety of mechanisms to moderate the effects of forfeiture, particularly for real property. Devices such as entails, uses and trusts all served primarily to allow landholders increased flexibility in long-term estate planning, but also served to obstruct the forfeiture of estates.[12] While forfeiture of real property became increasingly rare over time, the forfeiture of goods and chattels continued right up until abolished by statute in 1870.[13] Like coverture, criminal forfeiture survived in both theory and practice well into the nineteenth century.

---

[11]   See, for example, *The Treatise on the Laws and Customs of the Realm of England Commonly Called Glanvill*, ed. G. D. G. Hall (London, 1965; repr. Holmes Beach, FL: W. W. Graunt, 1983), 90–91. Note that technically, land 'escheated' for lack of an heir, while personal possessions and the year, day and waste of the land were 'forfeit'. A final caveat about terminology: recently a number of governments have revived forfeiture provisions, but this now tends to be civil rather than criminal forfeiture – *in rem* versus *in personam*, based more on the tradition of the deodand than on the criminal forfeiture provisions discussed here. See, for example, Leonard Levy, *A License to Steal: The Forfeiture of Property* (Chapel Hill: University of North Carolina Press, 1996), for an overview of the development of modern forfeiture law. Also pertinent to the topic of this chapter is Amy D. Ronner, 'Husband and Wife Are One – Him: *Bennis v. Michigan* as the Resurrection of Coverture', *Michigan Journal of Gender and Law* 4 (1996): 129–69, which argues that a 1996 case in which a wife lost her claim to an automobile seized for her husband's 'gross indecency' resurrects and fuses both coverture and civil forfeiture provisions. (My thanks to Tim Stretton for this reference.)

[12]   For entails, see Biancalana, *Fee Tail*; for uses, see J. M. W. Bean, *The Decline of English Feudalism, 1215–1540* (Manchester: Manchester University Press, 1968); for the device of using trustees to preserve contingent remainders and its emergence in the Interregnum, see John Habakkuk, *Marriage, Debt and the Estates System: English Landownership, 1650–1950* (Oxford: Clarendon Press, 1994). All three argue that a desire to frustrate the law's forfeiture provisions played a part in the development of these devices. On their immunity from forfeiture for treason and/or for felony, see also C. D. Ross, 'Forfeiture for Treason in the Reign of Richard II', *English Historical Review* 71 (1956): 560–75; J. R. Lander, 'Attainder and Forfeiture, 1453–1509', *Historical Journal* 4 (1961): 119–51; and John G. Bellamy, *The Law of Treason in England in the Later Middle Ages*, Cambridge Studies in English Legal History (Cambridge: Cambridge University Press 1970), 192–97.

[13]   For more on the mechanics of forfeiture and its longevity, see K. J. Kesselring, 'Felony Forfeiture, c. 1170–1870', *Journal of Legal History* 30 (2009): 201–26; 'Felons' Effects and the Effects of Felony in Nineteenth–Century England', *Law and History Review* 28 (2010): 111–39; and 'Felony Forfeiture and the Profits of Crime in Early Modern England', *Historical Journal* 53 (2010): 271–88.

The effects of coverture and criminal forfeiture thus shared a number of similarities.[14] What happened when they coincided? An unmarried woman who committed a felony was treated the same as a man: all possessions both real and personal were forfeit. A married female felon had already lost most of her property to her husband, and thus had less to lose. The personal property and chattels real she had owned before marriage were then her husband's and thus safe from seizure for her own offence; her real property was forfeit, but by the custom known as 'the curtesy of England' her husband could continue to use it until his own death if the couple had had children. In contrast, if a woman's husband committed felony, only whatever separate property she may have had remained safe from forfeiture; if she had had real property, it reverted to her upon her husband's execution. If she had had a jointure prepared for her upon marriage, it remained immune from seizure.[15] Until the mid-sixteenth century, however, everything else was forfeit.[16]

Throughout the Middle Ages, this included dower and any of the usual provisions for widowhood from the husband's movable goods. Common law typically entitled a widow to a dower of a life estate in one-third of the freehold lands that her husband had possessed during the marriage.[17] The entitlement for the widow of a copyholder, frequently known as freebench, varied significantly from one manor to another, but was commonly an interest in at least one-third of the lands of which her husband died seized, at least during widowhood if not for life.[18]

---

[14] Indeed, it is striking that the rights of the Crown and those of the widow followed a similar trajectory. The same devices that kept land safe from forfeiture for felony also made it immune to dower claims.

[15] See Biancalana, *Fee Tail*, and C. D. Ross, 'Forfeiture'. At least from the 1285 statute *De Donis Conditionalibus*, both entails and jointures were generally held to be immune to forfeiture.

[16] See, for example, Ferdinando Pulton, *De Pace Regis et Regni* (London, 1609), fols 229^r, 230^v, 231^v, 233^{r-v}, 237^v–38^r; T. E., *The Lawes Resolutions of Womens Rights* (London, 1632), 152–54; Edward Coke, *The First Part of the Institutes of the Laws of England, or a Commentary upon Littleton*, ed. Francis Hargrave and Charles Butler, 19th ed., 2 vols (London, 1832), vol. 2, 351a, 392b; Matthew Hale, *Historia Placitorum Coronae*, ed. Sollom Emlyn, 2 vols (Philadelphia, 1847), vol. 1, 253, 358; *A Treatise of Feme Coverts: Or, The Lady's Law* (London, 1732), 59, 59–60, 67–68, 75; and Blackstone, *Commentaries*, vol. 2, 130–31, 139, 433–35.

[17] See, however, the variety of dower claims made on different types of tenures in Sue Sheridan Walker, 'Litigation as Personal Quest: Suing for Dower in the Royal Courts, circa 1271–1350', in *Wife and Widow in Medieval England*, ed. Sue Sheridan Walker (Ann Arbor: University of Michigan Press, 1993), 82–83. See also her brief discussion of denials of dower based on accusations of felony, 91. See, too, Janet Senderowitz Loengard, '"Of the Gift of Her Husband": English Dower and Its Consequences in the Year 1200', in *Women of the Medieval World*, ed. Julius Kirshner and Suzanne F. Wemple (Oxford: Blackwell, 1985), 220, 220 n. 10, for the observation that by the early fifteenth century, 'judges were declaring confidently that English law had never permitted dower in chattels'.

[18] On freebench, see, for example, Barbara Todd, 'Freebench and Free Enterprise: Widows and Their Property in Two Berkshire Villages', in *English Rural Society, 1500–1800*:

A widow's allotment from the personal property also varied. Throughout much of the Middle Ages, she could expect 'reasonable parts': one-third if the couple had children, more if they did not. By the fourteenth century, men in much of the southern province of Canterbury gained the testamentary freedom to bequeath their personal property as they wished; between 1692 and 1725 statutes gave men throughout the country the same liberty. In cases of intestacy, however, the courts typically continued to bestow upon the widow one-third or more of her husband's personal property.[19] All of this – dower and the allotment of personal property, and depending upon local custom, freebench – disappeared if the husband was attainted of felony. Legally, the widow's entitlement began only at her husband's death, not at marriage; if he was found a felon before he died, he had no heir and no property against which his widow could claim.

This loss of the widow's entitlements prompted some criticism. Medieval petitions to have dower given the same protections as jointure produced no positive result, however. A petition put before the 1327 parliament, for example, had insisted that the right to dower ought to accrue to women through their marriages and not be forfeit for their husbands' misdeeds. The women were, after all, 'married at the great expense of their kinsmen'. But to this and to similar petitions throughout the Middle Ages, the various kings so addressed had always answered that the law ought to remain as it was.[20]

This did change in 1547, however, and by statute rather than by creative legal self-help. The councillors of the young King Edward VI introduced to his first parliament a bill with a striking proviso: that the wife of any man convicted of any act of treason or any felony whatsoever would thenceforth be entitled to her dower.[21] What prompted this measure at this time is unclear, given the paucity of relevant parliamentary sources. Men of the sort who sat in parliaments may well have become concerned about the security of their property after the contested passage of the recent Statute of Uses (1536), one provision of which held that land

---

Essays in Honour of Joan Thirsk, ed. John Chartres and David Hey (Cambridge: Cambridge University Press, 1990), 175–200. Note that some manorial customs preserved the freebench even of the widows of felons. See, for example, the successful claim of Jenet Haworth to a fourth part of her executed husband's messuage in 1543: *The Court Rolls of the Honor of Clitheroe*, ed. William Farrer, 3 vols (Edinburgh, 1913), vol. 3, 124. (My thanks to Paul Cavill for this reference.)

[19]   Amy Louise Erickson, *Women and Property in Early Modern England* (London: Routledge, 1993), 28, 178–80.

[20]   *The Parliament Rolls of Medieval England*, ed. C. Given-Wilson et al. (Leicester: Digital Scholarly Editions, 2004), 1327 January, 1:13, 1:14. See also 1399 October Part I, 6:130. It is sometimes erroneously claimed that 11 Richard II c. 5 (1388) protected the dower of the wives of traitors, but it protected only their 'heritage or jointure with their husbands'. See C. D. Ross, 'Forfeiture', 561.

[21]   1 Edward VI c. 12. On the passage and broader significance of this act, see A. F. Pollard, *England under Protector Somerset* (1900; repr. New York: Russell and Russell, 1966), 59–68.

put to use would no longer be protected from forfeiture for any crime, following the Henrician treason legislation that sought to ensure that entails and uses not bar forfeiture in such cases.[22] Given the political climate of the time, and recent history, criminal convictions of even the greatest men in the nation, and the deprivation of their families, loomed as possibilities.[23] MPs might also have intended the measure to put dower on a more even footing with the increasingly common jointure; the concurrent protections for the inheritance of heirs suggests, however, that a broader concern about the effects of forfeiture played a role beyond any simple desire to ensure consistent treatment of widows expecting dowers and those promised jointures.[24] A few years later, members of another of King Edward's parliaments decided against preserving the dower of the wives of traitors; but for the wives of felons, this protection remained.[25]

Thus, from the 1547 statute forward, both dower and jointure were protected from forfeiture for a husband's felonies. This was a significant development, and presumably a boon to many a widow. Its significance should not be overestimated, however, for all personal property remained forfeit. And the significance of personal property should not be underestimated. Leases and copyholds on land were considered chattels.[26] Indeed, the bulk of the population held the bulk of their wealth in such chattels and movable goods. As Erickson has noted, the value of much movable property is evident in the care with which each pot, sheet and

---

[22] 27 Henry VIII c. 10. See also 26 Henry VIII c. 1 and 33 Henry VIII c. 20.

[23] There had been one particularly high profile case in recent years: Thomas, Lord Dacre of the South, had been executed for murder in 1541, and his wife Mary had had no jointure. In the circumstances, the king's councillors authorized an emergency payment and Parliament passed a special act allowing her dower. See *Proceedings and Ordinances of the Privy Council*, ed. Harris Nichols, 7 vols (London, 1834–37), vol. 7, 207, and the act 33 Henry VIII c. 44 (Parliamentary Archives, HL/PO/PB/1541/33H8n44). See also Barbara J. Harris, *English Aristocratic Women, 1450–1550: Marriage and Family, Property and Careers* (Oxford: Oxford University Press, 2002), 139–43, and Anne Crawford, 'Victims of Attainder: The Howard and de Vere Women in the Late Fifteenth Century', *Reading Medieval Studies* 15 (1989): 59–74.

[24] Jointure acquired new prominence after the Statute of Uses, which barred women who had jointures prepared before marriage from also claiming dower. See Eileen Spring, *Law, Land, and Family: Aristocratic Inheritance in England, 1300–1800* (Chapel Hill: University of North Carolina Press, 1993), 43–58, and Staves, *Separate Property*, 29–30 and ch. 4. Strikingly, after Protector Somerset's own execution in 1552 on felony charges, his widow tried claiming her dower based on the 1547 statute but found that the Statute of Uses barred her from claiming both jointure and dower (73 *English Reports* 212–13 [1 Dyer 97a], and see also 73 *English Reports* 584 [3 Dyer 263b]).

[25] 5 and 6 Edward VI c. 11.

[26] The degree to which chattels real such as leases were subject to forfeiture seems to have differed over time, but for sixteenth-century practice, see, for example, the Elizabethan coroner's formulary, which specifically identified leases, copyholds and other chattels real as items to be forfeited by felons (Nottinghamshire Archives, DDE 67/1).

cow is listed in wills and post-mortem inventories.[27] For women in particular, personal property had an especial importance. Erickson has shown that early modern daughters inherited 'on a remarkably equitable basis with their brothers', but that the sons usually received the real property, while the daughters took their shares from the chattels. In one sample she found that wives usually brought to their marriages more than 50% of the total personal wealth of which their spouses died possessed.[28] Furthermore, any goods and chattels widows received from their husbands' estates, unlike dower or jointure, generally became theirs absolutely, not merely for widowhood or for life, and could in turn be willed by them to others. Thus, for the landless majority of the population and for women in particular, the forfeiture of personal property had the potential to pose significant hardship.

Many a wife presumably deemed it a rank injustice, too. The forfeiture of their husbands' goods and chattels did not just deny women necessary support, but denied them goods they may well have believed rightfully theirs. Margaret Hunt and others have shown that despite the dictates of coverture, women in the seventeenth and eighteenth centuries, at least, had a sense of ownership of the family's possessions and retained a particularly strong sense of personal ownership over whatever goods and chattels they had brought with them to the marital union. Their understanding of property rights differed from legal definitions of those rights. Women in the court cases examined by Hunt, for example, demonstrated a particular attachment to gifts from kin and to property obtained through their own work. They believed that in the event of marital collapse they were entitled to a sum equivalent to their contribution to the marriage.[29] Presumably, some such women believed they suffered a wrong when their husbands' offences resulted in the forfeiture of their property.

Certainly, in moving away from the generalizations and hypotheses derived from statutes and descriptive legal texts to concrete examples of women who faced the conjoined effects of coverture and criminal forfeiture, one finds much evidence of a sense of hardship and sometimes of injustice. The wives and widows of felons tried in various ways to avoid the loss of the familial possessions, sometimes

---

[27]   Erickson, *Women and Property*, 64–65.

[28]   Erickson, *Women and Property*, 19–20, 182.

[29]   Margaret Hunt, 'Wives and Marital "Rights" in the Court of Exchequer in the Early Eighteenth Century', in *Londinopolis: Essays in the Cultural and Social History of Early Modern London*, ed. Paul Griffiths and Mark S. R. Jenner (Manchester: Manchester University Press, 2000), 107–29. See also Joanne Bailey, 'Married Women, Property, and "Coverture" in England, 1660–1800', *Continuity and Change* 17 (2002): 351–72, and Amy Louise Erickson, 'Possession—and the Other One-tenth of the Law: Assessing Women's Ownership and Economic Roles in Early Modern England', *Women's History Review* 16 (2007): 370. Janet Loengard focuses on husbands, but suggests that in the sixteenth century, even they often demonstrated a sense that their wives retained a special claim to the goods they brought with them to the union ('"Plate, Good Stuff, and Household Things": Husbands, Wives, and Chattels in England at the End of the Middle Ages', *Ricardian* 13 [2003]: 328–40).

themselves transgressing legal boundaries to do so. Some petitioned. Alice Peete, for example, first petitioned for the life of her husband Francis, condemned for homicide, but when that failed, she begged for his forfeited goods. With four small children and a fifth on the way, she wrote that they were 'like to perish' unless relieved by the king's mercy.[30] Ellen Ewer thought she had secured a promise from the man who obtained her felonious husband's forfeited property that he would, in pity, give much of it back to her. When he failed to deliver, she implored the king's chief minister, Thomas Cromwell, for assistance. Ewer described herself as 'having by reason of her husband's late misfortune neither money nor goods wherewith to help herself and her said poor young children, but utterly is expelled and put from all comfort unless the great charity and goodness of your Lordship be unto her showed'.[31] Agnes Silkby combined similar invocations of poverty, maternal burdens and lordly clemency with an insistence upon her own innocence. Silkby petitioned the king to secure an estate valued at 6s, 4d per annum that her husband Robert had endeavoured to protect by putting it to use, as well as movable goods valued at 40s. Robert's execution for heretical, 'damnable opinions' left Agnes 'in great extreme poverty', even though she had 'never consented nor was privy to any of the said Robert's offences and hath three poor young children on her hand and hath not to sustain their living withal but only of charity and alms'.[32]

Instead of petitioning, Alice Avery turned to the courts. She based her 1547 Star Chamber suit against the undersheriff who seized 'her' goods on a rather distinctive claim: she maintained that she had never actually married her felonious partner and produced witnesses in an attempt to prove that she had lived in sin rather than lose her property. She described in great detail her household furniture, her red leather harness for her horse, her new velvet robe edged with parchment lace of gold and many other belongings that she insisted were hers alone. She and Thomas Kemmys had jointly kept an inn and victualling house in London until his execution for felony left her with nothing. A set of former customers deposed that Avery had kept a house very well furnished with items they believed to be hers, as Kemmys reportedly had a wife back in Wales. One said that he was 'very certain that the said Kemmys before he met with the said Alice had nothing more than he went in'. Others, however, reported that Avery and Kemmys 'was taken there amongst their neighbours as man and wife'. Indeed, witnesses said, when previously challenged about the 'evil rule' he kept with Avery, Kemmys angrily insisted that he had legitimately married her after divorcing the 'old forward

---

[30]   The National Archives: Public Record Office (hereafter TNA: PRO) SP 29/57, no. 8.

[31]   TNA: PRO SP 1/162, fol. 112.

[32]   TNA: PRO C 82/530/369. My thanks to Paul Cavill for this reference, and for sharing the draft of his forthcoming paper on heresy forfeitures.

woman' he had left in Wales.[33] Unfortunately, the outcome of the case is unknown, but divorce with remarriage being illegal at this time,[34] Avery may well have won.

While few proved quite so bold as Avery, other women who sought to protect 'their' possessions showed a significant degree of agency, assertiveness and legal knowledge. But they very often needed and found help from family and friends, too. This broad base of support itself suggests a degree of opposition to forfeiture's effects on the dependants of felons. When the constables of Cardiff came to seize the goods of a man convicted of manslaughter, his wife raised the hue and cry, and a serious melee seems to have followed.[35] When Anne Myles's husband committed murder in 1601, she immediately began distributing household items to friends and neighbours to keep them from being inventoried by the undersheriff: the vicar stored corn malt and other household stuff, and one Widow Malbye hid a brass pot. Once her husband was convicted, Anne and her father made suit to the man who had the right to forfeitures in their area that he would be good to her and her child, and grant her the goods she had not already managed to hide from him.[36]

When John Baynbrick committed an unspecified felony, it seems that the lease on his property was burned and a new one written up in the name of another individual in order to prevent its forfeiture, with money from the dubious sale paid to John's wife, Margaret.[37] Jane Shelley, the widow of a convict, went to court in 1606 claiming that some of the land seized from her husband had in fact been part of her jointure. The court awarded her some of the land, but not all. Shelley seems to have then cut her losses, selling her claim to the disputed parcels to another man, who then continued to fight the case in the courts.[38] In the same year, Margaret Ansley tried keeping £100 from the property of her husband Richard, executed for murder, by insisting that it had been intended long before the crime for her relief. She also maintained that there had been an error in her husband's indictment; having it overturned would be too late to save him, but might still save the money. Apparently, neither claim worked, but her brother-in-law then

---

[33]   TNA: PRO STAC 3/3/59. Of course, such court records cannot be trusted to reveal the facts of any particular case, with charges and depositions representing narratives designed to suit a litigant's best interests. Nor, in many cases, do the records reveal even what the court decided upon as the true course of events. Nonetheless, such records demonstrate the range of possible actions and believable claims open to the litigants in question.

[34]   For a discussion of the 'blurriness' between singleness and marriage, see Cordelia Beattie, '"Living as a Single Person": Marital Status, Performance and the Law in Late Medieval England', *Women's History Review* 17 (2008): 327–40; for self-divorce, see Tim Stretton, 'Marriage, Separation and the Common Law in England, 1540–1660', in *The Family in Early Modern England*, ed. Helen Berry and Elizabeth A. Foyster (Cambridge: Cambridge University Press, 2007), 18–39.

[35]   TNA: PRO, E 134/23 and 24 Chas I/Hil 2.

[36]   TNA: PRO, E 134/44 and 45 Eliz/Mich 39.

[37]   TNA: PRO, E 134/17 Eliz/Trin 4.

[38]   TNA: PRO, E 124/1, fol. 10d.

appeared in court with documentation which proved to the court's satisfaction that the £100 was his, pledged to him two months before the commission of the crime. One suspects that this was a ruse to keep the money for Margaret.[39]

Some such attempts proved particularly complex and cunning. John Honeywell was hanged for manslaughter in Essex in 1614 after unsuccessfully pleading benefit of clergy. Before his trial and execution, however, he and his wife, Alice, performed a jail-yard property conveyance. Thomas Tucker, an old family friend and a relative of John's, acquired the property in return for agreeing to pay off various small debts of John's amounting to £10, and a 'debt' of £110 to Alice's unmarried sister Mary Symonds. The agreement had the suspicious proviso that if Alice subsequently paid Thomas £120, she could secure the return of all the property in question.[40] One assumes that sister Mary – unwed and hence in full control of any assets that came to her – was simply to give Alice the money with which to repurchase the estate once Alice was safely a widow.

Evidence of such evasions is scattered throughout the records of various courts, as the grant-holders to whom the forfeitures were due launched suits when they believed themselves to have been cheated. Such evidence is easiest to find in respect to suicides, in part, perhaps, because of distinctive attitudes to self-slaying that made forfeiture for such a crime more contentious, but also because it is simply more easily located. As the King's Almoner typically had the right to collect the forfeitures of suicides, searching Star Chamber files for suits launched by the Almoner readily results in a trove of claims that widows, families, neighbours and coroners somehow obstructed forfeitures. A felony for much of its legal history, suicide occasioned the loss of only goods and chattels, not the real property, as the offender had not been formally attainted.[41] Yet even so, many a person risked the wrath of the Almoner by attempting to hide goods or to have a suicide falsely labelled a non-felonious death.

When husbandman Thomas Pink hanged himself in his cart house in 1608, for example, the coroner reportedly took a cow and £6 from the widow in return for his jury's verdict that Pink died a natural death. He thus saved her from the loss of all the family's personal possessions and made himself a sum well in excess of the usual fee for a felonious death.[42] Similarly, when William Ponder of Dodford killed himself in 1560, neighbour Thomas Baylie helped select and sway the coroner's

---

[39] TNA: PRO, E 124/1, fol. 255d.

[40] TNA: PRO, E 134/17 Jas 1/Mich 38. This case in particular suggests another possible indication of opposition to the law's forfeiture provisions, seen indirectly in the statutes against fraudulent conveyances, most notably 13 Elizabeth c. 5 (1571). See Charles Ross, *Elizabethan Literature and the Law of Fraudulent Conveyance: Sidney, Spenser, and Shakespeare* (Aldershot: Ashgate 2003), 29–31, 101–11; Pauncefoot's Case, 76 *English Reports*, 816–17 (3 Co. Rep. 82b); and *Shaw v. Bran*, 171 *English Reports*, 485 (1 Stark. 319).

[41] See, for instance, Hale, *Historia*, vol. 1, 412–13.

[42] TNA: PRO, STAC 3/2/77.

jury to protect Ponder's widow. Baylie reportedly assured her that 'I have been abroad and laboured of them of the inquest that dwell abroad out of Dodford ... be merry, for thou hast no cause to the contrary, for that thine own neighbours will be thy friends'. The jury found a verdict of accidental death, allowing the widow to keep her goods.[43] After Howell David killed himself, a bailiff inventoried and locked away his assets. Some 40 men subsequently broke in to liberate the goods. Whether truthfully or not, they later tried arguing that they had done so because they were 'near neighbours to the said poor distressed widow, came to comfort her in her heaviness'.[44] Michael Macdonald and Terence Murphy have studied thousands of records of coroners' inquests and Star Chamber suits and found that in addition to mislabelling deaths as non-felonious, juries often undervalued or failed to report goods for forfeiture.[45] Such cases reflect a variety of competing interests and admit a variety of interpretations. While one need not see all these people as 'principled defenders of family and locality', some of their actions and justifications suggest opposition to forfeiture, or at least a sense that the bereaved family had the greatest need of and entitlement to the goods in question in a given instance.[46]

Those with the legal rights to felons' forfeitures sometimes showed discretionary 'generosity', returning some of the possessions to the widow or allowing her to buy them back at a favourable rate. While such gifts do not demonstrate opposition to forfeiture as such, they do suggest the tensions that sometimes surrounded the deprivation of the wife of a felon of her husband's personal estate and a sense

---

[43]   TNA: PRO, STAC 5/A10/20.

[44]   TNA: PRO, STAC 8/24/10.

[45]   Michael MacDonald and Terence R. Murphy, *Sleepless Souls: Suicide in Early Modern England* (Oxford: Clarendon Press, 1990), 78. For the earlier history of jury discretion in respect to suicides, see Sara M. Butler, 'Degrees of Culpability: Suicide Verdicts, Mercy and the Jury in Medieval England', *Journal of Medieval and Early Modern Studies* 36 (2006): 263–90.

[46]   Cf. R. A. Houston, *Punishing the Dead? Suicide, Lordship, and Community in Britain, 1500–1830* (Oxford: Oxford University Press, 2010), quotation at 112. Macdonald and Murphy, *Sleepless Souls*, had used such cases of evasion primarily as evidence for the effective decriminalization of self-slaying, only secondarily as evidence of opposition to forfeiture. In responding to their argument about a growing sympathy for suicides, Houston has also inverted their depiction of the almoners and their opponents: Houston sees the almoner as bringing 'love, charity or Christian amity' (111) into tense situations, and those who opposed his efforts to seize the property of suicides as self-interested people with a narrow sense of community who sought to deny creditors their just claims. (Houston privileges the claims of creditors over those of widows and heirs, but neither had a legal 'right' to the goods in question.) While he prefers to see forfeiture as 'a means of enforcing trust and community among survivors through the mechanism of lordship', he does now allow that it was at least partly punitive (2). Yet, he claims that complaints about resulting familial hardship were (and are) unfounded (131). He seems to mistake the complaint that 'forfeiture should not affect the guiltless survivors' for an established principle, and later or localized evidence of exceptions for general practice.

that whatever the law, the widow might merit some recompense. When Henry Rookeby killed himself in Newcastle in 1617, for example, the town agreed to take only £40 from his widow, despite the estate being valued at some £500.[47] The audit books for the town of Great Yarmouth record a few such compositions for more modest estates, noting the receipt 'from the widow of Samuel Feake, her husband being executed this year, 5s' and from the wife of another felon, 'for the like, 5s'.[48]

The Crown occasionally gave pensions to the widows and children of executed traitors or returned to them some fraction of the seized property; the wives and widows of felons sometimes received royal bounty, too.[49] Anthony Horseman, a yeoman of Great Wolford, Warwick, fled after murdering a man in 1587. Queen Elizabeth granted the £33 worth of forfeited property to one of her gentlemen-at-arms, expressly for the relief of Horseman's wife and family. According to the text of the grant, 'being credibly informed of the poverty and great misery of the wife of the said Horseman and seven poor comfortless children, and taking thereupon great pity and compassion toward the said wife and children', the Queen granted the forfeiture to her servant, 'to the only end and intent that he ... shall dispose the same to the use, relief, and maintenance of the said wife and children as by him and them shall be thought most meet and convenient'.[50] Interestingly, these discretionary gifts sometimes amounted to one-third of the personal possessions of the felon, echoing the allotment of dower and 'reasonable parts'. When the Bishop of Peterborough acquired the forfeitures of convict John Browne in 1549, for example, he bestowed two parts on one of his servants but returned the third part to Browne's wife, Alice.[51]

Such gifts were just that, however – gifts. They were discretionary and by no means guaranteed. As with discretionary acts of grace more generally, they had the potential to lessen the sense of a disjunction between justice and legality and thus to secure support for the norm even while making an exception. (And sometimes, too, the gifts may have constituted bribes for compliant behaviour: when investigating Philip Witherick's involvement in a murder, for example, the bailiff told Witherick's wife that he would secure the return of all the forfeited goods if she cooperated, urging her to 'help herself as much as she could'.[52]) Nor did recipients necessarily see the return of only a fraction of the family goods – goods the women may well have seen as their own – as generosity. Even when the grant-holder did return a portion of the property, the widow may well have felt

---

[47]   TNA: PRO, STAC 8/29/15.

[48]   Norfolk Record Office, Great Yarmouth Audit Books, Y/C 27/1, fol. 283.

[49]   For examples of such grants to the families of traitors, see, for example, K. J. Kesselring, *The Northern Rebellion of 1569: Faith, Politics and Protest in Elizabethan England* (Basingstoke: Palgrave Macmillan, 2007), 136–41.

[50]   TNA: PRO, C 66/1320, mm. 11–12.

[51]   TNA: PRO, SP 10/8, no. 49.

[52]   John G. Bellamy, *Strange, Inhuman Deaths: Murder in Tudor England* (Sutton: Stroud, 2005), 95–96, citing TNA: PRO, SP 1/131, fols 208ᵛ–9ᵛ.

robbed. Despite receiving a third of her husband's forfeiture, Alice Brown still complained to William Cecil about the seizure of the other two-thirds and about the way in which the goods had been divided, noting among other things that she had lost her best down bed.[53] Yet these gifts, such as they were, along with the obstructions and evasions by women and their friends and family, may indicate a sense among some that the wives of felons retained a moral claim to the familial property at odds with the fiction of marital unity.

Certainly, the most common and enduring complaints about forfeiture throughout its history centred on its effects on family members imagined as innocent. Medieval petitioners lamented abuses, such as false convictions to secure the property of innocent men; nineteenth-century MPs drew on Benthamite principles to argue that it was an irrational, disproportionate punishment that 'produced pain without any corresponding advantage'.[54] The most frequent complaint, however, was that the punishment applied not only or even primarily to the offender, but to his or her innocent family members as well. The sons must not suffer for the sins of the father, nor the wife for those of the husband, these critics insisted. In the early 1540s, Protestant reformer and social critic Henry Brinkelow reserved a prominent place for forfeiture in his pamphlet, *The Complaint of Roderyck Mors ... unto the Parlament House of Ingland ... for the Redresse of Certeyn Wycked Lawes*. He exclaimed, 'O merciful God, what a cruel law is this? ... that when a traitor, a murderer, a felon or an heretic is condemned and put to death, his wife and children and his servants and all they whom he is debtor unto should be robbed for his offence, and brought to extreme poverty ... Alas what can the poor wife, the children, the kinsman or creditor do withal, being not culpable in the crime; if any of them be faulty, then let them have also the law, that is death, which recompenseth the crime'.[55] Similarly, William Tomlinson, a would-be law reformer of the Civil War era, complained in his attack on forfeiture that 'It is not enough that the wife hath lost her husband and the children their father, but to increase their misery, their livelihood must go with his life'.[56] When Englishmen abroad in the colonies had the chance to create law codes to their own liking, they sometimes abolished or restricted forfeiture. The Rhode Island law code of 1647, for example, explicitly declared the colonists' intent in getting rid of forfeiture that 'the wives and children ought not to bear the iniquities of the Husbands and Parents'.[57]

---

[53]   TNA: PRO, SP 10/8, no. 49.

[54]   For such medieval complaints, see *Parliament Rolls*, 1343 April (3:38, 3:42); 1354 April (262:51); 1365 January (2:14); 1372 November (3:22); 1376 April (10:71). For examples of nineteenth-century complaints, see Kesselring, 'Felons' Effects'.

[55]   Henry Brinkelow, *The Complaint of Roderyck Mors ... unto the Parlament House of Ingland ... for the Redresse of Certeyn Wycked Lawes, etc.* (London, 1548), sig. C3^{r-v}.

[56]   William Tomlinson, *Seven Particulars* (London, 1657), 18.

[57]   *Records of the Colony of Rhode Island and Providence Plantations*, ed. John Russell Bartlett, 10 vols (Providence, RI, 1856–65), vol. 1, 162.

A variety of sources, then, suggest that many people believed that the conflated effects of coverture and criminal forfeiture represented an unwarranted hardship or active injustice against the wife and family of a felon. From the statutes protecting jointure and dower, the obstructionist tactics of women and their confederates, through to the literature of complaint, evidence mounts that some contemporaries viewed the combined effects of forfeiture and coverture as a problem. Yet, it was precisely the effects of forfeiture on the wives and families of offenders that came to serve as the main defence of the practice. The deterrent value of the impoverishment of the felon's family came to justify the retention of a practice that had outlived the feudal context of its birth.

Sixteenth-century legal writers extolled the admonitory value of forfeiture. Ferdinando Pulton opined of a potential offender that 'if concern for his own life could not stay him from the committing of felony, or treason, yet the love which he did bear to his wife and children should restrain him thereof, whom he was assured by that wicked act to undo and utterly to deprive them of all livelihood wherewith to maintain them'.[58] William Staunford offered a similar argument, and in a bit of dubious legal history noted that this had been the 'intent' of forfeiture from its inception.[59] The author of the late sixteenth-century *The Lawes Resolutions of Womens Rights* observed that 'The first Solons of the English Law belike thought that tender regard of a wife's estate should restrain a husband from all enormous transgression'. He recognized the error in this assumption – 'would God it might', he observed – but could do no more than quote Staunford's assertion that 'men will now eschew those capital crimes when they shall see those persons who in nature and affection are nearest and dearest unto them, and most to be beloved, shall be punished with themselves, yet they should the rather refrain for the love of their wife and children upon whom they bring so perpetual loss and punishment'.[60]

This insistence upon the deterrent value of forfeiture as a punishment, this embracing of the deleterious effects on wives and children as a rationale for the retention of the practice, may have been new to the early modern period. The late thirteenth-century legal text known as *Britton* opined that the loss of dower was just, insofar as a wife 'may be fairly supposed to know of the felony of her husband'.[61] A wife might have diminished responsibility for her own petty crimes thanks to the effects of coverture, but could also justly be expected to

---

[58]   Pulton, *De Pace Regis et Regni*, 237d–238.

[59]   William Staunford, *Les Plees del Coron* (London, 1560), 194d.

[60]   T. E., *The Lawes Resolutions of Womens Rights* (London, 1632), 152.

[61]   *Britton: The French Text Carefully Revised, with an English Translation, Introduction and Notes*, ed. and trans. Francis Morgan Nichols, 2 vols (Oxford, 1865; repr. Holmes Beach, FL: W. W. Graunt, 1983), vol. 2, 279–80. Bracton, however, had simply treated the loss of dower as a technical consequence of the felon dying without an heir against whom the widow could claim (Henry Bracton, *On the Laws and Customs of England*, trans. S. E. Thorne, 4 vols [Cambridge, MA: Harvard University Press and the Selden Society, 1968–77], vol. 3, 360; see also vol. 2, 428). A widow's dower was, at various points, conditional on her being sexually available to her husband and to no others.

share the responsibility for her husband's offences. Early medieval law codes assumed notions of collective guilt and responsibility that only slowly waned.[62] The justification being offered by early modern writers was not an assertion of shared guilt, however; Pulton, Staunford and the rest made no mention of implied consent or even 'unity of person', otherwise so frequently invoked to explain the deleterious effects of marriage. Instead, they assumed the wife's innocence and the injustice done to her by her husband's actions.

Whether new to the early modern period or not, this emphasis on the ruining of a family as a valuable deterrent continued to be offered as a primary justification for forfeiture for many years. William Eden, for example, had somewhat contradictory views on the subject but of a sort that made his final endorsement of felony forfeiture all the more striking. In his influential tome on the *Principles of Penal Law*, first published in 1771, he expressed his belief that the forfeiture of the goods of suicides was 'ineffectual and absurd'. An individual who had no concern for his or her immortal soul presumably had no care for family. 'It is cruel also', he wrote, 'and unjust thus to heap sufferings on the head of innocence by punishing the child for the loss of its parent, or aggravating the distress of the widow, because she hath been deserted by her husband'. But he argued that forfeiture for other felonies and for treason served important functions: 'The mere execution of the criminal is a fleeing example; but the forfeiture of lands leaves a permanent impression. It is indeed one of our best constitutional safe-guards, when applied with discretion to the preservation of moral conduct and used without violence to the correction of guilt.' He acknowledged that 'on a superficial glance', it might seem harsh to 'involve a whole family in the punishment of one criminal'. Ultimately, though, he concluded that 'it is neither unjust nor unwise to convert human partialities to the promotion of human happiness'.[63]

One nineteenth-century attorney general, however, expressed some doubts about the effectiveness of this deterrent. Reporting to the 1819 Select Committee on Criminal Laws, he observed that a felon's forfeiture of property 'is attended with a visitation of poverty on the family, and proceeds upon a principle which I am afraid has little operation upon the depraved minds of felons, which is the well-being and comfort of their families. ... It is too refined a principle to be acted upon by such persons'.[64] And indeed, over the 1800s, opposition to felony forfeiture – and to the effects of coverture – mounted from a number of fronts. Over the

---

See Paul Brand, '"Deserving" and "Undeserving" Wives: Earning and Forfeiting Dower in Medieval England', *Legal History* 22 (2001): 1–20.

[62] Lawrence Stone, *The Family, Sex and Marriage in England, 1500–1800* (New York: Harper and Row, 1977), 126.

[63] William Eden, *Principles of Penal Law*, 3rd ed. (Dublin, 1772), 37–38, 48, 249–50. Eden drew much of his argument from Charles Yorke, *Considerations on the Law of Forfeiture for High Treason* (London, 1745).

[64] *Select Committee on Criminal Laws Relating to Capital Punishment in Felonies. Report, Minutes of Evidence* (London, 1819), 49.

preceding centuries, families generously endowed with land had found ways to protect it, through strict settlements and a variety of other equitable devices. But personal property remained prone to seizure, and as personal property came to acquire greater significance for more significant components of the population, calls to do away with its forfeiture grew louder.[65] Finally, in 1870 – the same year as the first Married Women's Property Act – Parliament abolished felony forfeiture.[66]

Throughout much of their histories, the conjunction of the effects of coverture and of criminal forfeiture had, and was seen to have, unfortunate effects on the wives or widows of felons. But rather than being merely a regrettable side-effect of the punishment, this impoverishment of the wife and family came to be one of its chief justifications. The patriarchal structure of property law impinged upon the criminal law in ways that posed hardship for many an individual woman; moderated by the equitable protections for the well-to-do, it also helped perpetuate the ancient sanction of criminal forfeiture through the years in which private property became sanctified. As Erickson has argued in other contexts, 'the shape of marital property law had multiple and far reaching ramifications ... well beyond issues of possession'.[67] The gendered nature of property rights under coverture provided a powerful rationale to retain the practice of felony forfeiture. English jurists liked to claim that women were a 'favourite' of the law, noting as evidence married women's diminished responsibility for their own criminal misdeeds. Given that wives and widows were for so long subject to punishment for their husbands' more frequent criminal acts, some might have thought this a very fictive kind of favouritism indeed.

Works Cited

Primary Sources

Manuscript Sources
National Archives. Public Record Office, SP 1/131; SP 1/162; SP 10/8; SP 29/57; C 66/1320; C 82/530/369; E 134/17 Eliz/Trin 4; E 134/44 and 45 Eliz/Mich 39; E 134/17 Jas 1/Mich 38; E 134/23 and 24 Chas I/Hil 2; E 124/1; STAC 3/2/77; STAC 3/3/59; STAC 5/A10/20; STAC 8/24/10.
Norfolk Record Office, Y/C 27/1.
Nottinghamshire Archives, DDE 67/1.
Parliamentary Archives, HL/PO/PB/1541/33H8n44.

---

[65]   See, for example, Theodore Barlow, *The Justice of the Peace* (London, 1745), 215.

[66]   See Kesselring, 'Felons' Effects', for the broader context of forfeiture's demise.

[67]   Erickson, 'Possession—and the Other One-tenth of the Law', 382, and Amy Louise Erickson, 'Coverture and Capitalism', *History Workshop Journal* 59 (2005): 1–16.

Printed Primary Sources

Barlow, Theodore. *The Justice of the Peace*. London, 1745.

Blackstone, William. *Commentaries on the Laws of England*. 4 vols. Oxford, 1765–69.

Bracton, Henry. *On the Laws and Customs of England*. Translated by S. E. Thorne. 4 vols. Cambridge, MA: Harvard University Press and the Selden Society, 1968–77.

Brinkelow, Henry. *The Complaint of Roderyck Mors ... unto the Parlament House of Ingland ... for the Redresse of Certeyn Wycked Lawes, etc.* 'Geneva' [i.e., London], 1548.

Britton: The French Text Carefully Revised, with an English Translation, Introduction and Notes. Edited and translated by Francis Morgan Nichols. 2 vols. Oxford, 1865; repr. Holmes Beach, FL: W. W. Graunt, 1983.

Cobbe, Frances Power. 'Criminals, Idiots, Women and Minors'. *Fraser's Magazine*, December 1868, 777–94.

Coke, Edward. *The First Part of the Institutes of the Laws of England, or a Commentary upon Littleton*. Edited by Francis Hargrave and Charles Butler. 19th ed. 2 vols. London, 1832.

The Court Rolls of the Honor of Clitheroe. Edited and translated by William Farrer. 3 vols. Edinburgh: Ballantyne Press, 1913.

Eden, William. *Principles of Penal Law*. 3rd ed. Dublin, 1772.

The English Reports. Edited by Alexander Wood Renton. 176 vols. Edinburgh, 1900–1932.

Hale, Matthew. *Historia Placitorum Coronae*. Edited by Sollom Emlyn. 2 vols. Philadelphia, PA, 1847.

Married Women's Property Committee Report of the Proceedings of the Annual Meeting, 1876. Manchester, 1876.

The Parliament Rolls of Medieval England. Edited by Chris Given-Wilson et al. Leicester: Scholarly Digital Editions, 2004.

Proceedings and Ordinances of the Privy Council. Edited by Harris Nichols. 7 vols. London, 1834–37.

Pulton, Ferdinando. *De Pace Regis et Regni*. London, 1609.

Records of the Colony of Rhode Island and Providence Plantations. Edited by John Russell Bartlett. 10 vols. Providence, RI: 1856–65.

Select Committee on Criminal Laws Relating to Capital Punishment in Felonies. Report, Minutes of Evidence. London, 1819.

Staunford, William. *Les Plees del Coron*. London, 1560.

T. E. *The Lawes Resolutions of Womens Rights*. London, 1632.

Tomlinson, William. *Seven Particulars*. London, 1657.

A Treatise of Feme Coverts: Or, The Lady's Law. London, 1732.

The Treatise on the Laws and Customs of the Realm of England Commonly Called Glanvill. Edited by G. D. G. Hall. London, 1965; repr. Holmes Beach, FL: W. W. Gaunt, 1983.

Yorke, Charles. *Considerations on the Law of Forfeiture for High Treason*. London, 1745.

Secondary Sources

Bailey, Joanne. 'Married Women, Property, and "Coverture" in England, 1660–1800'. *Continuity and Change* 17 (2002): 351–72.

Bean, J. M. W. *The Decline of English Feudalism, 1215–1540*. Manchester: Manchester University Press, 1968.

Beattie, Cordelia. '"Living as a Single Person": Marital Status, Performance and the Law in Late Medieval England'. *Women's History Review* 17 (2008): 327–40.

Bellamy, John G. *The Law of Treason in England in the Later Middle Ages*. Cambridge Studies in English Legal History. Cambridge: Cambridge University Press, 1970.

———. *Strange, Inhuman Deaths: Murder in Tudor England*. Sutton: Stroud, 2005.

Biancalana, Joseph. *The Fee Tail and the Common Recovery in Medieval England, 1176–1502*. Cambridge Studies in English Legal History. Cambridge: Cambridge University Press, 2001.

Brand, Paul. '"Deserving" and "Undeserving" Wives: Earning and Forfeiting Dower in Medieval England'. *Legal History* 22 (2001): 1–20.

Butler, Sara M. 'Degrees of Culpability: Suicide Verdicts, Mercy and the Jury in Medieval England'. *Journal of Medieval and Early Modern Studies* 36 (2006): 263–90.

Cioni, Maria. *Women and Law in Elizabethan England, with Particular Reference to the Court of Chancery*. New York: Garland, 1985.

Crawford, Anne. 'Victims of Attainder: The Howard and de Vere Women in the Late Fifteenth Century'. *Reading Medieval Studies* 15 (1989): 59–74.

Doggett, Maeve. *Marriage, Wife-Beating, and the Law in Victorian England*. Columbia: South Carolina University Press, 1993.

Dolan, Frances. *Marriage and Violence: The Early Modern Legacy*. Philadelphia: University of Pennsylvania Press, 2008.

Erickson, Amy Louise. 'Common Law versus Common Practice: The Use of Marriage Settlements in Early Modern England'. *Economic History Review*, 2nd ser., 43 (1990): 21–39.

———. 'Coverture and Capitalism'. *History Workshop Journal* 59 (2005): 1–16.

———. 'Possession—and the Other One-tenth of the Law: Assessing Women's Ownership and Economic Roles in Early Modern England'. *Women's History Review* 16 (2007): 369–85.

———. *Women and Property in Early Modern England*. London: Routledge, 1993.

Habakkuk, John. *Marriage, Debt and the Estates System: English Landownership 1650–1950*. Oxford: Clarendon Press, 1994.

Harris, Barbara J. *English Aristocratic Women, 1450–1550: Marriage and Family, Property and Careers*. Oxford: Oxford University Press, 2002.

Holcombe, Lee. *Wives and Property: Reform of the Married Women's Property Law in Nineteenth-Century England*. Toronto: University of Toronto Press, 1983.

Houston, R. A. *Punishing the Dead? Suicide, Lordship, and Community in Britain, 1500–1830.* Oxford: Oxford University Press, 2010.

Hunt, Margaret. 'Wives and Marital "Rights" in the Court of Exchequer in the Early Eighteenth Century'. In *Londinopolis: Essays in the Cultural and Social History of Early Modern London.* Edited by Paul Griffiths and Mark S. R. Jenner. Manchester: Manchester University Press, 2000. 107–29.

Jones, W. J. *The Elizabethan Court of Chancery.* Oxford: Clarendon Press, 1967.

Kesselring, K. J. 'Felons' Effects and the Effects of Felony in Nineteenth-Century England'. *Law and History Review* 28 (2010): 111–39.

———. 'Felony Forfeiture, c. 1170–1870'. *Journal of Legal History* 30 (2009): 201–26.

———. 'Felony Forfeiture and the Profits of Crime in Early Modern England'. *Historical Journal* 53 (2010): 271–88.

———. *The Northern Rebellion of 1569: Faith, Politics and Protest in Elizabethan England.* Basingstoke: Palgrave Macmillan, 2007.

Lander, J. R. 'Attainder and Forfeiture, 1453–1509'. *Historical Journal* 4 (1961): 119–51.

Levy, Leonard W. *A License to Steal: The Forfeiture of Property.* Chapel Hill: University of North Carolina Press, 1996.

Loengard, Janet. '"Of the Gift of Her Husband": English Dower and Its Consequences in the Year 1200'. In *Women of the Medieval World: Essays in Honor of John H. Mundy.* Edited by Julius Kirshner and Suzanne F. Wemple. Oxford: Blackwell, 1985. 215–55.

———. '"Plate, Good Stuff, and Household Things": Husbands, Wives, and Chattels in England at the End of the Middle Ages'. *Ricardian* 13 (2003): 328–40.

MacDonald, Michael, and Terence R. Murphy. *Sleepless Souls: Suicide in Early Modern England.* Oxford: Clarendon Press, 1990.

Pollard, A. F. *England under Protector Somerset.* 1900; repr. New York: Russell and Russell, 1966.

Ronner, Amy D. 'Husband and Wife Are One – Him: *Bennis v. Michigan* as the Resurrection of Coverture'. *Michigan Journal of Gender and Law* 4 (1996): 129–69.

Ross, C. D. 'Forfeiture for Treason in the Reign of Richard II'. *English Historical Review* 71 (1956): 560–75.

Ross, Charles. *Elizabethan Literature and the Law of Fraudulent Conveyance: Sidney, Spenser, and Shakespeare.* Aldershot: Ashgate, 2003.

Spring, Eileen. *Law, Land, and Family: Aristocratic Inheritance in England, 1300–1800.* Chapel Hill: University of North Carolina Press, 1993.

Staves, Susan. *Married Women's Separate Property in England, 1660–1833.* Cambridge, MA: Harvard University Press, 1990.

Stone, Lawrence. *The Family, Sex and Marriage in England, 1500–1800.* New York: Harper and Row, 1977.

Stretton, Tim. 'Coverture and Unity of Person in Blackstone's Commentaries'. In *Blackstone and His Commentaries: Biography, Law, History*. Edited by Wilfrid Robinson Prest. Oxford: Hart, 2009. 111–28.

———. 'Marriage, Separation and the Common Law in England, 1540–1660'. In *The Family in Early Modern England*. Edited by Helen Berry and Elizabeth A. Foyster. Cambridge: Cambridge University Press, 2007. 18–39.

Todd, Barbara. 'Freebench and Free Enterprise: Widows and Their Property in Two Berkshire Villages'. In *English Rural Society, 1500–1800: Essays in Honour of Joan Thirsk*. Edited by John Chartres and David Hey. Cambridge: Cambridge University Press, 1990. 175–200.

Walker, Sue Sheridan. 'Litigation as Personal Quest: Suing for Dower in the Royal Courts, circa 1271–1350'. In *Wife and Widow in Medieval England*. Edited by Sue Sheridan Walker. Ann Arbor: University of Michigan Press, 1993. 81–108.

Wormald, Patrick. *The Making of English Law: King Alfred to the Twelfth Century*. Vol. 1: *Legislation and Its Limits*. Oxford: Blackwell, 1999.

Index